NOT SO SLPPY

IAN HYSLOP

To Lyn, Gordon, Rhonda and an airline called Qantas

CONTENTS

Preface		vii
Chapter 1	"You Have to Write a Book"	1
Chapter 2	Where to Begin	4
Chapter 3	Coconuts and Kings	8
Chapter 4	On the Road Again	19
Chapter 5	Aunty ABC	31
Chapter 6	Nicknames and All that Nonsense	50
Chapter 7	It's a Boy!	53
Chapter 8	Born in the USA	55
Chapter 9	Welcome to the Green Room	70
Chapter 10	Up, Up and Away	77
Chapter 11	Top Gun I'm Not	89
Chapter 12	Sphincter Testers over America	97
Chapter 13	Tegucigalpa – How Do You Spell That?	102
Chapter 14	Medical Mysteries	109
Chapter 15	Heart to Heart	113
Chapter 16	A Day at the Office	116
Chapter 17	Taiwan Travails	120
Chapter 18	The Mother Finder	125
Chapter 19	Tears before Bedtime	131
Chapter 20	Beer Money	139
Chapter 21	A New Start	145
Chapter 22	Lady Barnett	156
Chapter 23	What To Do Now?	163

Chapter 24	Here Comes the Bride	168
Chapter 25	Honeymoon Hangover	175
Chapter 26	Hijinks on the High Seas	180
Chapter 27	Big Seas, Big Fears	186
Chapter 28	Beef Jerky and Blackjack	190
Chapter 29	Barging in Burgundy	195
Chapter 30	Checking out the Chef	198
Chapter 31	Bruised Buttocks, Battered Testicles	202
Chapter 32	Getting Down and Brown in DC	205
Chapter 33	Royal Rat	207
Chapter 34	And You Thought You Were Fit	210
Chapter 35	Jurassic Park	213
Chapter 36	Gophers in Paradise	216
Chapter 37	Out of Africa	219
Chapter 38	A Hole in None	223
Chapter 39	Beer O'Clock in Prague	229
Chapter 40	Terrible Travel 'Tails'	233
Chapter 41	Coping with a Colonoscopy	237
Chapter 42	And On It Goes!	242
Photography Credits		246

PREFACE

What's in a nickname?

After three decades of working in the fiercely competitive world of Australian television, Journalist Ian Hyslop reflects on a news career that spanned the globe, reporting on major breaking stories that shaped a generation.

From a cadetship with the ABC in the 1970s to his time as a foreign correspondent in the United States and Asia, Hyslop interviewed celebrities, politicians and newsmakers about their time in the headlines.

'Sloppy' to his colleagues, Ian was Channel 7's correspondent in Los Angeles in the 1980s, reporting on everything from the antics of Hollywood legends to the power plays of American politicians.

Witness the world through Ian's eyes as he finds himself at Cape Canaveral, grappling with the aftermath of the Challenger disaster, and aboard the 'press plane' during the 1988 Presidential campaign, where he somehow managed to keep up with George Bush and avoid a brush with death. Feel the ground shake beneath your feet as Ian recounts his time in San Francisco covering one of America's most powerful earthquakes, and a threat to his own mortality in Taipei during another quake that claimed 2000 lives.

Not so Sloppy chronicles a career in journalism and business that started with a small boy's pledge to his parents, "When I grow up I'm going to be a journalist!"

CHAPTER 1
YOU HAVE TO WRITE A BOOK

"You have to write a book!" Beware of this phrase. When you hear it, run and hide! Resist being tempted to make public the salient points of an undoubtedly fascinating life. It has to be fascinating, right? Why on earth would someone suggest you write a book unless they think you have plenty to say? Pause for a moment. Keep your ego in check. Take a deep breath and rein in the self-satisfied instinct that accepts most humbly that you are indeed an interesting character, with a bucket load of stories to share.

Now admit it. You are flattered that someone thinks you've done enough in life to be cajoled into sharing the fascinating details, but I repeat, beware! Writing isn't easy. I spent the best part of a lifetime penning stories for television news in countries around the world, but that isn't an instant qualification to write a book. Writing involves a lot more than churning out words. A whole new dimension comes into play – discipline, application and time – and we all know they aren't always easy to come by.

Who better to enlighten me on the subject than bestselling author Robert Ludlum, who I asked during my foreign correspondent days in the 1980s, what it took to be a successful writer? He was succinct and to the point; "the daily consumption of a tumbler of gin, but only after six hours of writing!" That simple formula certainly worked for the former high-flying ad-man turned bestselling author, judging by his palatial estate in Connecticut.

It was purchased with the proceeds of his scribbling, which, interestingly, he did on thick yellow legal pads to be transcribed by a secretary. The author of a long list of bestsellers translated into thirty-three languages, he was well qualified to express his views on the subject.

Fortunately, I caught Mr. Ludlum before midday, after a lengthy writing session, and was in time for a quick sit-down interview and the tumbler of gin – or was that tumblers of gin! I remember thinking at the time, "this writing business ain't half bad!"

For an Australian journalist, it was made even better when the writer's neighbour, comic Rodney Dangerfield, called by the gated estate, to join his pal in an afternoon tipple. The crew and I were invited to join the two in what was, for them, a common ritual.

With the camera safely put away to avoid any embarrassing missteps by these two very public figures, the group settled into a convivial and ultimately, quite drunken conversation about nothing in particular, though I suspect Dangerfield derived a few new ideas for his comedy act. His poor attempts at mimicking an Australian accent certainly matched Meryl Streep's 'a dingo has taken my baby' moment.

I recall little of the drive back to New York that evening, but the interview did ignite my interest in one day writing a book. It also set in motion a lifelong love of Bombay Sapphire Gin. If Robert could do it, I concluded, so could I. The name Hyslop and bestselling author was destined to be uttered in literary circles around the world. I was perplexed, however, by Mr. Ludlum's punishing regimen. How on earth could he be up writing at five am, as he claimed he did every morning, after consuming so much gin?

Nevertheless, his example offered me hope and inspiration, and since that meeting in the summer of 1986, I have become a prodigious consumer of gin, but alas, that first bestseller eludes me. Still, I endure the chorus from well-meaning family, friends and casual acquaintances, "Ian, you have to write a book!"

Little do they know I have started one or two, only to watch them fizzle out, interrupted by a punishing travel, golf, and drinking regime over my retirement years, and of course the odd bout of writer's block. Leading the chorus has been my beloved wife, Rhonda Margaret Rose Stewart Barnett, whom I often refer to as Lady Barnett because of her regal disposition and imperious demeanor. She is my rock and greatest supporter. She thinks I am quite brilliant on occasion, but seriously lazy.

While in one breath, she urges me to write a contemporary classic, she is also busy organizing the next overseas jaunt, somehow failing to understand this may keep me away from the writing desk. That's my excuse anyway. She would prefer my company on long ocean cruises, where I am once again bombarded by fellow travellers with that now famous phrase, "Oh Ian, you must write a book!"

So, I now find myself poised at a battered laptop, marshalling my thoughts and 'girding my loins' in anticipation of writing and hopefully completing the above-mentioned book. Remember my warning – writing is not easy! Neither is 'girding one's loins'.

For years, I have regarded with mild disdain so-called celebrities and public figures who write books about their fascinating lives, only to bore the living bejesus out of us. A lifetime in journalism has qualified me for little, but endowed me with a liberal sprinkling of cynicism. I find it embarrassing to think that years in front of a television camera or decades in public life should provide an automatic entree to a publishing house. Do we need to read the inane ramblings and allegedly hilarious anecdotes of celebrities, politicians, and jumped-up journalists intent on giving us a running commentary on their terribly interesting lives?

Now, about this book I'm writing. The inane ramblings of an old journo intent on leaving a record of his fascinating life to children most likely not interested, and a wife happy to finance a print run of millions, to distribute to friends, family and anyone who'll read it. Yes, it is the lazy way out. No complex storyline, fascinating plot, or intriguing use of fictional characters that will take the reader on a journey of discovery into the wonderful world of literature. In other words, the safe option! Read on McDuff!

CHAPTER 2
WHERE TO BEGIN?

In the grand and often disreputable universe of journalism, it was almost preordained that I, a curious concoction of Welsh and Australian parentage, would find my footing.

Born to a diminutive Welsh lass, Hester Eileen Hodder, and an Aussie bloke, Gordon Alexander Hyslop, it was nearly a cosmic certainty that their sole male offspring would sidestep the humdrum world of so-called 'normal professions'.

My destiny, it seemed, was a thrilling career that would involve skirting the edges of societal norms, poking fun at those who chose respectable and proper paths, like medicine, law or finance. My genetic cocktail was a fascinating brew, not unlike that of countless other Australians with ancestry scattered across the globe.

I must tip my hat, or rather, wag my finger, at my dear Mother for introducing the influential Welsh element to our little family. It would play a significant role in shaping her son's character, a son who shared the womb with sister, Diane. She ended up with more of her father's progeny.

Being a twin had a profound impact on the man I would become. Arriving on the planet twenty minutes after my sister, I was labelled either a gentleman or a lazy little bugger, depending on one's perspective.

The Hyslop twins, Diane Elizabeth and Ian Phillip, were born on 8th February, 1953, in the posh Sydney suburb of Cremorne. However, my parents were not residing in one of the luxurious harbour-side mansions. They lived in a private boarding house, after returning from Singapore, where my Father had worked as an aircraft engineer for Qantas.

Eileen Hodder had arrived in Singapore not long after the end of the war, as a young Women's Auxiliary Air Force (WAAF) volunteer. She came to help rebuild the shattered city, and brought with her bucket loads of wanderlust, and a keen appetite for adventure.

Years earlier, as war raged in Europe, she was forced to leave school and start work. Just weeks after her sixteenth birthday, she became the personal assistant to the boss of a munitions factory not far from the family home in Abersychan, South Wales. It was a prime target for German bombers, intent on diminishing Britain's firepower.

It was in that factory she took up the life-long habit of smoking. "Didn't know when it would be your last ciggy," she told me. "It was very tense; every time the siren wailed, the thought of all those bombs was beyond frightening. You grew up very quickly during wartime."

In Singapore, she carried out clerical duties by day, and at night was the featured lead in musical productions, to entertain the military and expatriates working to get the British colony back on its feet. The striking brunette with the wonderful, lilting Welsh soprano voice had no shortage of suitors competing for her charms. Gordon Hyslop was acutely aware of this, telling me years later, "There was one bloke, a Royal Air Force pilot I really had to watch. Bastard looked like a movie star and had the inside running."

Gordon rarely had the inside running, but grit and determination were character traits well suited in the contest for the woman he would one day marry. The year was 1947, and he was still recovering from malaria, contracted during his wartime service in New Guinea and Bougainville.

His main adversary in the battle for the affections of my soon-to-be Mother, the good-looking pilot, roused a special kind of resentment in the aircraft engineer, as Gordon had failed flying school due to colour blindness. He surely must have felt inferior to the boys who got a chance to take to the skies.

Such was his desire to become a pilot before the war, the story goes, he would 'shovel shit' in horse stables in Ashfield, an inner Sydney suburb, so he could earn money for flying lessons. He would cycle the twenty-kilometre round-trip to the airport to learn to fly in a flimsy Tiger Moth, and flew solo after only 5 hours training! That persistence would later come to the fore, as he competed for the attentions of the much sought-after Welsh bombshell who had so captivated him.

Their backgrounds could not have been more different; he, the product of a loveless union, that ended in divorce as the world entered the roaring 20s; she, from the warm bosom of a large, 'well to do' family from the Welsh valleys.

Gordon grew up in the Sydney home of his grandparents, strict disciplinarians who constantly reminded him of how lucky he was to be embraced by family. His two younger brothers had been placed in foster care after their mother ran off with her lover. He rarely spoke of his early years or his parents, but it was clear he was the product of a dysfunctional family life, that influenced his ability to be demonstrative with his own children. No doubt he loved us, but hugs and kisses were not generously handed out. He had no such problem, however, with the woman he married. He was besotted from the start. He knew he would have to work hard, or his confident, strong-minded bride would return to her family, who were eager to welcome her back to their version of 'God's country'. In post-war Wales, little was known of Australia. When news reached them that 'their Eileen' had taken up with an Australian there were rumblings, and genuine concern that she'd lost her senses. Was he an aboriginal they all asked; could he speak English?

'Working class' was the term used when referring to my Father's upbringing. It was a struggle from the start. His grandfather was showing the first signs of senility, sitting in the back yard of their small house in Rose Street, Ashfield, killing ants with a stick. His grandmother struggled with the job of raising a young boy, having already brought up twelve children of her own! He experienced the privations of the great depression and endured life in a loveless household. His family history was a 'closed door'. However, my better half, Rhonda (family history buff extraordinaire) pried it wide open to discover convicts from the First and Second Fleets on both sides of his family. Despite the fact that the First Fleeter, Mary Davies ended up Housekeeper at Government House in Parramatta, the guilty past would, in the early 1900s, have been considered shocking and kept firmly locked in the cupboard!

My Father left school at the age of fourteen to work as a bicycle messenger in Sydney's CBD, and later as a factory hand in the old AWA electronics plant. His prospects were not good. In many respects, the war did him a favour!

He joined the Royal Australian Air Force in November 1940, not long after the outbreak of World War 2, and just a month before his 21st birthday. Knowing his dream to be a pilot was just that, he signed on anyway, and was drafted into the construction of airstrips in the jungles of New Guinea and Bougainville.

It was there he also worked on aircraft engines, securing an occupation for the future.

My Father was a man of few words, in stark contrast to the eloquence of his bride. He never talked about the war, but one story did emerge on Anzac Day sometime in the 1960s. I was in primary school, and had long wondered what had caused a deep, ugly scar on his back.

Lubricated by a few beers, he launched into a story that stunned his wide-eyed young son. For a man who was not good with words, he painted a highly colourful story of hand-to-hand combat with the enemy, in the jungles of New Guinea.

"And that's when the little Jap stabbed me in the back with a bayonet", he said, grimacing with long remembered pain.

From that day on, I looked at my Father through changed eyes. He was a war hero! 'Still waters run deep', I remember thinking. For weeks, the story of Hyslop's 'Hero Father' did the rounds of the school. I swaggered around the playground with newfound confidence.

Time and again, I tried to draw my Father out for more detail on his near-death war experience, but he clammed up and would say no more. I judged his reticence to talk about it as the mark of a humble man, not wanting to 'big note' himself.

It must have been ten years later that the truth finally came out! That deep, ugly scar was caused by the removal of a large cyst from his back. I can't remember who laughed louder when the story unravelled, my Mother or Father. I learnt a valuable lesson from that epic war story: the power of storytelling, even if it is bullshit! Stories can change the way we look at life. The seed was planted! I wanted to be a storyteller, a bullshitter, a journalist!

CHAPTER 3
COCONUTS AND KINGS

They say travel broadens the mind, and if that's true, by my mid-teens I should have been a genius!

The Hyslop family was constantly on the move. The Qantas aircraft engineer worked on 'Super Constellations', the distinctive three-tailed aircraft that carried the 'Flying Kangaroo' to Europe, the United States and Asia. It also flew to Africa, and to get there the 'old Connie' had to refuel on Cocos Island, a fourteen square kilometre speck in the middle of the Indian Ocean.

When, in 1955, my Dad was asked to take his skills there, a more remote place on earth was hard to find. His Welsh wife was aghast at the thought of doing a 'Robinson Crusoe' with 2-year-old twins, on an island of which she knew nothing. But of course, she acquiesced, and found herself a world away from the rolling green valleys of her native Wales.

The remote posting followed almost eighteen months in Darwin, the wild frontier town on the top end of Australia. Hundred plus degree temperatures, and oppressive humidity tested her will to 'press on' and dedication to the role of Mother. She was not sad to leave. Little did she know what was in store for her in the middle of nowhere!

The Cocos Keeling Islands were the personal fiefdom of the Clunies-Ross clan, who first settled there in 1827 after their Scottish sea captain ancestor surveyed the islands and decided to stay. Five generations called themselves King, and ruled the tiny island group and the small native population for nearly one hundred and fifty years. In 1836, the *HMAS Beagle* with noted naturalist Charles Darwin onboard, dropped anchor and it was here he studied and wrote scientific journals about the formation of coral atolls.

In post WW2 years, a handful of Qantas and Civil Aviation personnel, mostly single men, had the pleasure of calling it home, before Australia took over the Islands as a special territory in 1955.

Gordon and Eileen, or 'Lyn' as he called her, settled into an idyllic lifestyle on the sun-soaked islands about halfway between Western Australia and Sri Lanka. The hair of their small twins was soon burnished a deep gold, from hours of play on the beach under a hot sun.

The fortnightly visits of the big Super Constellation inconveniently disturbed the engineer's daily ritual of fishing, drinking beer and spending time with his family. It was a close-knit group of workers, and like most expatriates in isolated communities, they found little difficulty in enjoying an active social life.

The Welsh soprano took on the role of chief entertainment officer, her experience on stage a crucial qualification in leading the 'sing-songs' and bringing a little class to social occasions.

The King of Cocos Island, John Clunies-Ross, was thrilled to have another Celt 'at court'. It was a welcome break from listening to the nasally twang of the blokes from Australia, who he joked were 'a bloody rough lot'. Queen Daphne, originally from England, was also happy to welcome the demure, young woman of obviously good breeding to the isolated outpost. Gordon and Eileen were often invited to the King's grand home, where the charming newcomer was prevailed upon to play the piano and sing. The aircraft engineer, who had no musical skills, was happy to drink the King's beer and bathe in the glory of his wife's glowing talents.

The royal abode was named 'Oceania House' and had eight bedrooms, a ballroom, music room and grand spiral staircase. It sat on manicured gardens enclosed by a high wall; only the best for royalty. Four previous generations of the Clunies-Ross clan had enjoyed the home, built from bricks shipped from Glasgow. It was an impressive structure that stood in stark contrast to the ramshackle huts and shacks of the copra workers and expatriate employees.

On a still night, the sound of music could be heard resonating across a stretch of water to the single men's quarters near the airstrip. It reinforced the fact that the Hyslops had gained a privileged position in the social hierarchy of the tiny island group. The boys didn't mind though, as Gordon's wife was a 'real good sheila' and 'not stuck up at all', despite her ties to the 'old country'.

It was on Cocos Island that a noteworthy incident happened that would be talked about for years. As it concerned me, I feel a special pride in recounting the colourful tale.

As I was only 2 years old at the time, my memory of the incident is somewhat hazy, however my Mother swore by her account, and so I have adopted it, and feel confident of its factual content.

The two atolls and twenty-seven coral islands that make up the Cocos-Keeling group have long been the breeding ground of crabs, millions of them. So profuse are they, that documentaries have been filmed detailing the life cycles of a wide variety of species. They include the purple land crab, red hermit crab, horn-eyed ghost crab, and one lot called, appropriately, the huge robber crab, nicknamed 'The Prince of Thieves'!

I was apparently fascinated by these multi-legged critters and became quite the explorer. As we spent most days on the beach, unencumbered by swimwear, the opportunities for naked exploration were endless and I apparently wandered around under the watchful eye of my Mother, to my heart's content.

The free-range roving, however, ended one day after she spotted me running down the beach crying hysterically, a crab clinging firmly to my little penis. As the story goes, I had been observed before this painful episode, thrusting my willy into crab holes. Speculation as to why I indulged myself in this curious pastime flourished over the years; practicing for the big world and its endless possibilities was my later defense.

The incident gave me the excuse of telling future love interests that I had lost a couple of inches, snipped off in an unfortunate childhood accident!

I told the story unashamedly into my teens and early twenties hoping to pique the interest of girls wanting to take a look, and try it out. The crude ploy worked from time to time.

It also honed my story telling ability. I figured if I was to be a journalist when I started work, I'd have to be a prodigious bullshitter. The accumulation of stories and anecdotes was an inevitable by-product of the Hyslop family wanderings through those early years.

My Mother, or the 'Welsh Witch' as she became known, was a tremendous influence in my life. She spoke with what my friends described as a 'plum in her mouth'. It was a lovely, lilting, Welsh accent not generally encountered in Australia in the 50s and 60s. It was 'proper Queen's English' and she continued speaking it, stubbornly refusing to succumb to the terrible Aussie accent spoken by the much of the population. Her eloquence and well-mannered ways made her a target for some, but she didn't care. She was from Wales and proud of it!

Sitting on a beach in the middle of the Indian Ocean, a long way from family and friends, she must surely have wondered where it all went wrong. Having to stop her son thrusting his penis down crab holes must also have given her pause about the Australian genes pulsing through his tiny body.

It was a rude introduction to the ways of the world. She wanted to travel and got her wish, but Cocos Island, really!

Home for the Hyslop family was a timber shack not far from the beach, surrounded by louvered windows and verandahs, which allowed gentle ocean breezes to take the edge off swelteringly hot days. They also permitted the odd intrusion of cyclone winds, whipped up over the sea and flung at the fragile buildings, constructed with little regard to building codes.

Eileen was soon to experience the ruthless power of nature. A fast-moving storm cell with cyclone-force winds lashed the island chain creating a storm surge that sent ankle-deep water into the house and blew out windows.

The island on which they lived was only three metres above sea level, and the water on a sunny day was a short walk from their doorstep. It was a frightening introduction to life in paradise, made worse by the fact that she had to deal with it on her own. Gordon was hunkered down at the airport, prevented in the worst of the storm from coming to his family's rescue. When he eventually arrived home, he found his excited children floating paper boats through the house, while a tired and emotional Mum was looking at the Qantas schedule for the next flight out.

It was in the quickly repaired house the couple went on to share the challenging parenting duties. When he was not at the airport awaiting the arrival of the Qantas 'Connie', Gordon tried hard to make his bride's life easier. He had plenty of time. Conscious of the massive readjustment she was undergoing, he organised a surprise, to lift her flagging spirits. It took six barefooted workmates several hours to transport the piano from a barge at the water's edge, over hot sands into the house.

Their reward was a generous flow of beer and a stirring rendition of the latest show tunes. The party went long into the night. The young, Welsh Mother was happy, well happier.

But life was not easy feeding and nurturing two active young kids, and coping with their never-ending demands. Nor was it easy for the man of the house, who had little experience of children or siblings throughout his dysfunctional early family life. Gordon was ill equipped to deal with these strange new circumstances, though he tried hard. Never more so than when entrusted to look after the kids, when his wife went off to visit the King and Queen of Cocos, for what had become regular afternoon teas.

The twins had been put to bed before Eileen left. It was her husband's job to make sure no accident befell them in her absence. He took the job seriously, and so when the first screams were heard, he rushed into their room, to be confronted with perhaps the most shocking sight in his 36 years of life.

There, sitting in her cot was Diane, her face, arms and body smeared in human excrement. Across the room in the other cot was brother, Ian also patterned in poo, and painting the walls in broad hand strokes, creating a stunning brown artwork. On the floor between them was enough excrement to suggest the presence of a couple of large bulls, clear evidence of a heated battle between the twins.

The story was recounted many times over the years, with Gordon reminding his children that they were full of shit!

When he did work at the seldom-visited Cocos Island International Airport, the hours could be long and exhausting. This was the early days of aviation. The huge propeller-powered engines of the Super Constellation were not as reliable as the jet engines that would soon replace them. It was not uncommon for him to pull an 'all-nighter'. Passengers were offloaded and accommodated in the sparse and rudimentary housing on the island, while he and his colleagues worked on the mechanical problem.

He formed a strong bond with the pilots and crew of these aircraft, and felt an exaggerated sense of responsibility in making sure they crossed the huge expanse of ocean safely. At the time, the flight leg between Cocos Island and Mauritius was the longest in the world without an alternative emergency landing strip.

The Super Constellation carried a navigator whose job it was to locate the tiny speck of Cocos Island in the middle of the Indian Ocean, no mean feat of airmanship and navigation.

My Father may have been denied his dream of becoming a pilot, but he had no doubt that he would make a thorough and conscientious engineer. This noble aspiration was threatened not long into his posting. He had worked on a mechanical problem long into the night, before giving the pilots the all-clear to depart.

But as the huge engines roared into action, and the plane began taxiing out to the only runway, the young engineer's stomach churned and he was gripped by an overwhelming sense of panic.

He jumped into an old jeep and sped after the aircraft to flag it down before take-off. With a crooked smile and a sweating brow, he asked the pilots to wait while he retrieved a couple of tools he remembered leaving in a wheel well.

It may not have affected the flight of the aircraft, but Gordon Hyslop had no wish to have the incident reported in an engineer's logbook in Mauritius or Johannesburg.

Though flights into Cocos were infrequent, one arrival aroused more than a little nervousness in the small group of Qantas workers. As part of a world tour, French leader, Charles de Gaulle flew in for a visit in 1956, and they were on hand to service his personal Douglas C-54.

The tall, arrogant Frenchman was feted by the Australian government and the King and Queen of Cocos. They organised a reception to which my Mother was invited, confirmation that she was now part of a select few, deemed sufficiently sophisticated and well-mannered to meet visiting dignitaries.

Her 'grease monkey' husband, however, received no such invitation, though he maintained he had more important things to do; making sure the Big Frog's aircraft could fly out of the place, just one.

There was deep suspicion surrounding the President's visit. A nuclear power, it was no secret France was looking for remote areas to test its bombs. The Clunies-Ross clan made it very clear that they were vehemently opposed to having any part of their kingdom turned into a bomb site!

Ten years later France would stage dozens of atomic explosions on isolated islands in the Pacific Ocean – nowhere near the Cocos Islands.

Engineer Hyslop was happy to see the back of the big Frenchman. The next day he celebrated by going fishing – just one bonus of working and playing in the tropical paradise. The message went out early in the morning; the sharks are running!

Visitors to the isolated island group were generally limited to passengers on the Qantas and South African Airways flights that landed for refuelling, and in some cases forced by mechanical problems to stay over. One notable and most welcome visitor was Sir Edmund Hillary who, three years earlier, was the first man to climb Mount Everest. He was an honoured guest in the single men's bar, and was asked to pose for a photograph next to a sign on which Cocos Island's altitude was posted. A man familiar with heights, the towering adventurer smiled broadly, as he stood a full 10 feet above sea level.

Another surprise visitor left a lasting impression. He was one of a group of passengers invited to go fishing by Qantas staff, after their aircraft, en route from Johannesburg to Perth, was delayed. After a fine day of swimming, sun bathing and fishing in the sparkling waters off Cocos, the man, who spoke with a broad South African accent, bid his hosts a fond farewell. However, it was not the last they would hear from him.

Months later, a large wooden crate arrived containing a wide range of fishing rods, tackle and assorted gear worth hundreds of pounds; "Thanks for the great day" read the note. It was signed by the grateful South African, who, they later found out, owned one of the biggest diamond mines in Pretoria and was a multi-millionaire.

Sadly, my Mother, a staunch monarchist (hence the twins middle names), had missed Queen Elizabeth's visit in 1954, shortly before their stay in the tropical paradise.

The arrival of the fortnightly service from Sydney and Perth was always much anticipated by the workers and especially my Mother, who was desperate for news of her Welsh family. The big 'Connie' carried the mailbag, and was her only link to the outside world. Most necessities were shipped in from Singapore, including beer supplies, an indispensable staple for the thirsty expatriate workers, who one day drank the island dry!

It was a crisis long remembered by my Father, but it was how the problem was solved that was perhaps more memorable. Tipped off that a Royal Navy destroyer was soon to visit Cocos from its base in Singapore, the call went out. The island was dry!

Two weeks later the Navy obliged, and beer supplies were replenished, considerably more, in fact, than was normally shipped on the small trading vessel that made its monthly visit. It was good news for Qantas employees, but not so for a young sailor who was caught sampling the amber fluid. When the ship anchored, he was confined to the brig.

After the mail deliveries, my Mother would sit in a rattan chair on the veranda of their small house, cigarette in hand, reading the latest gossip from Wales. There was no shortage of it, as she had two sisters, three brothers and a vast network of friends up and down the Welsh Valleys. Sister Elsie was married to a big rugby player from Griffithstown, Jack Bryant and was Mum to Pamela. Jeanne had tied the knot with a cocky little engineer, Graham White, and was also a Mum to girls, Lynne and Trish. Meanwhile her youngest sibling, Phil, the cheeky little devil who she had spent much of her teenage years looking after, had so far, kept out of trouble.

You could take the girl out of Wales but not Wales out of the girl. Many a tear, I suspect, was shed on the front veranda of that little shack on Cocos Island. All this family business was foreign to Gordon. He lived vicariously through my Mother's stories and, a while later, met and formed a strong bond with his Welsh in-laws.

Her siblings must surely have wondered what on earth their sister had gotten herself into, marrying an Australian who had selfishly spirited her off to some god-forsaken island in the middle of nowhere.

Her letters to them would paint an impossibly colourful picture, romantic visions of swaying palm trees, nut-brown natives and sparkling tropical lagoons. It was a far cry from the damp, dark winters of Wales.

"I hope our Eileen is alright," they would whisper at family gatherings, "those Australians are a strange lot."

They were a strange lot, but Eileen soon found a generosity of spirit, and an outrageous sense of fun that made the Cocos experience more than bearable. She became mother-confessor to a number of the single men, who were a valuable asset in helping entertain the hyperactive twins and an enthusiastic audience when she played the piano and sang at social gatherings. They would tell Gordon he had a 'bonza' wife and were careful to be perfect gentlemen in her company.

No doubt my Father kept a close eye on them. After all, he was one of the only men on Cocos who reaped the benefits of married life. It was not difficult to identify a sense of longing in their eyes.

The friendships forged in those years in the tropical paradise would last a lifetime, and provide more than a few hilarious stories to be recounted over a drink well into the future.

There was a colourful cast of characters on the Island, including the doctor who liked a tipple and became firm friends with Eileen. Doctor Goodly was his name, but an angel he was not. Gordon's gin was his drink of choice, and most surgical procedures were undertaken with the assistance of a few nips to steady the hand.

A young cook, Jimmy Parker, found this out after he sliced off a finger while chopping up ingredients for the evening meal.

An inebriated Parker was later heard in the single man's bar tearfully telling mates, "That bloody drunk, Goodly sewed me finger back on crooked."

"At least it's not on back to front!" reportedly shot back one wit in the crowd.

No doubt aware of the doctor's proclivities my Mother was, nonetheless, comforted by the fact that medical treatment was on hand for the children if needed. He lived on Home Island, one of only three habitable land masses in the group, and would have to clamor aboard a small boat to visit patients on nearby West and Direction Islands. With a few gins 'on board' that was not always easy, and fraught with potential calamities.

His nurse became a prime target for the single men, who suffered from a common condition known as 'sexual starvation'. There was much consternation among the Aussies when she favoured a Royal Marine, who was stationed on the island with a group of British nationals. Although an Australian herself, she apparently viewed many of her fellow countrymen with contempt; overheard on occasions complaining they were a 'bloody uncouth bunch'.

Few of the 'larrikins in residence' would deny the claim.

On one occasion, the good doctor was summoned to the Hyslop household by my Mother, who found her son and another small child in the kitchen, scuttling about in search of the huge winged cockroaches that flourished on the island.

The neighbour's little boy had developed a voracious appetite for the bugs and would swallow them whole. Her son was guilty by association, and even though she had not seen him eat one of the filthy critters, she was taking no chances.

It later emerged that her son's little mate had been doing this for ages with no apparent ill effects. His mother had been unable to break him of the unpalatable habit of devouring the loathsome bugs. The crunchy cockroach story was added to a long list of 'believe it or not' tales in the Hyslop household.

Medical advice was also sought for Gordon, after he broke a toe chasing his offspring around the house. The twins had developed a devious strategy, in their never-ending quest to mess with their Father's head. After committing a punishable offense, they would run in different directions and lay in wait to slam the door when his face loomed large. The inexperienced Father's toe paid the price of Ian's torment, a condition the doctor could not treat.

An ever-present danger on the islands throughout the Cocos-Keeling group were coconuts. Contrary to common belief, the nut-laden trees were not native to the windswept islands. Soon after deciding to settle, Clunies-Ross had planted hundreds of coconut palms, and brought in Malay workers to harvest the nuts and produce copra; their job title was 'nutter'. The King of Cocos was a savvy businessman, but to critics he was almost a slave trader; a claim subsequent generations of the family vigorously rejected.

It was with Queen Victoria's blessing in 1886, that the Clunies-Ross benign, if eccentric dictatorship was established. One early 1900s report described the Scotsman's unconventional rule as follows: "There are no police, no crimes, no trade unions and no strikes. Mr Clunies-Ross is king, doctor, parson, magistrate and merchant all rolled into one. The friendliness, well-being and content of his subjects afford a lesson to many more enlightened kingdoms."

The King's copra plantation prospered, but when the winds blew, so too did the coconuts; air-born missiles quite capable of causing death and serious injury. For newcomers, particularly the uninitiated Australian airline workers, who thought the trees were charming, the warning was ever-present. Keep an eye on the sky!

Eileen did, to the point she walked around with a permanent crick in her neck. All she needed was for news to get back to Wales that she or 'one of hers' had been killed by a flying coconut – not the most dignified demise! Thankfully, the Hyslop family escaped injury.

Dangers were ever present around the tiny islands, on land and in the sea. Favourite pastimes and the main activities available to residents were fishing and swimming. The bounty was rich, a huge variety of seafood available for the taking – and they took it. At sunset, the gentle breezes carried the tantalizing aroma of frying fish or boiling crabs, lobsters and prawns that became the staple diet. Imported beef was a rare treat indeed. The Malay workers' predilection for curry powder also carried on the wind, and provided an enticing culinary experience for many a palate.

One of Gordon's preferred dishes was shark steak. He and his mates would take to the waters most days hunting tiger sharks that were plentiful offshore, and in the glassy lagoons popular with swimmers. The sight of my Father catching a thrashing shark and tying it to a small wooden boat was common!

A popular fishing area was not far from the wreck site of the German cruiser, Emden sunk by the *HMAS Sydney* in 1914. The enemy ship had steamed to the island to destroy radio equipment set up by the British. It was a considerable 'feather in the cap' of the Australian Navy. One hundred and thirty-three German sailors died in the battle, many consumed by the sharks that swam in big numbers around the area. Decades later, the area would attract the boys from Qantas, eager for a bit of sport and a good feed.

The resident doctor was kept busy sewing up hook wounds and nasty gashes, inflicted by the jagged teeth of these large, dangerous predators.

It was around this time that Eileen became very careful about taking photos of her husband. His skin had been burnished the colour of dark teak, and if seen by relatives back in Wales would only confirm their fear that she had run off and married a native.

The lack of things to do, and places to go on the tiny landmass necessitated particularly creative and inventive minds. Stir craziness was a common malady among the young workers who, because of language differences, seldom mixed with the small Malay population. Followers of Islam, they were loath to join the hard-drinking Australians. The king also actively discouraged social intercourse between the groups. They were his subjects and he didn't need any of them corrupted by the larrikin Aussies.

As unofficial entertainment director, Eileen threw parties and staged musicals to relieve the boredom. The distinct lack of women on Cocos meant that single men were drafted into female roles, a sight and sound that caused much hilarity. A rough, bushy beard looked singularly unattractive on a costumed 'young lass', and the odd bulge in the wrong anatomical position also caused a stir. A firm favourite on the entertainment schedule was the all-male revue, 'The Queen of May', which found participants seeking out copious quantities of alcohol before donning girly costumes.

Their Royal Highnesses, the King and Queen, made regular appearances at these productions, and my Mother's standing in the small community grew with each song she sang, and each laugh her ingenuity provoked. This is what you did in isolated outposts, and it made for unforgettable memories and great fun.

It was a sad day when the Scottish rulers of the tiny fiefdom said goodbye to the Welsh wench and her young family.

Eileen's stint of being a 'beach bum' on one of the smallest inhabited islands in the world had come to an end, after just over two years. Her children were growing and would soon be ready for school. The engineer's skills were required elsewhere.

The Hyslop family's nomadic lifestyle was about to take another turn that involved more travel, and more stories to be stored away by a young son who would one day become a journalist.

CHAPTER 4
ON THE ROAD AGAIN

Australia's population in 1957 was nudging 10 million when the Hyslop family returned from their Indian Ocean exodus. Sir Robert Menzies was the liberal party Prime Minister and pounds, schillings and pence was still the legal tender.

Television broadcasting had started just months earlier, and Australians were transfixed by this exciting new form of entertainment. Little did Lyn and Gordon know, the medium would play a major part in their son's future.

Beer drinkers were prohibited from imbibing in hotels past 6 pm, and a loaf of bread cost one shilling. Danish architect Jørn Utzon had just won the design competition for the Sydney Opera House, and Australian country singer Slim Dusty picked up his first gold record for the iconic hit song, "A Pub with No Beer".

The basic wage was around fifteen pounds a week and Qantas engineer, Gordon Hyslop returned to accept not much more than that.

The lazy days of sunbathing, fishing and occasionally working on an aircraft were soon forgotten, as the family settled back into life in the 'big smoke'. First purchase was new clothing for the twins. Their days of naked beach romps were over, an attempt to educate them looming.

After almost four years of living in two of the most isolated places on earth, Eileen was back in civilized surroundings. Sydney boasted fashionable dress standards, temperate weather and a ready supply of potential female friends, denied her in the male-dominated Qantas outposts.

Gordon's employer was on the cusp of rapid expansion. The third oldest airline in the world, formed in 1920, it linked the isolated continent with the rest of the world, and had ambitious plans for expansion.

He had watched the fledgling airline's development in the late 1930s. It was the old Empire flying boats that took off from the waters of Rose Bay, bound for Singapore, which had first ignited his desire to become a pilot.

As an engineer in the late 1950s, he would work on the fleet of sixteen Super Constellations, which carried the 'privileged few' to the United States, Asia and Europe.

However, the jet age was soon ushered in, and the days of the old propeller-driven workhorses nearing an end. That day came in 1959, when the first Boeing 707 jet was introduced into service, sealing the fate of the airline's propeller-driven planes, which finally left service in 1963.

This development directly impacted my Father, as it meant he would have to upgrade his engineering qualifications, transiting from propellers to jet engines. For my Mother it would lead to an extended separation from her husband. He was one of a group of engineers chosen to fly to the Boeing factory in Seattle, to obtain licenses required to work on the new jets.

It was just one more test for the diminutive Welsh woman who had few friends in Sydney, and two children who were a handful at the best of times. But her hardship stints in Singapore, Darwin and Cocos Island had toughened and shaped her strong sense of independence. That didn't, however, rid her of the lingering thought of how much easier motherhood would have been closer to a loving family in Wales.

That thought translated into action, and she was soon able to show off the twins to an eager Welsh clan, who had not seen their daughter, sister, cousin and friend for more than ten years.

As Gordon headed for the west coast of the United States, his wife and kids boarded a Super Constellation for the long flight to London. It would be a six-month separation and the twins' first meeting with the colourful branch of the Welsh family.

It would also be the start of a life-long love of travel, and a decisive factor in my decision to become a journalist.

In the late fifties, international air travel was only for the privileged few. The cost of a return ticket from Sydney to London on the Kangaroo route was 585 pounds, equivalent to thirty weeks average pay at the time. Staff rates, of course, were considerably cheaper, and I was forever thankful for my Father's employment with Qantas, as it afforded me amazing travel opportunities.

Flight time to London was nearly sixty-four hours, and exotic transit destinations included Singapore, Karachi, Cairo and Tehran.

It was the early era of international aviation. Qantas was a very different beast. Small staff numbers made the airline a family affair. When the word went out that Gordon Hyslop's 'mob' was on board, the welcome was warm and friendly. There were eleven crew to look after twenty-nine 'all first class' passengers on the Super Constellation.

Travelling with two four-year-old children was never going to be easy, but that first long distance flight to London would test my Mother's ability to keep it together, and resist the urge to kill her offspring.

If it were not for the kindness and support of the Qantas flight stewards and stewardesses (as they were called in those days), she would most likely have ended up on charges.

They played hide and seek with the children for hours in a less than full aircraft, and set new standards in going above and beyond the call of duty.

Cockpit security was virtually non-existent in the early years, and I have vivid memories of being taken up to meet the captain. It was in the dead of night, and thousands of feet below, snow-capped Mount Ararat, in Turkey was eerily illuminated by a full moon. It was an image that has stayed with me to this day; just one of the many I have been lucky enough to see in my travels. The impact of exotic overseas destinations on a young mind cannot be overestimated.

A delay in Singapore had the Super Constellation arriving in London almost seventy-five hours after leaving Australia! It was a marathon, and more than three times what it takes an Airbus 380 to fly the Sydney/London route today.

They may have been the early, glamorous years of air travel, but the elite passengers inevitably emerged from the aircraft looking and feeling like they had been put through a meat grinder.

I remember as a 13-year-old on a subsequent trip, sitting in an oppressively humid airport in Tehran waiting to board the aircraft to London, when I first thought of becoming a journalist. It must have finally dawned on me that I was close to retarded in the academic areas of science and mathematics, and far more suited to a vocation in humanities.

The incident sowed the seed, and from that day, in answer to many adult questions about what I was going to do when I grew up, I was emphatic; having no idea, of course, how I would realise the goal, but there it was, and it would be achieved!

London is considerably colder than Darwin and the Cocos Islands, where swimsuits and short pants were de rigueur, but the welcome could not have been warmer. Nanny Hodder, the substantially built and highly intelligent mother of a brood of six, was the first to fly into the arms of her adventurous eldest daughter.

It had been over ten years since they last saw each other, an eternity for the Welsh, for whom travel apparently held little appeal. Eileen was the first and only one to leave the nest, and her disappearance all those years ago remained a mystery to many. Her brothers Tom, Brian, Philip and sisters, Elsie and Jeanne had all stayed close to home. The concept of someone leaving Wales to live elsewhere was difficult for the locals to comprehend: 'Why would you leave God's country', a common question?

To 4-year-old twins exposed to the warm embrace of extended family for the first time, the experience was overwhelming, along with the musical lilt of Welsh accents, so different to the sound of Australia.

"C'mon on then boyo, come to your Uncle Phil!" "No bloody kangaroos here, son, plenty of pit ponies, though!"

The jokes, the laughter, the seemingly never-ending parade of uncles, aunts, cousins and neighbours flooded into my Grandmother's house in Hanbury Road, Abersychan. They all wanted to take a 'sticky' at the little kids from Australia, who spoke English with a funny accent.

It would be the first of many visits to Wales through the 1970s and 80s, thanks to the Qantas staff discount extended to the Hyslop family.

The 4-storey row house was set among dozens of others, nestled into the contours of the valleys for which South Wales was renowned. It was always full of noise and frenetic activity, and the ever-present scent of burning coal. The front part of the house, close to the road, served as a butcher shop, run by my Grandmother. The dull thud of meat being whacked on the chopping block, and the banter of customers chatting resonated throughout the property. The family also operated a thriving stall in nearby Pontypool Market, which my uncle and aunt ran with great success.

It was in the cellar of this old home that I would be introduced to some of the great mysteries of life, particularly the darkened coal chute where I was to discover the 'tooth fairy'.

Uncle Phil, always the joker, was my chief tormentor and best mate. After losing my front tooth during one visit, he was there to proffer advice.

"In there, son, in you go, she always leaves the money in a small tin buried under the coal." I had been instructed to leave my recently unhinged tooth in a tin the night before.

Terrified, my eyes squinting in the dark, and armed with a small shovel and torch, I attacked the pile of coal with an energy fueled equally by fear and greed.

Besides the noise of my digging, I could hear muffled laughter outside the coal chute, no doubt an uncle highly amused by his nephew's fevered exertions.

The sound of shovel hitting tin was followed by a jubilant shout. It signaled the end of the frantic search. For my efforts, the tooth fairy rewarded me fifty pence, no small amount in those days!

However, the cellar of the Hanbury Road house would be remembered for more than fairies. It also housed the huge refrigerator in which haunches of beef were hung, along with up to a dozen pigs and lambs, some of them all the way from New Zealand.

"Bloody like wet rag," my uncle would rage, "only get it because it's cheaper than our premium Welsh lamb!"

The sight of dead animals held great fascination to a kid from Australia, who'd spent most of his short life on a beach.

It was also in the cellar that black pudding and faggots were made; favourites with many of the locals, some of whom lived in public housing and could ill afford the more expensive cuts of meat.

On my first trip to Wales, I was 'treated' to the horrific sight of my uncle pouring buckets of blood into a huge tub set in the middle of the floor.

Later visits had me roped into helping him prepare the well-known delicacy. It was my job to sit beside the tub to hold and separate the slimy pig's intestines (or strings as they were called), into which my uncle would pour blood and bread. I would tie off the strings and voilà – scrumptious blood sausage! Suffice to say, it was something I could not stomach.

It was not long after my 18th birthday, and graduation from high school in Sydney that I returned to Pontypool, and brought along a mate I'd met in London. He would soon be introduced to the ancient art of Welsh sausage making.

We arrived at the house to a warm welcome from my Grandmother who told me Uncle Phil was in the cellar, hard at work.

"C'mon down and meet him," I told my friend. "He's a wag" I warned.

On entering the sprawling work area, we were treated to the sight of him bent over the huge tub, mixing bread into the bloody mess.

Caught by surprise, he spun around to shriek a cry of welcome and dispense a bear hug that could have killed a small horse. He surveyed the young bloke standing by my side.

"Who is this then?" he enquired his eyes twinkling with mischief.

"Meet my mate, also an Ian, from Sydney," I said.

"Well, boyo, welcome to Wales," he said and with that he bent down scooped up a handful of blood, pulled out his false teeth, and took a big slurp before extending a bloody hand in welcome!

Armed by my earlier warning and a couple of stories I told him on the train coming down from London, Ian's handshake was firm, despite a nervous laugh and a barely heard expletive.

The name Phil Hodder was well known in the Pontypool area. He was a prosperous local merchant with a wicked sense of humour, and a respected name. My grandfather had been a highly decorated soldier in World War 1, who had started up several businesses in the area and bought large tracts of land. He was gassed in the 'Great War' and came home with a chest full of medals – and a fragile mind. He 'took to the drink' throughout his life; haunted, my Mother told me, by his experience in the bloody battle of the Somme. It didn't, however, affect his ability to make money, or rule with an iron fist and a leather strap when it came to disciplining his large brood. My outspoken Mother was no fan of her father's parenting style, and they often clashed; a compelling reason, I think, for her decision to leave Wales and travel. The Hodders were butchers and jewellers. They lived in a large house on the hill called 'The Oaks' and looked down on a population that predominantly worked in the coalmines, from where 'black gold' had been extracted for centuries.

My uncle would hold court in the George Hotel, adjacent to the markets where he conducted business and played cards, liberating many a mate of their hard-earned money. To his nephew from Australia he was a larger than life character, hugely charismatic and very funny. I would make the trip into the George a few times in my teens. It was in the smoke-filled bar, as a 13-year-old that I would be treated to my first pint of Black and White Lager.

"Sit here, boyo," he instructed me, "Meet me nephew from Orstralia," he would say to his group of cronies at the card table, before producing, with a flourish, a roll of bank notes you couldn't jump over with a running start.

He was an unabashed show-off, but my Mother's brother made me proud to claim Welsh heritage. He took me under his wing, but that close bond would be tested when he decided to introduce his young nephew to scrumpy cider, a potent brew dispensed in a little village pub in Pantygasseg. It was perched on top of a windswept mountain, not far from my Grandmother's home, but some distance from the prying eyes of regulators.

This would be my first and last encounter with the toxic brew that few grown men could stomach, let alone a callow youth just into his teens. The introduction was in the company of two other uncles, big men who could consume 10 pints of beer easily in one sitting. It turned out they were much more cautious around scrumpy!

One pint was enough to render my skinny young legs useless, and my senses scrambled, a condition Uncle Phil found hilarious! The wrath of my Mother on seeing her drunken son, however, provoked a 'tongue lashing' long remembered in the Hodder household. I would be reminded through the years, of the day I got pissed on scrumpy. It was just one more 'Right of Passage' story, written and orchestrated by a mischievous uncle who quickly became my best mate.

He had a big heart, as he proved when he brought home an old fellow by the name of Hayden, who had fallen on hard times and been 'sleeping rough' under a bridge. A full house required me to share a bed with the old guy on one of our visits. It was my Grandmother's job to make sure he took a bath every Saturday, a pastime it appeared he had not bothered with for years, judging by the whiff of him.

The old boy must have thought his Christmases had all come at once, as Phil would pick him up in a flashy, bright blue Jaguar and take him off to the pub for the odd outing.

"Bloody good man, your uncle," he would tell me, though I never found out why it was that Phil showed such generosity to the old man. He remained in the house and was looked after by my Grandmother for years.

While Phil had his own house a short distance away, he was always at Hanbury Road, along with a steady stream of uncles, aunts and cousins who would drop in for a catch up, before we flew back to Australia.

Used to sunshine and beaches back home, the dark, cold and snowy winters made for quite a change. Things were done differently in Wales; meal times for one. Supper was around ten o'clock at night in front of a blazing fire, with the steady sound of rain and snowflakes hitting window panes.

Food was never in short supply, especially meat prepared by either my Grandmother or Uncle, who would be on hand to cook up a feast. One dinner was particularly memorable.

"C'mon then, dig into these," he said, carrying a big platter of breaded balls.

"What are they?" I innocently inquired.

"Sweetbreads," he said, rolling a couple on to my plate.

Sweetbreads, I thought, never heard of them. The first bite dislodged the breadcrumbs to reveal a slippery, grey mass crisscrossed with what looked like blood vessels.

"What are sweetbreads?" I tentatively asked my uncle, fearing I knew the answer, but hoping he would not confirm it.

"Sheep balls," he said, "Bloody delicious, go on dig in!"

It was the first time in my life I had munched on a sheep's testicle, or any testicle for that matter, and I still remember the shocked looked on the cook's face when I told him I had no intention of consuming any more.

I was ten years old at the time, and the thought of eating an animal's genitals was just not on!

Along with my introduction to the butchering business, came a good lesson in human nature. I was assigned to ride 'shotgun' in the company delivery van with Don, aptly named, 'The Butcher Boy', who worked for my uncle. We would make the daily runs to such exotic destinations as Talywain, Trevethin, Blaenavon, Abergavenny, Pontnewynydd; small towns that housed some of the warmest and friendliest folk you could find anywhere in the world. From them I received a crash course in the Welsh sense of humour.

"Meet Phil Hodder's nephew from Australia," Don told one old bloke, "here on holidays".

"Well, then, very white for an Australian, he is. I thought they were all black down there!"

"How are you boyo, speak a bit of English, do you?"

The banter was always accompanied by a twinkle of the eye and a crooked smile, even though they really had little to smile about. The Welsh valleys at the time were in deep depression, with the region's primary industry, coal mining in decline. Maggie Thatcher was locked in battle with union boss, Arthur Scargill, who she would succeed in breaking. It spelt the end of coal mining in South Wales. Many were doing it tough, and my uncle's black pudding and faggots, which sold for pennies were a cheap weekday favourite. Roast pork, beef or lamb were a real treat, and usually reserved for the family meal on the weekend.

My 'apprenticeship' in the butchering trade also included early morning runs to the abattoir, invariably made in freezing, drizzling and one-time, blizzard like conditions. If it wasn't bad enough being forced out of bed at 4 o'clock in the morning, I then had to watch the brutal killing of a whole range of animals. To a young kid it was quite a shock!

"Don't look away son," my uncle would say, "it's all a part of the life cycle."

One image would stay with me for years. I watched as abattoir workers corralled an enormous sow into a pen over which the executioner stood on an elevated platform holding a bolt gun, which he fired into the animal's brain.

The side of the pen was swung open and the huge beast rolled out onto the wet, concrete floor covered with blood, oozing from dozens of sheep lying on nearby racks, their throats cut and bleeding out.

"Look, it's not dead," I yelled over the din of distressed animals, as the body of the enormous beast appeared to take flight, rising in jerky movements off the floor. This went on for what felt like minutes and held my rapt attention for every second.

It was explained to me that involuntary nerve spasms made it appear the huge pig was still alive, but in fact it was quite dead.

The sights and sounds I experienced in that death house in South Wales confirmed that the time-honoured trade of butchering was not for me. I simply did not have the stomach for it. Playing with words and writing seemed a much better way to make a living. Even then, I had an inkling of what I wanted to do in the future.

The butcher's shop was also not the preferred choice for my young cousin, Phil, or Pip as we called him, Uncle Philip's son. Earmarked by his father to take over the family business, he chose, in his early twenties, to go back to school and study law. To the surprise of all in the family, it turned out he had a photographic memory, passed the exams, and still practices as a highly successful barrister. It was a career change not welcomed by his father. Relations between the two were frosty for many years, until at last big Phil recognized what a remarkable achievement it was. It would not have happened at all if it wasn't for the family dog.

An argument with a neighbour over his pet ended up with an appearance in the Pontypool courthouse, where Pip got his first look at the machinations of the legal system. He represented himself in the dispute, won the case, and decided it was an occupation he would like to try. And so, the unlikely journey started; from butcher boy to barrister. Anyone who knew the strong and domineering personality of Uncle Philip Hodder, were in no doubt about what it took to defy and ultimately win the battle of wills between the two.

There were few people to whom my brash uncle would defer. My Mother was one. Family was hugely important in the small villages up and down the Welsh valleys.

It was a tribal, clannish lifestyle, so different to Australia, where the vast continent and small population often resulted in family members moving interstate for job opportunities or lifestyle change. In Wales, they lived in each other's pockets, sharing the ups and downs of life, and jealously protecting the unity and reputation of family members.

When referring to an uncle, an aunt, or cousin it was always 'our' Eileen or 'our' Brian. It is a delightful tradition, and I well remember how warm and fuzzy I felt when referred to as 'our Ian'.

To a cocky, well-travelled kid it was easy to underestimate the folk who had never left the small villages of Wales. I soon found out how stupid was the assumption that travel somehow provided one with a more informed insight into human nature. The Welsh, like their Celtic cousins in Ireland and Scotland, are a highly perceptive people, who quickly work out the myriad intrigues motivating human behaviour. They didn't need to acquire 'worldliness' and travel to New York or Sydney to work out the bloke next door was a crook, or their daughter's suitor was a no-hoper. They just knew it and took the necessary action.

Very few of my Welsh relatives had travelled by the time I met them in the 1960s, only the odd one for military service, so when my uncle Phil announced that he was flying to Washington DC, as a supporter of the local rugby team, surprise and envy were common reactions. However, the fact that he was undertaking the trip in the company of a rowdy bunch of rugby-loving mates was no surprise. The likelihood of him doing it on his own were 'slim to nil', as he'd never owned a passport, never been on an aircraft and had no experience of travelling abroad.

He was blissfully ignorant of the world away from his little patch in Wales, but he wasn't going to let that intimidate or scare him. He was a big man in town, a successful merchant and the prospect of showing the Yanks how to play rugby was irresistible.

It all went spectacularly well until the flight back home. They had won the rugby. The Americans, he informed everyone, were a delightful bunch, and much fun was had by the boys on tour.

Nevertheless, one experience shook him to the core, and would leave a permanent scar that put him off flying for years. While in the American capital, he was delighted to find some of the cheapest and best Scotch whiskey and Cuban cigars money could buy – much cheaper than back home; a bargain!

He was unrestrained in his purchases, even splashing out on a new suitcase to accommodate the haul.

After a boozy flight, the bedraggled bunch of rugby tragics filed off the aircraft, retrieved their bags and made their way to the Customs Hall, where a uniformed officer asked Phil if he had 'anything to declare'.

It was a question he had never been asked before. On seeing my uncle's look of confusion, the efficient officer directed him to open his suitcase, sparking a chain of events that left the Welsh butcher severely shaken. He was invited to a room, stripped searched and asked to account for his actions in smuggling the illegal booty into the country. It was a confronting experience with officialdom, which highlighted how little he knew about the workings of the world. He had difficulty curbing his tongue in the course of the interrogation, and was 'stuck dumb' when the customs man threatened to digitally penetrate him in the search for more contraband. This was not a common occurrence in the Welsh Valleys!!

After paying a fine of more than 200 pounds, a fortune in those days, an ashen-faced Philip Hodder made his way to the waiting coach. He was met with unsympathetic murmurings and ribald comments from his mates, forced to wait for more than three hours.

For years as he plied his trade as a butcher in the Pontypool markets, he would be approached by those familiar with the story and asked if he had any Cuban cigars for sale!

I couldn't help myself, quizzing him on his first trip to Australia many years later, if he'd declared anything coming through customs!

My uncle's connection to Welsh Rugby, the reason he'd fallen foul of British authorities, remained strong through the 1970s and 80s. The Welsh National Team was virtually unbeatable at the time, winning six Triple Crowns and dominating the international scene. He was an enthusiastic supporter, but very careful not to follow his team anywhere an overseas flight would be involved. His face would pale every time family members laughingly referred to his run-in with the customs men at Heathrow airport.

"Bloody terrible," he would tell them, "scared the shit out me!"

One of my fondest memories as a kid was when three of my uncles took me to Cardiff Arms Park to watch Wales play. I stood sandwiched between them in the packed stadium as the Welsh National Anthem was sung with a passion I have never heard matched. To this day, it still brings a tear to my eye when I hear it.

The stalwarts of rugby during this period were three forwards, who gained fame as the 'Pontypool Front Row' and played with distinction and ferocity for the national team. They were tough men, who worked in the mines and steel mills in South Wales, when rugby was an amateur sport.

The names Graham Price, Bobby Windsor and Charlie Faulkner would be forever remembered by a rugby mad nation.

As a teenager, I had the great privilege of meeting the hooker, Bobby Windsor in the toilets of the Pontypool Rugby Club. He was urinating into a washbasin at the time as the trough and stalls were busy. A legend could apparently do that, and certainly, no one was going to criticize him for the small indiscretion.

My uncle approached him and proffered the introduction. "Bobby, meet my nephew from Australia".

"Well," he said, "A little Wallaby, how are you, son?"

It was an encounter not conducive to a long conversation, as I found it hard to look him in the eyes. Years later, in 1978, I would go to the Sydney Cricket Ground to watch Wales play Australia. The home side won the match 19 to 17.

In the first minutes of the game, Wallaby front row, Steve Finnane, threw a punch that broke Graham Price's jaw. The action was widely regarded as a turning point in Australian rugby. For too long, seen as the 'easy beats' of the world game, the brutal action garnered instant respect; Graham Price later describing it as a 'bloody good punch'.

Punches also flew during one of my visits to Pontypool, and I was at the centre of the action. The year was 1966, and I was 13 years old when I returned home to my Grandmother's home covered in blood, after a street fight with one of the local boys. Fearing I had been seriously hurt, given the amount of blood on my shirt front, family members crowded around trying to find the source. It turned out to be my opponent, whose head I had repeatedly hit while secured in a headlock. This revelation was met with great enthusiasm by my uncle, happy his nephew had acquitted himself well, but my Mother and Grandmother took a rather different view.

It coincidentally turned out that the boy I had come to blows with, was the same lad with whom I'd clashed three years earlier. On that occasion, however, I had bled profusely. After another street skirmish in which insults were exchanged revolving around my Australian origins, I made the mistake of calling him a 'Pom', a grievous allegation, given his Welsh heritage. He set his large Alsatian onto me, and the resulting gash ripped just above my lip required a trip to the hospital and ten stitches. I was apparently not the only one who had history with the dog's owner.

The kid was a well-known bully from a family described by my uncle as 'lowlifes', whose reputation was well established in the small town. Times were tough. Pontypool, like many other places in the Welsh valleys, was struggling due to the turmoil between the union movement and the government. I was witness to the resultant social unrest on my many visits to South Wales, and the birthplace of my Mother has always held a special place in my heart.

CHAPTER 5
AUNTY ABC

It was the much anticipated job application I had been waiting years to write.

Australia's national broadcaster, the ABC, was the lofty target of my quest for employment, as it offered cadetships to aspiring, young journalists.

In 1973, six were up for grabs. I was just one of hundreds seeking the opportunity to work for the country's most high-profile news organization, affording arguably the most comprehensive training program in journalism.

For 6 months after matriculating from high school in Sydney, I had sold women's shoes to earn funds for a working holiday to England and Spain. Six months later, I was back, ready to embrace full-time employment in my chosen field. Problem was, who in my chosen field would offer me a job? It was another six months before I would discover whether I was destined for a career in journalism.

In the meantime, I stumbled across an opportunity that gave me a viable alternative to my preferred career path. It was in the tawdry world of advertising (almost as tawdry as journalism). I took on the role of assistant to an industry veteran recruited from an international ad agency, McCann Erickson to head up the advertising department of Prouds, a nationwide jewellery chain. It was our job to help flog wedding rings to the brides of Australia. I found myself not writing news stories, but advertising copy under the direction of a boss who showed great generosity in showing me the ropes. To a 19-year-old kid it was heady stuff.

A notable collaboration that garnered widespread industry recognition was a musical jingle we wrote, that ran for many years. "From any little thing to diamond ring," was the catchy sales pitch that brought many a loving couple into Prouds, to choose their wedding bands.

Much of my work, however, revolved around the more humdrum area of media placement, collating photographs of the vast array of jewellery stock, and writing simple copy for various publications.

It was about 3 months into the job that I saw the ABC advertisement for the next intake of cadet journalists. Little was to be lost, I thought, in applying for the opportunity. I had accidentally found my way into advertising, but the prospect of working in the serious world of journalism was much more enticing. I sent off the job application and settled in for the wait. It was a long one. Just when I had given up all hope, I received a reply asking me to report to the William Street offices of the ABC, in Sydney for an interview.

Six cadetships were on offer, four for university graduates and only two for matriculates. As I was in the latter category, I knew the competition would be fierce. My higher school certificate results were less than sparkling, barely enough to get me into university to do an Arts Degree, something I regarded as a waste of time anyway.

However, I had scored in the top one percent of English exam results in New South Wales, which I hoped would place me in good stead. The fact that I had totally ignored mathematics and science only highlighted my success in other subjects, and would hopefully be overlooked by those on the selection panel.

Academically I may have been 'behind the eight ball', but years of international travel, and growing up in four states of Australia had equipped me with ample confidence, a good grasp of general knowledge, current affairs, and a fast mouth. The fact that I had a Welsh Mother, 'hell bent' on stopping her son speaking with a broad Aussie accent would be a plus, I prayed, for the good gentlemen of the ABC. I assumed they would be intent on recruiting applicants who spoke 'proper English'.

The first step towards that goal came when, full of trepidation, I walked into the voluminous, buzzing newsroom to be introduced to the three-man panel who would decide if I had what it took to be given entrée to the wonderful world of journalism. Apparently, I did.

Weeks later, as I worked at my desk at Prouds, I answered a call from an excited Mother, informing me a letter had arrived at the family home. It was from the ABC, she said, raising the prospect that steam may have played a part in her knowledge of that fact. I would ask that question another day, but in the meantime wasted no time catching a train to the leafy North Shore to learn my fate.

It indeed contained the offer of a job, and the house erupted in great celebration. They all knew how important this news was to a son and brother who had been declaring since his early teens that he wanted to be a journalist.

The 1973 intake of cadets included Oxford University graduate, Mark Colvin, who went on to have a long and distinguished career with Aunty.

Three other Australian university graduates were chosen and two matriculates, including a very excited Ian Phillip Hyslop. As it turned out, I was one of the last non-university graduates employed as a cadet journalist. I had won the job over more than 450 applicants.

As pleased as I was to be given the chance of employment with the national broadcaster, I now faced the daunting task of telling my boss and mentor, David Kinsman, that I was quitting advertising to go into journalism. For more than six months, he had worked hard to bring me up to speed and the working relationship had been progressing well. To my embarrassment, he mounted a spirited campaign to dissuade me from leaving. Journalists were poorly paid, he declared, his voice full of contempt. There was good money in advertising and I had the potential to succeed in the field. I had heard the same argument before from Raymond Castle, the shoe retailer, who tried to recruit me as a store manager, when I had worked for him for a brief period.

They were both right, of course, the job was poorly paid, but it was a start, and would lead to great adventures and a good wage in commercial television in the future. Vindication came years later when I received a message from my old advertising boss, congratulating me on my appointment as the U.S. correspondent for the 7 Network.

I couldn't have picked a more fertile time to enter the field of journalism. Nationally Gough Whitlam had come to power as Prime Minister, promising to achieve wide-ranging changes to the administration and structure of Australian government. In NSW, Premier Bob Askin was at the centre of corruption allegations that he had received bribes from casino operators and bookmakers, while in Queensland, Joh Bjelke-Petersen was on his way to becoming the longest-serving Premier in the state's history. On the economic front, we were in a deep recession, and the country's best-known tourist attraction, the Sydney Opera House was officially opened by Queen Elizabeth.

Internationally, the Nixon Administration was imploding due to revelations about Watergate, the Vietnam War ceasefire agreement was signed, and a CIA backed coup in Chile led to the suicide of President Allende. Idi Amin's murderous regime was in full swing in Uganda and the UK formally joined the EEC.

Like the BBC in Britain, the ABC charter was to 'provide an innovative and comprehensive broadcasting service at a high standard across the country'. Founded in 1929, it was expressly deemed independent from government and party politics, though funding flowed from the government of the day, leading many to claim political interference.

When I first started work, the national broadcaster was commonly referred to as 'Aunty', a term of affection first applied in the 1950s, to contrast the old broadcaster with its newer and more 'swinging' rivals. Similarly, the BBC had an image as a prudish, puritanical broadcaster, very different to its much brasher competition, and was also called 'Auntie'.

The cadet journalist program in both organizations was virtually identical. The eager young journalists in my intake were in for a busy training schedule, which involved long sessions of voice training. We also learnt Pitman shorthand, equipping us with the skill to write at the impressive speed of 120 words a minute. For some unfathomable reason I took to this strange, squiggly language, and graduated top of the class, which was full of attractive young women. The ABC paid for our tuition at Miss Hale's Secretarial College in Sydney's CBD, and it proved to be a refreshing break from the serious business of the newsroom. Though I embraced shorthand enthusiastically, it was lost in the ensuing years, as tape recorders and television cameras made it redundant. The only time it came in handy was in a courtroom or parliament.

Cadets spent most of their time in the ABC newsroom in William Street, but as training unfolded, we were rotated to the television studios in Gore Hill. This gave us the chance to work on the Nightly News, read at the time by veteran broadcaster, James Dibble.

There was great competition between the two divisions, and the crusty old journalists on the sub-editor's desk in William Street would lambast cadets returning from a stint at Gore Hill as 'pretty boys', more concerned about getting their faces on television than becoming serious journalists. The newsroom politics was ferocious.

It was the cadet journalist counsellor's job to recognize the strengths and weaknesses of his charges, and make recommendations to management about where best to use their skills. I soon found myself spending more time at the television studios, resulting in a frosty reception from some of my William Street colleagues. The irony though, was that you worked twice as hard when assigned to Gore Hill, as you had to file copy for the radio bulletins, and prepare the report for the nightly TV news.

It was the challenge of every cadet to impress the older newsroom journos, many of whom worked on the sub-editor's desk, where some of the most high-profile foreign correspondents would end up. It was a 'rite of passage' for cadets to man the police radios on the graveyard shift from midnight to dawn. I was in this tiny room in the early hours of Christmas Day in 1974, when Cyclone Tracy wiped out the city of Darwin. The category 4 cyclone blasted the city with 200 kilometre an hour winds that ultimately killed 71 residents. The police and emergency services radio network carried the latest details of the impact, and I was kept busy filing copy for the radio bulletins to broadcast around Australia.

It was during the overnight shift that all domestic and overseas copy was edited for broadcast in the all-important morning news bulletins. Once these went to air, the sub-editors would walk out 'en masse' and head to Old Fitzroy or Bells Hotel in nearby Woolloomooloo, where they would stand shoulder to shoulder with wharfies and eager early drinkers, to toast the new day.

These sessions could run into lunch, and were the proving ground for many young journalists, including yours truly. The grizzled old veterans enjoyed nothing more than getting their younger colleagues hopelessly drunk, and watching them throw up outside the pub. I had no doubts I was held in higher esteem each time I hurled the contents of my stomach after a marathon session. Australian machismo was alive and well in the 1970s.

It was welcome news to be taken off the 'midnight to dawn' shift and rostered to work alongside senior journalists. We were assigned to dedicated rounds in the Courts, Parliament House, Police Headquarters or at the International Airport. A part of their job was to school their younger colleagues in the finer points of news reporting. Some were generous, but others highly territorial individuals, who jealously guarded their bailiwick, and saw cadets as a potential threat.

Not only would the trainees get a well-rounded education in all facets of journalism, but valuable life lessons were learnt in the many country towns where we were stationed. The tentacles of the national broadcaster were far-reaching. In the course of my cadetship, I worked in the regional cities of Orange, Bathurst, Kempsey, Grafton, Tamworth and Darwin. They were generally six-week postings, during which time I would write the news bulletins for local radio presenters to read. For a 'city slicker', unfamiliar with cattle yards, sheep dip methods and local politics, it was quite a challenge. Never more so than when the newsreader called in sick, and you would have to fill in and read your own copy. The disproportionate number of complicated aboriginal place names was a recipe for disaster, and after getting 'off air' you were sometimes forced to field phone calls from angry locals correcting your appalling pronunciation.

This would often play out in the pubs at night, when you were fair game.

"Are you that ABC bloke who doesn't know shit about this area?" the occasional one would ask.

"Yep, that's me," I would reply with a crooked smile, hoping I wouldn't receive a smack in the head.

By the end of the stint, you had just about got a handle on the place, and started to know and usually like the locals. It was a great training ground, and taught me the valuable lesson of accountability. You would try awfully hard to get your facts right, for fear of being confronted later by a big-boned farmer, intent on pointing out the error of your ways. Country folk are plain talkers, and generally have highly refined 'bullshit meters'.

In big city journalism, feedback was never so direct, and led to many scribes playing loose with the facts. To a young journalist it was a valuable lesson. The country postings were character-building. Trudging through freezing snow, at four o'clock in the morning, to open the radio station in Orange and write the morning news bulletin was a grim task.

The ABC would put you up in a local pub and pay a modest daily 'per diem'. Suffering sleepless nights, generally on the weekend, was an inevitable consequence of rowdy, drunken locals celebrating their week-long endeavours on the land. A six-week stay allowed you to become very familiar with the pub owners. An unexpected experience in Grafton, in northern New South Wales, provided a perfect example. I was posted there to replace another young journalist, who had almost completed his stint under the tutelage of ABC broadcasting veteran, Reginald Bultitude. Reg had run the radio station for many years and was used to hosting cadets from the 'mother ship' in Sydney. He recommended they stay at the Australian Hotel, a typical rickety and charming old pub, surrounded by latticed balconies.

It was a pub I will never forget, for as I drove up to the front door, a heavy porcelain washbasin sailed over the balcony and crashed onto the bonnet of a sexy MGB sports car. Seconds later, a young man ran out, jumped into the car and sped off. The fellow I was replacing had apparently 'got to know' the publican's wife a little too well, and I was left to pick up the pieces. In his haste to leave, an introduction to his successor was not possible.

Suffice to say, the 'gentleman host' who threw the basin was not well disposed towards ABC journalists. I would work hard to win his approval in the coming weeks, and assiduously avoided eye contact with his wife for the duration of my stay. I never did find out whether Reggie Bultitude reported my colleague's antics to head office, but I was determined not to succumb to the temptations of the flesh, particularly with the publican's wife.

I much preferred to stay in hotels occupied by a host with a large family who would provide a special kind of hospitality. A full country breakfast consumed in the pub's kitchen was one of the rare treats of travelling in the bush.

It was here, over a mountain of bacon, steak and eggs, that I would gather vital intelligence about the movers and shakers, and get valuable gossip about 'who was who' in town. Younger members of the family were a fertile source of information about where best to look for female company. The town's pharmacy or hospital, were for a reason that never became apparent, often the employers of the prettiest, young women.

After years of travelling in the bush on assignment, I found this to be an indisputable fact, and I would always call by the chemist shop on my arrival in town and ask how best to treat a sore throat. The soothing lozenges purchased, for the most part, remained untouched. Buying condoms was also another conversation opener, but one had to be careful about the resultant gossip. The local male population believed they deserved first crack at the best-looking girls in town, and would be quick to point it out, if word got around the ABC bloke was up to no good.

Driving in country areas also presented its challenges to a city boy, and I was careful to heed the local's advice on how best to avoid the ubiquitous kangaroos. They were in plague proportions in many places, and would come out to feed at dusk and early morning. I learnt the hard way one night near Tamworth, when the car I was travelling in hit a big, grey kangaroo. We went off the road at 90 miles an hour, rolled and very nearly hit trees, which would have meant certain death. My mate, the driver, was a local, but not immune to this country hazard. We were both shaken and cut up, but largely uninjured.

Kangaroos would also play a major role in another story that emerged from my working days in the bush. Many farmers culled them, as they would sweep across their properties, devouring crops and grasslands. They were considered vermin, which contrasted dramatically to city folks' perception of them as cute symbols of Australia. Having grown up mostly in the 'big smoke', I somewhat naively held this view, and it wasn't until I spoke to farmers that I realized what a destructive pest they could be. Killing them, however, seemed a little extreme. I would find this out, after being asked by a publican's teenage son if I wanted to join them for some nighttime 'spotlighting'.

It was a term I was unfamiliar with, but soon got the idea when handed a rifle and invited into the back of a battered, old ute equipped with huge spotlights. Had my companions known I'd rarely used a gun, they may have thought twice about handing me one, but they obviously believed I was up for it, and would enjoy the unique country pastime.

Wisely, one of them positioned himself nearby, as chief advisor and protector, should I inadvertently try to shoot myself or anyone else. The hunt was on, and it wasn't hard to find a mob of kangaroos. They were everywhere!

My first shaky attempt to line one up was greeted with howls of laughter.

"Yer dickhead, that's a bloody cow!" he screamed, grabbing a hold of the rifle to make sure I didn't let off a shot and make a costly mistake.

To a novice this was not as easy as it looked. From a distance, the eyes of the mesmerized animals were illuminated by the lights, but the body shape was not always clear. For the country boys it was like shooting fish in a barrel. They could easily discern the difference between cow, sheep, kangaroo and assorted other animal's eyes. In short order, the bodies of dozens of 'skippies' were scattered around the paddocks.

The whooping and a hollering continued well into the night, as our little convoy left a trail of death behind us. Empty beer cans formed a small mountain in the back of the ute, where I had easy access to the amber fluid and found it helped me distance myself from the reality of what we were doing. I was certainly no 'Crocodile Dundee', but careful to disguise my disdain of the activity from the boys who had asked me to join them in the kill fest.

I have no idea how many kangaroos I shot that night, if any, but the episode demonstrated starkly the differences between country and city folk, and the way we are conditioned to look at things.

Life on the land has never been easy. Floods and droughts are a constant threat to the men and women who work hard, growing crops or raising sheep and cattle destined for export or Aussie supermarkets.

Good years often followed by bad, homesteads decimated by floods, crop yields and livestock numbers cut by drought. They are a tough, pragmatic lot, blessed with an inner strength and fortitude seldom matched by their city cousins. I was to see many examples of this in the bush. Record floods in the 1970s in the Northern Rivers of New South Wales, were followed by killer bushfires in the Blue Mountains, west of Sydney. Standing in the ashes of someone's home talking to them about losing everything, or surveying the damage of a flood-ravaged house was a sobering experience to a young journalist just starting out in the business. Working for the ABC afforded cadets the regard and respect of people, who depended on the national broadcaster to bring news to the bush. They may have been leery about your lack of experience, but they cut you a break because you worked for 'Aunty'. We were just blow-ins, but it was the long-term ABC employees, invested in the bush who were held in highest esteem by locals. They were experienced men and women, well acquainted with growing crops and raising livestock. They would prepare the all-important market reports, and interview farmers, livestock agents and government regulators. Many a cadet would go on to work as a foreign correspondent, reinforced and strengthened by their experience in the Aussie bush. It was a crucial part of the training required to produce a well-rounded journalist. When I later went to work in the United States, I visited many small towns and cities in the mid-west, and was struck by the similarity to Australia. Not so much in the geography, but the commonality of spirit among the country folk. They were plain talkers and good neighbours, without the affectations and bullshit of many of their city counterparts.

In my early days with the ABC, competition between the cadets was fierce. The Australian university graduates trying desperately hard to gain the upper hand over the Oxford boy, while the two high school underdogs were determined to show a degree meant absolutely nothing in the scheme of things.

It was a 2-year cadetship for the graduates, and up to 5 for matriculates. As I was employed as a mature age candidate, not common in those days, I found myself being elevated to the lofty position of D grade journalist along with the graduates. I'd like to think it had something to do with my performance over that time.

Young journalists eagerly awaited the opportunity of being assigned a high-profile story, generally given as a matter of course to the more experienced reporters. If one came your way it was a real coup, and a chance not to be squandered. My moment came in July 1977, four years after joining 'Aunty', when prominent businessman, Donald Mackay disappeared in the Riverina town of Griffith, in southern New South Wales.

McKay had been making sensational allegations about marijuana cultivation in the area. He had implicated several local Italian families, alleging they ran a mafia-like organization, growing and distributing the drug throughout Australia.

Media flooded into the town, to report a story that promised to uncover a criminal conspiracy involving murder, drugs and police corruption. McKay's wife, Barbara pointed the finger at a local man, Tony Sergi, a winemaker, who she alleged headed a secret organization, called variously The Honoured Society, La Famiglia or N'Drangheta.

His was just one of several immigrant families who had settled the area to plant grapes and produce wine in the 1950s and 60s. They were none too pleased to be at the centre of drug trafficking allegations, and made known their displeasure to newsmen intent on reporting the story.

I was soon to find myself a target of their wrath. Accompanied by one of the ABC's oldest and most experienced cameramen, we drove to the Sergi family farm, in the nearby town of Tharbogang. Al Grassby, flamboyant minister in the Whitlam government, had officially opened the winery on his property two years earlier.

Like all fair reporters, I was going to give Tony Sergi a chance to tell his side of the story, and refute what I was sure he thought were scurrilous allegations.

A locked gate at the front of the property should have given us the first clue that he was not keen to talk, but full of youthful enthusiasm, I persuaded my older colleague to hop the fence and we headed for the homestead.

Our progress, however, was short lived. A stocky man emerged from the front door and posed threateningly with a shotgun. Before I was able to say a word, he let loose a blast aimed at stopping us in our tracks. It did, at least momentarily, until my elderly colleague 'hit the toe', making a mockery of his advanced years. He hurdled the fence well ahead of me with all the grace of an Olympic athlete!

We were later dissuaded from reporting the incident, as we had technically trespassed on private property.

Donald McKay's body was never found. Tony Sergi died in 2017 aged 82, almost four decades after Justice Woodward found that he was the pivotal figure behind the Griffith marijuana industry, and a member of the secret organization known as N'Drangheta.

It was a memorable story, pursued by an ambitious, young journalist keen to get ahead in the 'dog eat dog' business of TV news.

The ABC was intent on exposing its young men and women to experience all over the country. Darwin, the wild frontier town at the top end of Australia, was where I had lived as a toddler. I found myself serving two tours of duty there, coming across some of the most bizarre characters and interesting stories you could find anywhere.

At the time, the Vietnam War had just ended, and refugees were flooding out of the war-ravaged country, headed to Australia in leaky boats. They were coming ashore all along the coast, creating a humanitarian nightmare for a government, ill prepared for the influx. Thousands more had died on the high seas, while attempting to find a new life in the safe and peaceful south.

It was a fertile time for journalists, and I found myself spending many hours in a light aircraft flying out of Darwin in search of refugee boats. The 'Top End' was always a popular destination for young pilots, accumulating flying hours to qualify for jobs with Qantas. It was no comfort at all, sitting in a hellishly hot light aircraft watching a sweating pilot, who looked younger than most high school kids. I dare say he would have preferred to see an older journalist in charge of a notebook as well.

Darwin airport was at the centre of one of the more memorable stories I came across in the sweltering city, where temperatures rarely vary off 32C.

"You want me to get into that?" I asked.

'That' looked like a tiny biplane resembling the aircraft flown by the German air ace, Manfred Von Richthofan, in the First World War.

I posed the question, with a note of incredulity, to a senior journalist in the Darwin newsroom, who had just assigned me to report on a local, who had represented Australia in International Aerobatic Competitions piloting the quirky little plane.

The year was 1976. I was 23 years old, and was seconded to the northern extremes for the usual six-week stint from the ABC Sydney head office. The conversation went something like this.

"It looks like the Red Baron's plane," I said, examining the photo he proffered, "It's bloody ancient and you want me to fly in it?"

"What better way to get a feel for the story?" he replied, "besides, it's not an old plane, it's a Pitts Special, designed for aerobatics."

"Oh great," I replied, "loops, rolls and dives; I can hardly wait!"

"Yeah, of course, but you don't have to. Just thought a young gun like you would welcome the chance. This bloke's a national champion and it'll get a run on the shows in Sydney."

The sly, old bugger, I thought, knew what buttons to press; probably wanted to see the smart arse from the big smoke fall flat on his face.

I accepted the assignment somewhat diffidently, thinking it was a setup. The Darwin boys would get a good laugh when reports filtered back that I had filled up the cockpit with vomit.

Back in the 70s, the city was a pretty wild place. ABC management must have thought a short posting was a good way to toughen up its young reporters. Everyone there was escaping from something; either the law in the southern states or life in general. Alcoholism was rife and fisticuffs flew frequently. A perfect environment to hone a young man's journalistic skills!

Just the place, I thought, to die in a fiery crash.

Darwin was a hellishly hot city at the best of times, but the morning I met champion aerobatics pilot, Guido Zuccoli you could fry an egg on the airport tarmac.

I had done my research. The man was an immigrant success story; a civil engineer who had built tunnels through the Italian Alps, before coming to Australia in 1961. He had started up his own company, Steelcon Constructions, which was responsible for major civil engineering projects in the outback.

When I arrived at the airport, it was not hard to find his distinctive, little plane. Guido found me minutes later. His first words I will never forget.

"So, you wanna go up in my little plane, eh?"

It was a loaded question, which I desisted from truthfully answering. I could have said, "No bloody way!" but I think I mumbled something like "let's have a talk first, shall we?"

From the outset of the interview, which was for ABC radio, it was clear this man was an exceptional character. When he talked about flying and his interest in vintage warplanes, his face lit up and his arms spun like the propeller on his plane. He was Italian, after all! With all that passion, he would go on to win national and international aviation awards, and forge a successful business career.

Guido Zuccoli was a very likeable man, whose enthusiasm was contagious, and I was soon eager for an invitation to take to the skies.

That came in short order, and I was to discover what it was like to have my anus just inches from my throat, or that's what it felt like. The man showed no mercy, throwing the small plane around the skies and, no doubt, relishing the thought of scaring the bejesus out of the youngster from Sydney. For all I know my ABC colleagues put him up to it. Either way, they would most definitely hear that I had lost the contents of my stomach somewhere over Darwin Harbour.

I did not, however, fill the cockpit!

It is a story I have told for years and one of the many aviation related assignments I have had the pleasure, albeit with a bit of pain, of doing for a range of broadcasters.

It was with sadness I heard twenty years later, that Guido was killed at Tindal Airbase, near Katherine in the Northern Territory, taking off in one of the warbirds he had so lovingly restored. He was only 57 years old.

My two work stints in Darwin more than 40 years ago exposed me for the first time to our indigenous population. Having mainly grown up in cities, I had rarely seen aboriginals, and seldom considered the controversial issues and inequities that were a part of daily life in the Australian outback.

In the mid-70s, there were estimated to be around 33 thousand aboriginals scattered across the Northern Territory. Most lived in small communities, but the lure of the big towns was strong, bringing many to Darwin, where, in 1974, the Northern Land Council was created to campaign for aboriginal rights.

It followed recommendations of the Woodward Royal Commission, and had its origins in the struggle for fair wages and land, during a strike on the Wave Hill cattle station in 1966. The fight for land rights was a big story throughout the 70s. A prime mover and leader of the cause was Galarrwuy Yunupingu, an articulate and charismatic man, whose family also produced two famous singers. He came to national attention in the 60s for his role in the landmark Gove Land Rights case, the first by indigenous Australians to challenge the mining industry's exploitation of traditional lands.

It was ultimately unsuccessful, but the profile he gained in the struggle set the scene for him to successfully lead the Northern Land Council through the 70s and 80s. On several occasions, I interviewed the passionate advocate, and my stories were carried nationally. It was a controversial development, and many in the southern states were aghast at the thought of aboriginals demanding their land back, and payments from companies for mining it.

Aboriginal communities were beset with problems; a huge infant mortality rate, rampant alcohol abuse and a raft of other health and social issues, which were gaining publicity.

One story I was to attempt, highlighted a disturbing new trend among aboriginal youth, which had the potential to be a major 'thorn in the side' of government officials.

Acting on a tip-off from nursing staff at Darwin Hospital, the ABC discovered that kids in outlying areas were being flown in with severe brain damage, after sniffing petrol on aboriginal reserves. It was a shocking allegation, confirmed by the presence of several children, who had effectively fried their brains by inhaling these toxic fumes.

The practice was most widespread in the small township of Maningrida, about an hour by plane from Darwin. I was assigned the story, with a veteran ABC stringer cameraman, who knew the Northern Territory well, and better still, was acquainted with many law enforcement and government officials.

Because of the sensitive and controversial nature of the assignment, a cover story was concocted that bore no resemblance to the real purpose of our visit to the remote reserve. Aboriginal communities around the territory were serviced by light aircraft, which would fly in commuters and supplies. The coastal run to the mining towns of Nhulunbuy and Yirrkala would also call into Maningrida. On board were Aboriginals returning from picking up social security benefits and in many cases, beer supplies from Darwin. It was the sad reality of life in the Top End. Aboriginal alcohol abuse was rife in the 70s, and was fueled by government handouts, that resulted in tragic social consequences.

An old DC3 was used on the route, and the day we flew out ominous, black clouds promised a rough flight. We were travelling light. In our bags, an Arriflex film camera and more importantly, an infrared night scope, which would be crucial in filming the kids after dark. It was then, we were told, they would steal petrol, put it into cut-up coke cans and sniff the contents to give themselves a high.

The flight was a nightmare. A fast-moving storm cell produced conditions that flung the old aircraft around the leaden skies, and made many passengers violently ill.

The relatively short flight felt like an eternity, as vomit was liberally splashed around the cabin, making conditions far from ideal. It was a relief to step off the aircraft, but we would soon find a less than warm welcome. Waiting for us were two local policemen stationed on the reserve, who questioned us as to why we had come to Maningrida. Our answers failed to impress the constabulary, and they promptly confiscated the camera gear. The purpose of our visit had obviously been leaked, but we never found out who had warned the authorities.

An overnight stay on the reserve, until a flight the next day revealed little. Not one child was seen, and it was obvious the place had been locked down until the media people were sent on their way. The ABC did break the story later, but I was back in Sydney, left to rue the 'one that got away'.

Darwin was like no other city in Australia. It offered great recreational opportunities to a young man in his early twenties, but also severely tested anyone used to the more moderate climates of the southern states. 'Going Troppo' was a phrase commonly used to describe the erratic, drunken behaviour of locals, pushed to the edge by tropical humidity and high rainfall; the suicide rate consistently the highest in Australia.

My first visit to the city came just two years after it was virtually wiped out by Cyclone Tracy. Darwin was in a massive rebuilding phase, with an influx of thousands of tradesmen and builders from the southern states. It was a boom time with hotels full, and pubs overflowing. The Northern Territory police force was kept busy, with 'drunk and disorderly' the most commonly laid charge. A favourite tipple for the locals was a 'Darwin stubby', a huge bottle of beer brewed by Carlton & United Brewery, containing 80 fluid ounces (2,270 ml). It didn't take many to render the consumer blind drunk. The huge imbalance between male and female numbers led to fierce competition for the attentions of the few available ladies. Fisticuffs and heavy drinking were common – an ideal environment to find the odd story or two.

A decision to drive on Darwin roads had to be carefully considered, as a large percentage of the population was drunk at any given time. I decided the best way to get around was on a motorcycle, an odd decision, as I had never learnt to ride one, and had only clung to the back of an experienced rider. Undaunted, I went to a showroom on the busy Stuart Highway and entered negotiations with the owner, who agreed to buy back the bike at the conclusion of my posting. I settled on a Yamaha 250, and went on to ask him how the gear system worked.

"What do you mean?" he asked, "It's the same as all of them; one down four up!"

Before he had the chance to ask pertinent questions about my qualifications, I put it into first gear, and unfortunately released the clutch a little too quickly. It was not a good start to the test ride. The bike shot out of the parking lot, narrowly missing cars, before hitting the median strip, becoming airborne and barely managing to avoid the traffic stream coming the other way. In any other city in Australia, this would have been an extraordinary spectacle. In Darwin, crazy behaviour on the roads was commonplace.

I returned to the showroom 15 minutes later, having mastered the operation of the two-wheeled conveyance, and paid cash to the owner, who no doubt thought there was little chance of ever having to buy it back. As it turned out the little Yamaha offered the perfect air-conditioned solution to the sweltering conditions. It was not, however, great in the afternoon thunderstorms that were a constant feature of the wet season. It served me well, and was returned to the surprised bike shop owner six weeks later.

To a visitor, the city offered an extraordinarily colourful array of inhabitants. It was a multi-cultural melting pot, long before other Australian cities welcomed big numbers of overseas immigrants. The Greeks and Italians had cornered the restaurant trade, which was supplied by Chinese market gardeners. Added to this, was a sprinkling of Indonesian and Timorese workers, large numbers of Aboriginals and a constant flow of European backpackers, mixed with a nomadic selection of wandering Aussies. It was always a challenge re-adjusting to life back home after a spell in the tropical north.

On return to Aunty's headquarters in Sydney a de-briefing was always held with the cadet counsellor, who would have a written report from the news director or station manager where you had recently been posted. It would go towards the ongoing evaluation for your promotion to become a graded journalist. The ABC was a strictly hierarchical organization, and the procedures long established. Journalists were graded on a scale from D to A grade with a special 'A super' category for those who reached the dizzy heights.

Almost all were union members, and there was no such thing as work contracts, which was the norm in commercial media organizations.

Feedback was also sought from the experienced journalists who looked after the political, crime and court rounds, and would oversee training in these areas. Many valuable lessons were learned; most notably one I came across at Sydney airport, where I was assigned to file reports on the comings and goings of politicians, visiting dignitaries and famous entertainers.

American crooner, Frank Sinatra had just flown in to perform to sold-out concerts around the country. No doubt fortified by large quantities of alcohol on the long flight from the U.S., he faced a huge press contingent, of which I was one.

The first question came from a veteran reporter from the Sydney Morning Herald, who asked the star how he felt being in Australia. Without blinking, 'Old Blue Eyes' replied, "Very comfortable, thank you," gesturing to seat on which he was sitting.

From that day on, I resolved never to ask an interview subject how he or she felt. I still cringe when young reporters ask grieving parents how they feel about the loss of a child, or murderers how they feel about a long prison sentence after a brutal killing rampage.

Frank Sinatra's funny comeback line was for him, the first and last encounter with the Australian media. He issued a statement saying there would be no more press conferences for the remainder of the tour, a move that predictably led to a media 'feeding frenzy'. They chased his motorcades, mobbed his hotels and rehashed the old headlines concerning his mob connections, ex-wives and heavy drinking. At 59 years of age, the famous crooner was coming out of retirement, and the tour was supposed to be a soft re-entry into the entertainment business. It was anything but. His comments prompted union bans, and a second concert in Melbourne was cancelled. Frank Sinatra would never return to Australia, and left behind a tirade of foul-mouthed headlines directed at the media.

"They're parasites. They're bums and they're always going to be bums, a pox on them. The broads who work in the press are the hookers of the press. I might give them a buck and a half."

I was to write about 'Old Blue Eyes' years later, when posted to Los Angeles working for the 7 Network. He continued singing to nostalgic and loyal audiences almost until his death in 1998 at the age of 82.

Entertainment-related stories were the staple while living in America, but one of the more interesting assignments in that genre came months after becoming a graded journalist with the ABC, in the late 70s.

I was assigned the task of interviewing the famous British fashion model, April Ashley who had gained notoriety as the second man to have a sex change operation.

I remember detecting a twinkle in the eye of Chief of Staff, Len Annear, when he handed me the assignment. Transgender issues rarely garnered publicity in those days, and I was not sure of what to think when selected to do the interview. It no doubt got a few laughs down the pub later in the day.

April Ashley, born George Jamieson, in Liverpool in 1935 had written a book about her controversial journey, and come to Australia to promote the tell-all, which made for interesting reading. It chronicled her difficult teenage years, suicide attempts and incarceration in a mental institution. At the age of 25, having saved three thousand pounds, she had 7-hour gender reassignment surgery, performed in Casablanca in 1960.

George became April, and was soon working as a successful fashion model and actress in the film, 'The Road to Hong Kong' starring Bing Crosby and Bob Hope. Her film credit was dropped, however, after a Fleet Street tabloid outed her as transgender, sparking a scandal. It also put pressure on her marriage to Arthur Corbett, the Eton-educated son and heir of Lord Rowallan, which broke down not long after the revelations.

To a young, inexperienced, heterosexual journalist the story promised to be a challenge. April Ashley was quite a woman, who certainly made up for years of being trapped in the body of a man. Chic, attractive and sophisticated, the author of the best-seller had taken quite a risk coming to Australia. Our country, at the time, was not renowned for its enlightened attitudes toward sexual orientation and gender identity. 'Poofter bashing' and misogyny were popular attitudes for a good percentage of locals, and her visit was not going to be well received by many.

While I was miserably under-qualified to ask questions about the little-known subject of transgender experience, the interview was broadcast on both ABC radio and Television news and ultimately met with the approval of my interview subject. She was probably equally relieved to get through the experience, and showed her thanks by extending an invitation to dinner.

They say curiosity is a prime requisite in the make-up of a journalist and I wasted little time agreeing to dine with the poster girl of a largely underground, but emerging transgender movement. It turned out to be a fascinating introduction to a world I really had no idea existed. It would ultimately help extinguish any lingering prejudices I held towards such people.

April Ashley was the epitome of femininity, and appeared more than comfortable in the body she now inhabited. Dinner soon progressed to drinks, and then an offer that would forever qualify me to talk authoritatively about gender re-assignment surgery.

With all the assurance of an experienced older woman, she asked if I would be interested in going to her hotel room to familiarize myself with the subject of our earlier interview. I could say I was in the clutches of alcoholic inebriation, but that would be a lie. Curiosity once again won the day, though it must be said, grog helped!

It was in that room I examined the work of French gynecologist, Georges Burou, who owned the Casablanca clinic where April had become a woman, and was widely credited with innovating modern sex re-assignment surgery.

The experience was liberating, and taught me some valuable lessons about human nature. I would never fall into the trap of regarding trans genders as queers or perverts. April Ashley had found comfort and happiness in her new life, and helped educate a young, Australian journalist lucky enough to be in no doubt about his own sexuality.

It was the experience and training I received at the ABC that shaped my future, and equipped me to be an overseas correspondent years later. I had hoped to be posted to one of the national broadcaster's overseas bureaus, but before I had served what was seen by department heads as the 'required amount of time', commercial television came 'a calling'.

It was a familiar story. 'Aunty' would provide its recruits with the best journalistic training, but had no strategy to hold onto them when commercial rivals opened their cheque books. I had worked in the newsroom for just over five years, and been promoted to the level of a B grade reporter, when first approached by Channel 9 in Sydney.

The salary offered was considerably more than that paid to some of my more senior ABC colleagues, and when I went to discuss my future with management, was told they could not match the commercial offer. I was, they understandably argued, comparatively unseasoned, compared to others in the newsroom.

They were right, of course, but I held out the hope there was room for negotiation, suggesting they reward me with an A grade pay rate, well short of what I had been offered by Channel 9. After all, I was genuinely thankful for my training and time at Aunty, and really didn't want to leave. Sound logic, I thought, but singularly unconvincing to the two senior men, who thanked me for my service and, no doubt, went off to a long lunch to discuss the temerity of young Hyslop, the upstart.

The national broadcaster was not in the business of competition. Funding from the government assured its continued operation, unlike commercial rivals, who lived and died by their ratings success. The organization was full of empire builders, more concerned about their own survival than moving with the times.

And so it was in 1979, I left the warm bosom of Aunty and with great trepidation, headed to the 'brave new world' of commercial television.

CHAPTER 6
NICKNAMES AND ALL THAT NONSENSE

I can't remember exactly when I was tagged with the nickname, 'Sloppy', but it has followed me through life, blurted out by both friend and foe with no small amount of glee.

To some, it is a term of endearment, others a chance to cause embarrassment, particularly when used in front of those unfamiliar with the unique sobriquet.

I don't suppose I should have been surprised. Australians are well known for abbreviating names. It's all part of their quest to make the English language more informal, to dump all pretension and allow the words to roll easily off the tongue; a form of rebellion, if you like, against their stuffy colonial oppressors.

It starts early, when a kid's name like Daniel ends up a Danny or Dan, Robert, a Bobby, or William, a Billy. They are diminutives meant to convey informality, familiarity and friendliness. It also happens in later life when workmates have their fun. Laurence becomes 'Lozza', Daryl, 'Dazza', Warwick, 'Wocka' and it's not just names that undergo a dramatic makeover. An afternoon becomes an 'arvo', a television a 'telly', and breakfast, 'brekky'. It's all very confusing to non-Australians.

I became 'Sloppy', a diminutive of the surname Hyslop. No surprise then that with 'slop' on the end, a 'Y' was soon added.

I remember as a youngster going to my Father and asking where the name Hyslop came from. So sick and tired was I of the constant ribbing I received, I wanted to know exactly what it meant. He was not much help, muttering something about Scotland and little more.

Didn't he realise it was a bloody awful name to be saddled with and made me a target of every schoolyard bully? I was determined to discover the derivation of this 'millstone around my neck' and went to a library in Geelong, where the family was domiciled at the time, to solve the mystery.

There was no internet in those days and it was a long walk.

I found it in an old reference book; a coloured photograph of the Hyslop family crest and coat of arms, confirmation of my illustrious forbears. A green and silver coat of arms was adorned with the image of a knight in armor, and a stag with enormous antlers. But as impressive as it was, I wasn't sure it was worth all the grief I was copping!

I read with mild interest that the name was connected to the ancient Anglo-Saxon tribes of Britain. The surname Hyslop, it said, was derived from the Old English word 'haesel' and the Norse word, 'hesli', which both mean hazel. The book informed me that my name "was first found in Islip, Oxfordshire, birthplace of Edward the Confessor in 1005." Subsequent moves to Yorkshire in 1414, then Scotland from 1425 explained my Father's understanding of a Scottish link. Family history buff, Rhonda, more recently managed to trace my Hyslop family tree back to the 1700s, in Glencairn, Scotland, between Glasgow and the English border.

All this information may have filled in some of the gaps, but it was cold comfort to kid who changed schools like other people changed underwear. Diane and I were Qantas brats, and saw classrooms in four Australian states before our teens. No sooner had we settled into one place, than my Father would come home and tell us he had been transferred. It was an announcement not always welcomed, and would result in another long walk into an unfamiliar new school in yet another city. I have vivid memories of holding my sister's hand and bracing myself for a new round of abuse and ridicule over our silly name. Children can be extremely brutal.

In Brisbane, Hyslop became 'Dishmop". In Victoria, we copped 'Piss a lot' and 'Pisslop'. At no time, however, can I remember being called, Sloppy. That came later.

When we finally settled back in Sydney to attend high school, we were veterans of the Australian education system finding ourselves, because of the widely divergent curriculums, considered very bright in Brisbane, average in Melbourne and below par in Sydney, having to repeat a grade.

They say 'sticks and stones will break your bones, but names will never hurt you'. I'm not sure, as a child I could subscribe to that well-worn maxim. It did, however, serve a purpose. I learnt how to fight, and often found myself on the end of a teacher's strap or cane. It also provided a great window into human nature, and was pivotal in equipping me with what it took to cope in later life.

It can be said with great confidence, I would not have chosen my surname to take into the field of journalism, particularly television news, a medium where I was required after each report to tell viewers, who I was. Ian Hyslop, ABC News. In Los Angeles, Ian Hyslop, 7 National News. Ian Hyslop for Eyewitness News – get the idea!

The one compensation was that the name, being so unusual, was not likely to be quickly forgotten. I, as reporter, may have faded instantaneously from the viewer's consciousness, but the name, funnily enough was, and continues to be remembered.

I have thought long and hard about when it was that colleagues realized there was a 'Slop' on the end of the surname and came up with Sloppy, but I cannot pinpoint the timing.

I suspect it was a cameraman in my early career, probably so sick and tired of the large number of standups, or 'pieces to camera' I managed to stuff up.

"Ah, c'mon Sloppy, for Christ sake, get it right!"

At any rate, before I knew it, I was 'Sloppy' to all my workmates. Even crews working for other television networks called me the less than flattering name.

Now, to an ambitious, young reporter this was a disconcerting development. I took myself very seriously, and being referred to as 'Sloppy' was a far from desirable turn of events. After all, senior newsmen around the world were not burdened with so colourful a nickname, so why me? I was not sloppy in manner or demeanor, but there it was, a name I could not shake.

I would watch the confused look on the face of famous interview subjects, when they heard crew members refer to me by my nickname.

In time, I came to accept it, thinking it sounded friendly enough, similar to the name you'd give a small dog or cute kitten. However, I still didn't have to like it, and would have gladly accepted a nickname with more gravitas.

CHAPTER 7
IT'S A BOY

"That's what happens when you put a Shetland pony with a Draught horse!"

It is a phrase I will never forget. It was uttered by an obstetrician to a doctor early one morning in October 1982, in the maternity ward of St Margaret's Hospital in Darlinghurst, Sydney.

Just a few hours earlier I had been sitting in the Channel 10 studios reading the late news, when the beeper on my belt vibrated, alerting me to the fact that I was about to become a father.

My then wife, Kathy had been rushed to hospital while her husband was on the job. Months earlier, I had made the switch from Channel 9 to rival station, Channel 10, and by day was reporting the news, and at night, reading the late bulletin, Nightcast. Work started at 9 am and finished after 10 pm!

It was the price I paid for the job change. A chance to read the news and satisfy an impatient, overly ambitious streak, fueled by a news director who hired me with the flamboyant promise of, "Gunna make you a star, Hyslop!"

Before he could do that, however, I – with the help of Kathy – made a son. Daniel Lee Hyslop entered the world after a particularly traumatic experience, which saw his mother endure 18 hours in labor, an epidural, and a caesarian birth.

It was in the corridors of the hospital I was to overhear the birth doctors talking about the impending procedure, and using the equine descriptions of ponies and horses. The only possible justification for the colourful language was the fact my wife was considerably smaller than I. It would come home to 'bite them on the arse!'

Speaking to the obstetrician, just minutes after he pulled my son from his mother's gaping body, I watched him visibly pale after I thanked him profusely, suggesting the difficult procedure was probably due to putting a Shetland pony with a Draught horse!

It no doubt taught him a valuable lesson about how to conduct professional conversations with colleagues, particularly when you have curious journalists lurking in the shadows.

You would think with all the grief I copped regarding my surname, I would have been more sensitive when it came to naming my son. I couldn't do anything about his surname, but when he was born, I sat for long hours considering the options. I knew that Hyslop would be a 'character builder', but what else would help.

I contemplated 'Humphrey', followed closely by 'Horatio'. They had quite an understated strength to them, I thought, but when my Mother heard the choices, she read me the 'riot act'. Rarely had I seen her so agitated.

"You will not call your son, bloody Horatio," she told me with an icy chill that would quickly melt my resolve. And so, was born the name Daniel Hyslop, Dan or Danno, to his family, friends and colleagues.

It must be said, it beats the hell out of Sloppy!

CHAPTER 8
BORN IN THE U.S.A.

In the early 80s, it was not standard procedure for the father to be present in the operating theatre for the birth of his child, particularly when it was a caesarian procedure. Six years later however, that was not the case when we welcomed my daughter, Morgan into the world.

Once again, her father was stationed behind the news desk when word reached him that the birth was imminent. President Ronald Reagan was defending the American navy, which had just mistakenly shot down an Iranian passenger plane, and I was doing a live cross into Australia from the 7 Network's Los Angeles Bureau.

During the report, I got the 'thumbs up' from cameraman, Maurice Roper that the birth was about to happen in nearby St John's Hospital, Santa Monica. The company van was on standby and ready to go.

It was a minor miracle I was even in town for the event, as the daily travel schedule was hectic. Anticipating that to be the case, I had invited my parents, Lyn and Gordon to come over and be on hand for the birth, even if their son wasn't.

I arrived at the hospital just minutes before doctors performed the caesarian, which I was able to witness in all its gory detail. I remember being shocked to the core as the surgeon's scalpel made the incision that would release my tiny daughter. She emerged without the trauma of a natural birth and looked all the better for it, a beautiful little specimen, just like her brother, who had a full head of hair, and had been described by the obstetrician as the most beautiful baby he had ever seen. Given the doctor's Chinese origins however, I suspect he may have been biased in his opinion.

My daughter made her appearance appropriately enough on 4th July, 1988; American Independence Day. She remained in the hospital with her mother for two weeks, and shared the spotlight with actress Elizabeth Taylor, who had been admitted for treatment for heavy drinking and substance abuse.

Each time I visited the hospital, I had to pass a gauntlet of television cameras that were on standby to report on the star's convalescence. It was a story Channel 7 Australia could not ignore and I was asked to do an update on Miss Taylor's condition.

It was my first and only experience with the U.S. health system, and was relatively painless, given that I had full private health insurance. Just as well, because the bill for the birth and stay in hospital exceeded 80 thousand dollars!

I had been living in the United States for four years when Morgan was born, and had done several stories highlighting the inequities in the U.S. health system, which turned away poor, uninsured people from hospitals. I could not believe the world's most powerful country had failed to structure a health system to look after the less advantaged in their society.

My arrival in Los Angeles in 1984 came midway through President Ronald Reagan's tenure in the top job, and just months after the Olympic Games, which had been hailed as a financial and sporting 'thundering success'. I replaced broadcasting veteran Kerry O'Brien, who would return to the ABC in Australia, where he would remain and work with distinction for the remainder of his career.

The 7 Network bureau was located on Santa Monica Boulevard in Century City, just around the corner from exclusive Beverly Hills and Rodeo Drive. Our office was a short distance from the coast and on a clear day, (which in the 1980s was rare) you could see Catalina Island and some spectacular sunsets, turned blood red by the city's shocking pollution. The office also overlooked the exclusive L.A. Country Club, famous for excluding actors, blacks and Jews from membership. Its manicured, green fairways hosted the city's privileged few, who fell outside the aforementioned categories. The golf course featured in a notable story that I was to tell for many years.

Brisbane sports reporter David Fordham, an avid golfer, had been covering the Olympics and telling staff he intended to play on the Country Club course before flying home to Australia. He was duly informed that the famous links was off limits to virtually everyone but the privileged few, news he refused to believe.

Motivated to prove everyone wrong, he rang the Club and asked to speak to the manager. David informed him that he was an Aussie sportscaster who had a special interest in the great golf courses of the world, and would consider it a real honour if he was allowed to walk the course, inferring he had no expectations of being able to play.

Apparently charmed by the Aussie's direct and respectful approach, the manager asked if David was a member of an Australian golf club, to which he replied in the affirmative.

"I am a member of Royal Ashgrove in Brisbane," he said, somewhat exaggerating the status of the small municipal golf course and adding a regal tag that did not actually exist.

"Oh really," replied the gentleman, obviously impressed by the royal word, "I do believe I've heard of that club".

"What's your handicap, David?"

"I am an 8 handicapper," the Australian lied, obviously thinking the real figure of around 18 would raise serious concerns about the damage he may cause to the manicured fairways if allowed to play.

"And do you have your clubs with you?" he asked.

"Why yes I do," he again lied. "I always travel with them, love the game."

"Well, David we don't usually extend invitations for non-members to play on our course, but how would you like to come as my guest tomorrow morning."

After enthusiastically accepting the rarely proffered invitation, David faced the reality of trying to find a decent set of golf clubs. Not before, however, declaring to astonished colleagues that he had received an invitation to play across the road.

Later in the afternoon, he savoured success after phoning the nearby Rancho Park golf course, one of the busiest public courses in America. Again, using his prodigious persuasive powers he asked the golf professional if he could hire a set of clubs.

"What time would you like to play, Sir?" the pro inquired.

"No," David replied, "you don't understand. Can I hire a set of clubs, to take away," he stammered. "Look, I've just received an invitation to play at the L.A. Country Club tomorrow. I'm visiting from Australia and don't have my clubs with me," he explained.

"The L.A Country Club?" the pro repeated with a note of incredulity. "Well, Sir, I tell you what, you can use mine, that's about the only chance they'll get a hit there."

The kind offer was not the end of Fordham's famous golf tale. The following day he was met with great ceremony at the famous course, and went on to play admirably well, before being taken to the clubhouse for lunch and drinks.

In fine fettle and at his loquacious best, he thanked his hosts for their kind hospitality and presented the manager with a small token of his appreciation; a necktie from the 'Royal Ashgrove Golf Course'. It was, in fact, one of

David's many rugby ties, collected during his time as a commentator in Australia!

The 10100 Santa Monica Boulevard address was the backdrop for many funny stories to emerge during my years in the City of Angels. An up-market 26-storey building, it housed some of the city's most famous attorneys, and talent agents to the rich and famous. It was 'not unusual' to run into Welsh crooner, Tom Jones in the lift, which prompted me to use my affected Welsh accent, picked up on the many visits to the country of my Mother's birth.

"How are you, Boyo?" I once asked him. The cheeky enquiry received a hearty chuckle and sparked a short conversation that allowed me to boast to my Mother, a great fan of the singer, that I knew her idol well, and chatted to him frequently.

The lift was also the unlikely location for an episode involving CNN founder and America's Cup sailor Ted Turner. I was familiar with the legend of Turner, as Channel 7 was affiliated with the fledgling cable news network he founded, and I would make numerous trips to Atlanta to talk to news bosses there. To see him in our building, though was quite a surprise, but what he did was even more surprising. As he entered the packed lift, he let out one of the loudest farts I would have thought a human being capable of producing. Uncomfortable laughter rippled through the confined space, but none as loud as Ted Turner's own response to his flagrant (or was that fragrant) abuse of a captive audience. I would later find out this was a common action from the unabashed attention-seeker, who liked nothing more than to shock those around him. He thrived on cultivating his image as a renegade redneck, revelling in the nicknames, the 'Mouth from the South' and 'Captain Outrageous'. He swept into Hollywood and married Jane Fonda, one of the most recognisable, and variously disliked, actresses in the country. His business dealings were always aggressive and audacious.

Ted Turner was one of a kind and I have no doubt, if scientifically measured, would be credited with producing the loudest fart in the history of mankind. His larger-than-life persona was also famous for producing memorable quotes, among them, 'Life is a game. Money is how we keep score', 'You can never quit. Winners never quit, and quitters never win', 'The United States has got some of the dumbest people in the world. I want you to know that we know that.'

And, perhaps the one quote that truly sums up the man, 'The word impossible does not exist for me. I've got a lot of signal flags in my bag, but there is not a white one in there. I am going to keep fighting until the day I die, and might keep on fighting afterward…depends on where I am.'

All of them original and memorable quotes, but for me nothing he's done in life could possibly match the deliberate noise he made in that Los Angeles lift.

On the ground floor of the building that housed the 'Ted Turner Memorial Lift' was a small restaurant and bar that was of vital importance to the 7 Network's Los Angeles Bureau. It was run by a Russian Jewish refugee by the name of Alex Rosenblum, a man who would become a life-long friend. His little bar was warm and friendly, but I soon identified that it could also be a dangerous place for journalists. Particularly so for those who worked in television, and were expected to be sober when filing voice reports, or on-camera live crosses to Australia.

My drink of choice was a Bombay gin and tonic, a refreshing 'pick me up' that I would sometimes indulge in around cocktail hour. This was an infrequent occurrence as we found ourselves constantly on the road, travelling on various assignments. However, when in L.A., the long hours and non-stop pressure would require staff to take the odd short break. It was in the darkened bar I witnessed first-hand the unique expertise of American bar staff. These guys did not simply dispense drinks like their Australian counterparts. They took on the role of confidantes and pals to patrons, and in the process poured some of the most potent brews known to man and God. Free pouring was a common practice; drunken behaviour an even more common by-product.

My barman mate was a Bostonian by the name of Danny. He was a sports nut, like most Americans, and an ardent supporter of the Celtics Basketball Team, who were involved, at the time, in play offs with the Los Angeles Lakers. I had little interest in the sport, so when given courtside seats to one of the play-off games by contacts at CBS Sports, I headed downstairs and gave them to my Bostonian buddy. He was beside himself, and I later found out why! The prize seats were valued at over 15 hundred dollars, and placed the barman on the sideline, close to the action, and not far from actor Jack Nicholson, an enthusiastic Laker's supporter. The generous gesture unfortunately had unintended consequences. Forever in my debt, the only way Danny could show his thanks was by the heaviness of his hand!

I moved quickly to nip the practice in the bud, explaining to him my job depended on a clear brain and lucid tongue, and clearly alcohol did not encourage this condition. I asked him to measure my drinks in future, and only change that practice if I winked at him. He would eagerly await the signal, but it came infrequently, as I had no wish to lose my job because of a 'slip of the tongue' or brain fade. I can't imagine what fellow drinkers thought, on witnessing the Aussie winking at the overweight barman from Boston.

The 6pm Channel 7 news bulletins in Australia would go to air at 10 pm local time in LA. Depending on breaking news, we would often have to go 'live' and the days were long and stressful.

The news bureau, on the 20th floor of the building, provided stunning views of west Los Angeles all the way to the Pacific Ocean, but the height of the skyscraper raised questions about its vulnerability to earthquakes, a fact I found mildly disturbing.

My colleagues moved to allay those fears, explaining the building was on rollers that would allow it, and us, to survive even the worst 'shaker'. This would come into play during a live cross to Australia.

The lighting grid on the ceiling of the studio started shaking wildly, and I experienced a rolling sensation that confirmed the building's unique design features. The sight of me reacting to the seismic shift no doubt entertained viewers back home, but I at least avoided the humiliating action of diving under the desk, like American broadcaster Kent Shocknek, who worked for KNBC. It did not end his career, but it would provide rich fodder for comedians in Los Angeles at the time. His disappearance under the desk was accompanied by the commentary 'his mother had told him as a child that in the event of an earthquake at school, get under the desk'. He was a truly obedient son.

Earthquakes are a fact of life in California, and so it would seem are short memories. Residents live with the reality that 'The Big One' will almost certainly devastate their city at some point. The San Andreas Fault runs through the coastal state, but they still go about their life and business, apparently unconcerned.

Years of living in both Los Angeles and Taiwan exposed my family to their destructive power, and reinforced the appeal of Australia as a relatively safe place to live. They may have scared the hell out of me, but there was no doubting their importance to my career as a newsman.

I was to find that out on October 17th, 1989, when the Loma Prieta earthquake hit northern California. I had just returned to the office after a rare long lunch to farewell Ken Burslem, a journalist who worked for opposition broadcaster, Channel 10, and was headed home at the end of his posting.

It was just after 5pm, leaving plenty of time to decide on the story of the day to be filed for the folks back home. I settled into the office, feet on desk, when that question was dramatically answered. The building's aforementioned rollers came in to play, signaling another major seismic event. Within minutes, the bank of television monitors in the office carried the newsflash that a magnitude 6.9 earthquake had hit San Francisco and Oakland, more than 600 kilometres away. Less than an hour later, we were on a flight to nearby San Jose. San Francisco Airport was closed, freeways destroyed and suburbs reportedly on fire, leaving no doubt this was a major catastrophe!

It would be the start of one of the most intensive and exhausting reporting assignments of my career. Few natural disasters cause the shock and trauma of an earthquake. It was clearly written on the faces of survivors illuminated by the lights of our car, as it came off the Golden Gate Bridge shortly before midnight. We headed for the Marina District, one of the worst hit areas, which was ablaze after gas lines were fractured and power lines brought down. It had an eerie 'end of the world' movie-set feel about it, but this was real life and the images were a graphic reminder of the savage power of nature. For four days we broadcast non-stop into shows in Australia, reporting that 63 people had been killed and almost four thousand injured. The Nimitz Freeway accounted for the biggest death toll when a span of the top deck collapsed, crushing cars on the lower deck, while a section of the San Francisco-Oakland Bay Bridge was also damaged.

Four years earlier, I had reported on an earthquake that devastated Mexico City, killing more than 10 thousand people and injuring 30,000.

In both cases, my job was to report on these natural disasters, but in 1999, I found myself at the centre of a deadly quake in Taiwan, where I had moved with my family two years earlier. We were rudely awoken in the middle of the night by a magnitude 7.7 earthquake, that struck south of Taipei. Experiencing this awesome power was the most terrifying experience of my life. It is a reminder of how powerless we all are when nature decides to show its wrath.

During the years spent in Los Angeles, they were just one hazard. The city took some getting used to. The high crime rate may have been rich fodder for a journalist, but it was no comfort as a husband and father. Living in Westwood provided some reassurance, as it was adjacent to Beverly Hills, which boasted one of the biggest police departments in the country, but it was not immune to crime. I was given some unique advice when I first moved into the neighbourhood.

Not long after arriving at the comfortable three-bedroom bungalow we would call home, my next-door neighbour came by to introduce himself and offer some valuable suggestions.

Archibald Trout was a tall, gangling, extremely fit man somewhere in his late 70s.

"Call me Archie," he affably instructed the family, "welcome to Westwood." However, his next words caused more than a little concern.

"Got a gun, son?"

"Ah, no Archie, I don't."

"Good idea to get one" he casually suggested, and then went on to tell me why.

It turned out Archie was a veteran of both the Los Angeles Police and Fire Departments. "Retired after 20 years as a cop, and then went on to work as a fireman for another twenty years," he told me.

It would have been easy to dismiss Archie as an eccentric old guy, but when you're told by a pro to rush out and arm yourself, I was interested to find out why. Our little street was nestled in between two of Los Angeles busiest boulevards, Pico and Olympic. Close to the ocean, it was considered a 'good area'.

"Got much crime down in Australia," he inquired after finding out where we came from and what I did for a living.

"Not a lot," I replied, "at least compared to this place."

"Not saying this is the hotbed of crime, here, son, but it's always good to be prepared," he offered.

"You still carry," I asked, expecting him to pull out a magnum and do a Dirty Harry impersonation.

"No, but I got a small arsenal in the house" he told me with a smile and a wink. "Thing is, burglary's the most common crime you're likely to encounter. Lot of poor folks around, who would like what you've got," he said.

This comment resonated with me, as I had seen large groups of Mexican illegals just around the corner waiting to be picked up by businessmen or homeowners hiring cheap labour for short-term projects.

"If someone's breaking into your place, you have every right to defend yourself with deadly force," he informed me.

But it was what he said next that was truly shocking. "But remember, if you kill them in your house, it's alright, but if you shoot them dead in your yard, drag 'em inside. They can't charge you then".

For a second I thought he was joking, but his steely-eyed seriousness, and no-nonsense language had the ring of truth about it. He really did remind me of an older Clint Eastwood.

Archie failed in his attempt to get me to buy a weapon, but we became firm friends. He and his wife took on the role of surrogate grandparents to my two children, and it was mightily comforting knowing he had all the firepower needed if the neighbourhood erupted in violence, or a crime wave swept through the area.

It must be said that in the seven years we lived in L.A, crime stayed away from our doorstep. This was in stark contrast to other areas of the huge metropolis, which featured regularly on the nightly news for assorted incidents of murder, mayhem and disorder.

My only personal encounter with the seedy underbelly of crime in the City of Angels came when I was forced to spend a night in jail after a run-in with local traffic police. I was no stranger to the inside of some of the most notorious prisons in America, having visited San Quentin, Sing Sing, Rikers Island and Marion Supermax Prison in Illinois, but that was on assignment, not as an inmate.

My 'jail time' came after a phone call from my Mother in Sydney, asking me to take visiting family friends to dinner. The dining completed, I offered to drive them to the home of their friends in the San Fernando Valley, quite a drive from the restaurant.

Soon after entering one of the freeway ramps along the way, the sound of a siren interrupted conversation and I noticed the flashing lights of a police car. What's all this, I thought, feeling I had nothing to worry about, as I had only one drink over dinner and I certainly wasn't speeding.

Nervous giggles from my visitors rippled through the car, as I waited to find out. It was not long before a female LAPD officer asked for my license and instructed me to get out of the car.

"Have you been drinking, Sir," she inquired, as a second female officer provided back-up.

"I have had one beer in a restaurant in Westwood, and am taking my friends from Australia home to where they're staying," I informed her.

"Then you won't mind doing a sobriety test?"

"Not at all," I replied, thinking I had nothing to worry about, a statement I could not always feel comfortable making.

What followed must have been the most comprehensive test ever given to a motorist on a Los Angeles freeway. I walked the line, stood on one leg, performed pirouettes, did hand-eye coordination tests, everything that was asked of me, short of climbing trees at the side of the freeway.

As they appeared to be running out of tests for me to perform, I made the fatal mistake of showing my frustration.

"C'mon girls, it should be obvious to you I haven't been drinking, it's late and I have to get these ladies home!"

I have had many years to consider why the officers did what they did next, and can only put it down to my use of the word 'girls'.

Within seconds, I was handcuffed and being bundled into the police car, leaving the two Australian guests at the side of the freeway. My entreaties to one of the officers to drive them fell on deaf ears. She did, however, tell them where I was being taken, assuming they could drive and find the Van Nuys Police Station.

It was the start of a very long night! After being given a blood test, I was to experience the 'salubrious' surroundings of the 'drunk tank'. I joined a multi-coloured assortment of either very drunk or drugged 'gentlemen', whose company was less than compelling. I was told I could make a phone call, which I wasted on my wife, Kathy. I was later informed by one of the more articulate cellmates that I should have called a bail bondsman who, for a fee, would have got me out in no time.

My ignorance of the process led to one of the most frightening experiences of my life. About 2 o'clock in the morning, I was taken to another holding cell, the occupants of which were destined to be transferred to the notorious L.A. County Jail in the morning.

My entry into the cramped surroundings of the cell couldn't have come at a worse time. A pitched battle was in progress, with three very large African Americans beating the hell out of a couple of heavily tattooed Latinos. I took a seat on a bare concrete bench and immediately cast my eyes in the direction of the floor, assiduously avoiding eye contact.

These guys were not drunks and traffic offenders, but gang bangers and killers. The smell of dozens of bodies was overpowering, and not helped by the stench emitted by a small black man who sat on a toilet opening his bowels in clear view of everyone. Jive talk of the black ghettos was mixed with shouted Mexican obscenities and the dark, angry eyes of desperate men trying hard to outstare each other. It didn't take long for interest to fall on the well-dressed white gringo sitting, eyes downcast, and clearly trying to crawl into a crack in the floor.

Their fun finished with the two Latinos, who sat bloodied and nursing wounds in the corner of the cell, it appeared it was my turn to 'face the music'.

To this day, I still don't know what prompted my inspired response, but it most certainly saved me from a severe beating. Voice raised, I let out a foul-mouthed tirade aimed at the cops who arrested me, letting my potential attackers know I was an Australian, and the system in America was well and truly fucked. Each shouted expletive criticizing the system elicited a positive response from my potential adversaries. They were acting talents I never knew I possessed!

It was enough to diffuse their blood lust, and gave me a temporary reprieve, but it wasn't the end of the adventure. I had serious concerns about being taken to the County Jail in the morning. Added to that fear, was the fact that I was supposed to be on a 7am flight to Washington DC to report on the 'Wheat Talks' between U.S. and Australian government officials.

As I sat pondering the dilemma, I felt movement at my side as a thick-set, tattooed Mexican sat next to me.

"What you need, man?" he asked.

"To get out of here," I answered truthfully.

"You need to use the phone?" he inquired, looking over to where several tough looking guys were lined up to make calls.

"Yeah, but I don't think there's much chance," I told him, nodding at the queue.

"Don't worry," he said, getting up and walking over to the group gathered by the phone.

I watched in disbelief as he tapped each inmate on the shoulder and told them to 'fuck off'. Whoever this guy was, he had 'serious juice' and must have been the baddest dude in the cell. He would later tell me he was being arraigned on multiple murder charges, the result of a drive-by shooting that had dominated news headlines for months. Why he decided to help me, I had no idea.

He called me over and I again phoned my wife, who said she had contacted the police and was on her way. Hearing my name called out just before 5 am was the greatest relief of my life.

I was bailed out, and taken straight to the airport, where I barely made the flight to Washington. The temptation to drink proved too much, and I felt little pain several hours into the flight. The gentleman sitting next to me heard all about my brush with the law and night in jail, and enthusiastically joined me in the early morning tipple.

It was not the end of the story. Several weeks later, in court, the judge moved to dismiss the DUI charge, after evidence showed my alcohol reading was well under the limit. The two female officers who made the arrest were in court, and listened as I explained my side of story. In summing up, the judge roundly criticized the actions of the police officers, and apologized on behalf of the city of Los Angeles for the ordeal to which I and my family friends had been subjected.

It was just one of the many interactions I had over the years with U.S.

law enforcement and certainly the most negative, but in general I had huge respect for the men and women in uniform and appreciated just how difficult their job was. Many stories Channel 7 would select to broadcast in Australia revolved around the high crime rate in America.

I found myself in the company of police officers often. On one occasion early in my posting, I flew to New York City to do a story on the 'Crack Cocaine Epidemic'. In the research phase, we had lined up police officers to take the camera crew out at night to cruise the streets of Harlem, one of the most dangerous, drug-affected areas in the country.

Our three-man crew (reporter, cameraman, sound man/editor) usually travelled with a huge amount of gear and the rental car of choice was a Lincoln Town Car. It's a luxury sedan with an enormous boot (or trunk in America), that could accommodate all our equipment so it would not be visible, and therefore less likely to be stolen.

Our flight arrived in NYC shortly after 6am, and we quickly loaded the gear into a sparkling new car and headed to Harlem. It was my decision to get a head start on filming before we met up with the police, to do the potentially dangerous nighttime shoot.

I reasoned daylight would afford some protection, an opinion that later drew criticism from our friends in uniform. I had written a long 'piece to camera' explaining the drug problem in the area. For effect, I delivered it walking along a seedy sidewalk amid a sea of black faces, as cameraman, Scott Lipman, recently arrived from Australia, filmed from a distance. For all intents and purposes, it looked as though I was on my own, in an exclusively black, hostile neighbourhood.

In theory, it was a good idea, but like many seemingly good ideas, they are sometimes not.

Delivering my monologue through a radio microphone, it became apparent that there would need to be some serious editing, as the word 'motherfucker' could be clearly heard, with locals responding to the unusual sight of a white man on their street.

"What you doing, motherfucker?" was the most common inquiry, that never received a reply as I continued babbling, and appeared to be talking to myself. They must have thought I was mad, which probably afforded me some degree of protection.

After several attempts to get it right, I got the thumbs up from a highly amused soundman, and headed back to the car. We were probably lucky to only be missing four hubcaps, which had disappeared while the crew had been busy filming.

Our rendezvous with the police came several hours later, and when they found out we had already filmed in the area, they were none too happy.

"Are you guys goddamned crazy" was the response I remember. It came from a grizzled black veteran, who had been charged with the responsibility of helping out the Aussie crew.

He laughed at my defense that I thought daylight would provide a safer environment to film in the area.

"This is Harlem, man; the ass end of the world where you can get killed just looking at someone. It don't matter if its day or night, you don't want to be wandering around unprotected, especially when you got cameras. Then you're a target!"

He went on to brief us on what to expect during the nighttime shoot, and produced some telling crime statistics, showing graphically the impact the drug trade had had on the murder and crime rate.

Harlem had a special place in the history of New York. Originally, a Dutch outpost in the 17th century, the area was largely farmland. In the 1900s, it became the centre of African-American culture, known for its intimate jazz clubs and restaurants. Sadly, by the 70s and 80s, the drug trade had taken over and the murder rate was six times higher than the New York average. It had developed a dangerous reputation as an area to be avoided.

Businesses went into decline and urban decay set in. Drug-addicted squatters took over many of the abandoned buildings in the area providing the perfect environment for dealers and pushers to ply their trade. Competition for business sparked turf wars as rival gangs vied for dominance, and it fell to the police to try to enforce law and order. The war raged, not very far from downtown Manhattan, where real estate sold for mega millions and tourists walked the streets in relative safety.

The men who policed the area were a special breed, a hardened group, who had witnessed the worst of humanity, and the death and destruction caused by the drug trade. They used humour to mask the seriousness of their daily work regime.

"Put these on," the fat, black sergeant instructed us, minutes before hitting the streets to film a typical night in the life of a New York cop. The bulletproof vests, which we all wore, gave a hint of the life and death game played in the area every night.

Snugly tucked into them, it also gave the Aussie film crew a strong sense that this was serious business, and not to be taken lightly.

Crack cocaine had come onto the scene in U.S. cities in the early 80s, and was causing a major crime wave, as criminals cashed in on the hugely profitable trade. It was a highly addictive substance, and had the added 'advantage' of being less expensive than the white powder favoured in the more polite, professional circles of New York City. It quickly took hold in the poor working-class areas, with pushers targeting unemployed black youths. Use of the substance had reached epidemic proportions and was responsible for a mounting death toll in the 'city that never sleeps'.

The sights we witnessed in Harlem on that hot night in 1985 left a lasting impression, and a deep regard for the law enforcement officers charged with the responsibility of trying to stop a trade that seemed unstoppable.

New York would be a fertile hunting ground for stories over the years, and a base for assignments that would involve multiple shoots on the east coast. Channel 7 crews became familiar with a wide range of hotels in the Big Apple, and one would feature in a story that was told ad nauseam. We had just finished a 9-day swing through the east coast doing stories for a variety of programs, to be edited back in Los Angeles. The nighttime drive from LaGuardia Airport into Manhattan and the Omni on the Park Hotel was much anticipated, as the crew was exhausted, and in desperate need of a warm comfortable bed.

The upscale hotel overlooked New York's sprawling Central Park, and was a considerable upgrade to the Howard Johnsons and other medium price chains we were used to on our travels around America.

After checking in, the crew headed for their respective rooms, burdened with a mountain of television equipment, while I went in search of my accommodation. My room was on one of the upper floors and promised impressive views, but on opening the door, I was 'greeted' with the sight of a couple noisily 'doing the business' in a big king-size bed. So involved were they in the act that I doubt they would have heard my mumbled apologies.

Minutes later an angry Australian appeared at the front desk threatening to disrupt the high-priced serenity of the hotel lobby. The manager quickly explained that the hotel was full, and offered to relocate me into a nearby property. I rejected that solution, explaining that my two colleagues were already ensconced in their rooms, and our car parked in the hotel basement.

"You're only booked in for the one night, sir?" he asked.

An angry nod of the head appeared to help the manager make up his mind. He explained he was willing to offer me the Presidential suite for the night, but checkout time would have to be strictly observed.

"Is that alright, sir?"

"Yes, it is," I somberly declared, watching as a bellboy was summoned to take my bags and lead me to the luxurious suite.

New York City is without a doubt one the most exciting, vibrant and colourful cities in the world, and viewed from the wrap around balconies on the top floor of a luxury hotel, it certainly could be savoured and fully appreciated.

The Presidential suite was indeed fit for a serious Head of State. Two large bedrooms, three bathrooms, a dining room with seating for 18, and a bar and lounge area that led on to huge balconies offering 360-degree views. All exhaustion quickly fell away, as I made my way to the full bar fridge, and a phone.

I summoned my two workmates on the pretense of talking about the morning's schedule. They arrived with gaping mouths and looks of incredulity.

"You bastard, Hyslop!" It was the first expletive uttered by a cameraman, who cynically thought I had somehow secured the room and was lauding it over him.

Without a second thought, we put in a call to our NBC affiliates in the nearby Rockefeller Plaza, and invited a number of contacts over for a small impromptu party.

Years later they were still talking about how well those 'goddamned Aussies' lived while on assignment.

CHAPTER 9
WELCOME TO THE GREEN ROOM

He didn't look at all like the suave, sophisticated character that played America's most famous lawyer, in one of television's most endearing and longest running shows.

The man who stood before me must have weighed close to 150 kilos, albeit cleverly disguised by excellent tailoring and dark, slimming colours. The remnants of the rugged, good looks of his youth were there, but I was still struggling with thought that life had not been kind to the aging actor.

Raymond Burr had come to the Channel 7 studios in Los Angeles to be interviewed, before flying to Australia on a tour to publicize a one-episode remake of 'Perry Mason'.

"Meet my valet," he said, directing my attention to a younger man, who played the role of gentleman's butler perfectly. Years earlier, the actor had 'come out' as gay, making it more than likely his manservant was indeed his partner. Both Burr's on-screen characters, Perry Mason and Chief Robert Ironside, had enjoyed huge exposure in Australia over the years, and were being re-run decades after the series cancellations.

No surprise then that Network executives were keen to promote the famous actor, who had rarely lost a case in his fictional role as the famous Los Angeles attorney.

Raymond Burr was no stranger to transpacific flights, as he had bought an island in Fiji in the mid-60s, a long way from the prying eyes of Hollywood. He visited the South Pacific regularly. It was an interesting angle to be included in the interview, and he was happy to talk about it. More than 20 years later, I stayed in one of Burr's old homes that had been converted to a boutique hotel, near Nadi on the main island, Viti Levu. It was on the property the actor grew stunning orchids that remain a popular tourist attraction to this day.

Actors, comedians and entertainers were frequent visitors to the 'Green Room' of the Century City studio. I would be tasked to interview them for inclusion in stories to be aired later, or they would do satellite interviews with the hosts of shows in Australia.

It was hard not to be star-struck when some of America's funniest comedians and famous actors walked through the door to promote their latest movie or upcoming tour 'downunder'. Despite a small population, Australia was an important market to U.S. television networks and movie producers. Their product translated easily to a society, steadily and successfully Americanized over the years. Aussies were, per capita, among the biggest spenders at the box office. For many entertainers past their prime, Australia also became the 'go to' place to pick up some much needed cash, and revive flagging careers. The Aussie TV networks, with bureaus in Los Angeles, provided easy access to promote performers and programs.

When I arrived in the City of Angels in the mid-80s, many of the modern-day legends were getting their start in the entertainment business and 'cutting their teeth' in the stand-up comedy clubs on Sunset Boulevard, which I regularly visited. Years later, I would get a chance to interview the cream of the crop, funny men who had become household names.

The tragic suicide of Robin Williams in 2014 would shock a nation, and draw attention to the mental health issues of a brilliant man, who could take on a dramatic role as easily as stand on stage and make people laugh.

The diminutive actor with sad eyes was a well-established box office star when he walked into the Channel 7 studios in the mid-80s. I remember ushering him into the Green Room, before he was to front the cameras for a satellite interview.

His quiet, almost shy, demeanor was a far cry from the manic onstage persona, fueled in his early career by drugs and alcohol. He had none of the raging ego and demanding ways of performers far less talented, but when the time came to 'flick the switch', I have never seen such a dramatic transformation. One moment he was quiet and reflective, the next, a veritable cyclone of comic energy. I suppose, in hindsight, it was not hard to understand how being bipolar contributed to the highs and lows of an amazing career.

It was a common theme among fellow comedians. Billy Crystal and Steve Martin were William's contemporaries and 'brothers in arms' in the quest to make people laugh. I had occasion to interview both, finding them incredibly well balanced, humble and talented. An hour in their company, hardly made me an expert on the intricacies of their personalities, but my gut told me they were good guys. Both have gone on to stellar careers and longevity in the business matched by few.

Los Angeles was home to some of the biggest names in show business, who occupied flashy mansions and the most expensive real estate in the Hollywood Hills, Bel Air and West Los Angeles.

In the late 80s, I was to get a taste of quintessential Hollywood when I interviewed actor, Glenn Ford, one of the biggest stars of the Golden Era.

His huge 9-thousand square foot mansion was in palm tree-lined Cove Way, Beverly Hills, only a ten-minute drive from Channel 7's studio in Century City.

Ford was a major box office draw from the 1940s to the 1960s, and the epitome of the ruggedly good-looking leading man. His movie credits featured numerous westerns including '3.10 to Yuma', 'The Fastest Gun Alive', and 'The Sheepman'. However, his reputation as a 'lady's man' was cemented by his performance in the movie, 'Gilda', alongside Rita Hayworth, with whom he had a long-term relationship.

A Canadian by birth, the actor greeted the Australian television crew warmly, and I remember thinking at the time that life had been good to this aging star. He had recently celebrated his 70th birthday, and was not surrounded by 'handlers', just the one agent, who had spoken glowingly about his client. We figured we were in for a fascinating interview.

The notoriety of Ford's home had become a part of Hollywood folklore as the palatial backdrop of some of the most lavish and wildest parties of the Golden Age. Regular visitors included Gregory Peck, John Wayne, Ava Gardner and Cary Grant; the brightest stars of the time. On a tour of the huge house, Ford confirmed the basement bar became a regular hangout for Frank Sinatra and the 'Rat Pack'. He dropped names like an apple tree sheds fruit, all done with a wicked sense of humour, and a confidence born of years as the ultimate Hollywood insider. This would be an 'easy one', I thought as he led me around his personal fiefdom with a relaxed charm and lucid tongue that had likely savoured a 'wee drink' before our arrival.

Much of the interview was conducted on the move as we toured the enormous home. More than 150 autographed photos of his contemporaries adorned the walls, and provided an excellent opportunity to elicit a comment about the famous faces. Some of his opinions of fellow stars were not fit for broadcast, and confirmed he was at the epicenter of the halcyon years of Hollywood. He clearly knew where all the 'bodies were buried', and had no problem answering questions about his colourful love life.

Married 4 times, (only three at the time of my interview), he confirmed with a twinkle he had enjoyed a one night stand with Marilyn Monroe, a fling with Judy Garland, and a 40 year, on-and-off affair with his co-star, Rita Hayworth. He had, in the 60s, bought the neighbouring property to make their trysts easier and more discreet. His marriage to dancer, Eleanor Powell, lasted 16 years and produced one son, actor Peter Ford. He retired at the age of 75 and died at his home, aged 90.

Los Angeles's reputation as the movie capital of America also made it home to some of the biggest names in entertainment. Movie stars' residences dotted the Hollywood Hills, and provided rich fodder for tourist operators, while the streets of Beverly Hills boasted the world's most expensive shopping. Rodeo Drive was, and still is a magnet to the rich and famous, and the backdrop for some of Hollywood's most notorious stories. I was to report on one of them in 1989, when Hungarian actress and socialite, Zsa Zsa Gabor was arrested after assaulting a motorcycle policeman.

The ageing actress was pulled up for driving her Rolls Royce convertible with expired registration tags, but it was what she did next that made headlines. While policeman, Paul Kramer was checking for other violations, Gabor drove off, only to be chased and pulled up a second time.

When he confronted her, she slapped him, claiming it was 'in self-defense' after Kramer pulled her out of the car roughly. It was a slap heard around the world and provoked a circus-like court trial that attracted huge media coverage.

Producers in Australia were keen to get the story, so I was asked to chase it down with a call to her agent, who not surprisingly, said Ms. Gabor would be delighted to talk to Australian television.

The outrageous socialite, who had been married nine times and was famous for calling everyone, 'dahling', told me her side of the story while standing next to her two hundred thousand dollar Rolls Royce, at the scene of the alleged crime.

Efforts to garner sympathy and support apparently fell on deaf ears, as the judge fined Gabor some 13 thousand dollars for slapping the officer, driving without a license and possessing an open container of Jack Daniels whiskey.

The judge accused Gabor of milking the criminal justice system to publicise herself, and ordered her to serve 3 days in jail, perform community service, and undergo psychiatric evaluation.

The fascination with, and demand for, Hollywood celebrity stories kept the 7 Network bureau busy, and one in particular dominated headlines. It revolved around perhaps tinsel town's biggest star and established leading man.

In 1985, Rock Hudson found himself embroiled in a sensational court case after allegations surfaced that he had knowingly exposed his gay lover,

Marc Christian, to the Aids virus.

News that the aging actor, who had never 'come out of the closet', was stricken with the deadly disease, shocked the world and led to a media frenzy.

Australia was not immune to the salacious headlines and interest was intense. Decades of Women's Weekly articles portraying Hudson as a great lover to America's most beautiful starlets had not prepared readers for the shocking news that he actually preferred 'blokes'. The phones ran hot from producers wanting coverage of the court proceedings, and an interview with Marc Christian, the 31-year-old at the centre of allegations.

Representing Christian at the time was Hollywood celebrity lawyer, Marvin Mitchelson, whose office was coincidentally in the same building as the 7 Bureau.

An unabashed self-promoter, Mitchelson had gained fame representing the defacto wife of actor Lee Marvin in her quest to relieve him of half his fortune. He became known as the 'Prince of Palimony', describing the term as 'marriage with no rings attached', and was an advocate for clients including Bianca Jagger, Joan Collins, Robert De Niro and Zsa Zsa Gabor.

The interview with Marc Christian was organised after Mitchelson paid a late night visit to our studio. Half a bottle of scotch later, the details were thrashed out, and Christian agreed to tell his side of the story to television viewers in Australia.

Just months later, Rock Hudson died of the disease that was claiming a mounting toll of gay men in America. He was 59 years old.

Mitchelson lodged a 10-million-dollar claim against Hudson's estate, alleging his client had suffered severe emotional distress after hearing on a news broadcast that the matinee idol had Aids.

Although he tested negative to the virus several times after learning of Hudson's diagnosis, he contended the star had put him at risk of contracting the disease by concealing his illness, and continuing to have sexual relations with him.

Four years after Hudson died, the L.A. Superior Court awarded Marc Christian almost 22 million dollars, but it was later reduced on appeal to 5.5 million.

He would remain Aids free until his death from pulmonary problems in 2009, aged 55.

Celebrity lawyer, Marvin Mitchelson was jailed 8 years after the celebrated court case on Tax Fraud charges. He died of cancer in 2004.

One Hollywood movie icon whose sexuality was never in question was legendary tough guy, Clint Eastwood.

I had watched his movies as I grew up, and got the chance to meet him in 1986 in Carmel, on the Monterey Peninsula, in Northern California.

It was not his acting that attracted the attention of Channel 7, but his move into politics. At the age of 55, and at the height of his celebrity, Eastwood decided to run for office as Mayor of the small coastal town.

He campaigned on a platform of 'bringing back ice cream cones.' Only in America! A zoning law enacted in 1929 had banned them, and Eastwood thought it was time the archaic regulations were updated. He had history with the town's previous administration, winning a legal suit, after he was thwarted in erecting an office building on land he owned. He had an axe to grind with the local politicians.

Also the proud proprietor of the restaurant, Hog's Breath Inn, he argued his credentials as a business owner, not a famous actor, qualified him to seek office.

The story was an easy sell to producers in Sydney, and I was quickly on the phone to Eastwood's agent with a request for an interview.

He came back with a date and time, and our three-man crew found ourselves cruising up the Pacific Coast Highway, for an overnight stay before the 8am interview.

First call on our early evening arrival was the Hog's Breath Inn, where there was no shortage of interview subjects, prepared to voice an opinion on the movie star's political aspirations. Predictably, there was no sign of Clint serving behind the bar, probably off reading a script for his next multi-million-dollar movie, I thought.

His opponent was two-term mayor, Charlotte Townsend, who boasted she took phone calls from residents anytime, while Eastwood had an unlisted number. In response, the actor vowed to get an answering machine.

Next morning, we arrived at the Clint's beachside house, expecting to be received by a Malpaso Productions employee, but the door was opened by a disheveled Eastwood, clearly not expecting to find a TV crew on his doorstep.

My explanation that we were from Australia for an 8 am interview, set up by his agent, failed to impress the clearly 'out of sorts' actor.

"Goddamned leeches," he screamed as he pushed passed us and ran down the side of his house into a neighboring property.

We followed with camera rolling, trying to explain what I thought was an obvious miscommunication. Five minutes later, he emerged from the house, still in a frosty mood, and agreed to a brief stand-up interview.

I can only assume a quick phone call had confirmed my story, and he hadn't been kept in the loop by his agent. There were no apologies, not that

I expected one, and we went on our way with what I thought would be a highly entertaining story.

It was. The final cut went to air after the actor won a landslide victory, 2166 votes to 799. The new mayor's first act in office was to throw out the planning board, which had vetoed the ice cream prohibition repeal.

My story featured our exchange and wobbly shots of him on the run intercut with stock vision of his famous Dirty Harry character, uttering that famous line, "Go on punk, make my day!"

Little did he know, he had inadvertently made mine.

Clint Eastwood did not seek re-election two years later, and continues his legendary career as actor, director, composer and producer well into his 90s.

Entertainment related stories were the staple while based in L.A, and one reason the 7 Network initially resisted the urge to move to the East Coast, where politics provided content for news and current event shows. By the time my posting ended after seven years, the network had a presence on the East Coast and I had visited 46 of the 50 states in America. I believed I had a pretty good handle on the country and its people.

CHAPTER 10
UP, UP AND AWAY

As a journalist and foreign correspondent, a fear of flying is supposedly not an option.

A quick response to breaking news is essential, so whether it was in a helicopter, light aircraft, commercial jet or military plane, I often found myself jet-lagged and leery of flying.

As a Qantas brat, who had seen a large slice of the world by his twelfth birthday, airports and planes held little mystery. It was only when I was employed as a journalist that I got a real taste of flying in aircraft of differing shapes and sizes.

Whether as a passenger or reporter on assignment, planes had always both fascinated and frightened me. On long overseas flights to England as a boy, the family would 'run a book' on how long it would take me to throw up.

It was not uncommon for the captain's cockpit announcements during landing to be drowned out by the shocking noise of me 'losing my lunch' into a bag in the back of the aircraft. So loud was the commotion, verging on high-pitched screams that my sister would move away in embarrassment.

On one long haul flight to London, cabin crew were overheard by Di exclaiming, "It's that Hyslop kid again!"

Thankfully, by the time of my appointment as a cadet-journalist with the Australian Broadcasting Commission, I had taught my stomach to behave itself.

The first test came not long after starting work with the national broadcaster.

In 1977, a massive bushfire swept through the Blue Mountains, west of Sydney. Dozens of homes were destroyed, and two people died. I was one of a team of reporters assigned to cover the unfolding drama. To meet the 7 pm deadline, a small Hughes helicopter was dispatched to airlift me back to the ABC Gore Hill studios, to edit my report.

It was a quick 'in and out' operation. The agreed landing spot was on an oval, ringed by fires and buffeted by heavy winds. I jumped into the chopper and as we lifted off, the rotor blades of a nearby Army Iroquois helicopter slammed against our perspex bubble. While the pilot battled to control the flimsy craft, I battled to control my twitching sphincter! We barely managed our respective tasks.

Welcome, I thought, to the dangerous world of journalism.

On two other occasions over the next twenty years, I was in helicopters forced to auto rotate, or in layman's terms, crash!

The pilots' good timing and quick thinking, combined with plenty of luck resulted in no injuries, but the incidents provided another rigorous test for that twitching sphincter.

While flying in television station helicopters is generally safe, sourcing light aircraft in overseas countries is often problematic. A classy webpage or glossy brochure rarely gives a full picture or accurate flying record of the operator.

I found this out on two memorable occasions.

In October, 1994, I was dispatched to the Philippines with cameraman, Ian McGill and an assistant, to film reports ranging from pedophile priests, Aussie bar owners, and the re-enactment of the 50th anniversary of General MacArthur's landing on Leyte Island.

The latter was a complicated shoot, involving a flight to the outlying island, and a series of live crosses during the highly choreographed military exercises on land and sea.

A producer in the Channel 7 Melbourne newsroom told us that a pilot would meet us at Manila airport. No details were provided about the type of aircraft or the airline. We were 'flying blind' so to speak; we had the hanger number and not much else.

Loaded with heavy gear, a van deposited us outside the meeting spot at the assigned time. The sight that greeted us most certainly guaranteed a twitch or two.

Standing on the tarmac was a small Beechcraft Baron, that looked like it had come off the production line not long after the second world war; peeling paint flapping listlessly from an aging fuselage, two ancient engines had leaked dirty black oil streaks on both sides of the aircraft. It was a thoroughly disturbing picture, confirmed in the eyes of my cameraman, a consummate professional, who returned a look that said it all. You're joking, right!

The young assistant, who was new to the business, appeared on the verge of tears and no doubt ready to run. They both looked at me for reassurance.

However, before I could respond, a loud shout cut through the air. Striding out of a nearby hanger was a figure closely resembling a World War 1 air ace.

Within seconds, it was clear there were two figures heading towards us, one carrying an oversized toolbox, and another taller man wearing brown overalls, a leather helmet and goggles.

"Hello, welcome," the taller man bellowed, "I am Captain Rodrigo, and this is my mechanic, Carlos."

It looked like 'Biggles' had been hired to fly us to Leyte, by a faceless producer, who had no idea of the condition and safety of the plane we were about to board.

"We must move quickly," he authoritatively declared, "bad weather is coming, and the military has declared restricted airspace if we are not there on time."

The urgency with which he spoke succeeded in quashing any questions I may have thought to ask: probing queries like, "can this bloody thing fly?"

Furtive, nervous glances among the crew were replaced by frenetic activity. Camera and editing equipment was hoisted hurriedly into the baggage compartment.

A few seconds later, we were instructed to buckle up, followed by a deafening roar. It did nothing to placate our concerns or calm tattered nerves. Thick smoke belched from both engines, the fuselage shook, threatening to dislodge rivets holding the aircraft together. The pilot and mechanic exchanged what suspiciously appeared to be worried looks.

It was going to be a long two-hour flight, and what had he said about bad weather?

It was not long before we found out. Within twenty minutes, seriously black clouds enveloped the small plane, and began throwing it about the stormy skies, with no regard to its age or the terror of its occupants.

To be fair, the captain looked like he knew what he was doing, but when you have your eyes closed for most of the time, and your lips tightly clenched to guard against projectile vomiting, not too much rational thought gets processed.

We were battling not just the storm, but also the deadline. All media organisations had been instructed to be on the ground and ready to film the re-enactment by 11 am. We were cutting it way too fine, but when Captain Rodrigo turned to me and yelled that we had to land on an isolated island to ride out the storm, I was not at all conflicted.

"Get it down," I stammered urgently.

Once on the ground, though, rational thought returned and I began worrying about the ramifications of a missed deadline. Expensive satellite feeds had been booked into daytime programs in Australia, and the producers back home would not be happy if those live crosses were not forthcoming.

A quickly convened chat with Rodrigo, after a couple of even more quickly consumed beers to calm the nerves, elicited a promise to take off as soon as possible. However, he wasn't sure we could beat the landing embargo on Leyte.

His fears were confirmed as we neared the island in much-improved weather. Air traffic controllers had started the countdown on barring landings.

There was only one thing to do; an action for which I will be forever grateful.

In an appropriately panicked voice, Captain Rodrigo declared an emergency.

"Mayday, Mayday!" the call went out.

The battered old aircraft, which looked like it had taken a round or two of anti-aircraft fire, touched down minutes later to be followed along the runway by fire engines and military police, none too pleased by the late arrival.

First out of the plane was Carlos the mechanic who, with all the theatrical flair of a seasoned actor, flung the cowling of the right engine open to pinpoint the 'problem'.

We too played our part warmly congratulating our 'hero captain' for saving our bacon. Little did the authorities know, he really had, but in a different way. The military police were having none of it. They later grilled Captain Rodrigo, slapping him with an infringement and the threat of future action. It was a fine Channel 7 was happy to pick up. He was my hero!

Australian consular officials were waiting to escort us to the area where fellow media were assembled, to film the re-enactment of this historically important moment. Bemused looks were exchanged, confirming an understanding that our 'mayday' landing was deeply suspicious.

Once filming started, the actor portraying General Macarthur, stepped off a landing craft in his much-heralded return, only to fall head first into the water. It was the 'money shot' and a fabulously comical moment.

We later boarded an Australian Navy destroyer, which carried a group of veterans who had participated in the biggest naval engagement of WW2, together with their families.

In an emotional dawn ceremony, the old sailors cast wreaths into the water to honour mates, who were killed in action on 21st October, 1944. Most were on board '*HMAS Australia*', hit by a lone Japanese dive-bomber, which crashed into the ship's foremast killing 30 crew, including the Commanding Officer.

Being guests of the Australian Navy to record the emotional ceremony was considerably safer than our earlier adventure in the small aircraft flying to the island.

That frightening flight in stormy skies drove home the dangers of news organisations contracting small airlines, without any idea of their background and record.

It also bought into sharp focus the conflicting emotions journalists struggle with, when weighing up the dangers and rewards of proceeding with an assignment that could be life-threatening.

Another flight in a foreign land raised similar issues.

The year was 1988, and the 'land downunder' was getting ready to celebrate its Bicentennial. To titillate the nationalistic fervour of television viewers, I was sent to Rio de Janeiro, where ships of the First Fleet Re-enactment would call in, on their way to Sydney Harbour.

On the same trip, I would also interview Great Train Robber, Ronald Biggs and film an expose on a blood-selling racket that had left Brazil with the second-largest number of AIDS cases in the world. We would also shoot another story on the horrific crime rate in the famous holiday destination. It would be a very full schedule.

As part of the Bicentennial story, a helicopter was required to do aerial filming of the flotilla making its way into the sparkling harbour. The shots from the flying platform would showcase Sugarloaf Mountain and the majestic Corcovado, with Christ the Redeemer looking down on the breathtaking vista.

I tasked our translator with finding a chopper operator to carry out the assignment.

On the day of the tall ships' arrival, perfect weather bathed the city in bright sunshine, great conditions for filming.

We were driven in a state of high expectation to a park in a beachside suburb, to board the helicopter and take to the skies. I was not prepared for what awaited us. Sitting on the helipad was an aircraft from a different era; a very old chopper that looked, as they say in the classics, 'like it had seen better days' and none of them recent.

The Portuguese-speaking pilot met us with a firm handshake and a no-nonsense manner. I looked closely to see if he resembled the translator who had hired him, maybe a brother or a second cousin.

I had been in dozens of helicopters over the years, but this one was perhaps the most decrepit, invoking the same doubts encountered in Manila: do I risk the crews' lives in this aircraft?

However, as usual, time constraints prevailed, and the macho instinct of 'don't be such a sissy' won out. Cameraman Maurice Roper's anticipation of filming was apparently overruling any sensible or lingering doubts he may have had. He could have said 'no way', but peer group dynamic made that unlikely. Due to weight restrictions, the third member of our team was left on the ground, no doubt a huge relief to him after seeing the chopper.

We climbed into the old flying machine, my imagination working overtime. The door was removed, leaving Maurice to jerry-rig a makeshift harness that would allow him maximum mobility to capture the great shots we would soon encounter. And stop him falling to a certain death!

It was a sound I still remember, a noise resembling a clapped-out Volkswagen. Instead of the high-pitched, whistling scream of most chopper engines, this one was more like a dull rumbling of an automobile fueled by diesel.

It was disconcerting to say the least, but magically, the old 'rust bucket' lifted off and succeeded in staying aloft for the duration of the forty-minute flight, over some of the most stunning scenery imaginable.

The magnificent, tall ships were greeted, and escorted into the harbour by hundreds of brightly coloured vessels. Captain Cook's *Endeavour* replica proudly flew the British ensign, but from one of the masts flapped a less formal flag, featuring a boxing kangaroo.

The obligatory 'stand-up' was shot with sun-lit Sugarloaf Mountain in the background. Life was good, not a hair out of place; could it get any better?

The fact that I reflect and write about these incidents with attempted humour is a common way to cope with fear. It's a mechanism used by soldiers, emergency service workers and journalists who experience first-hand the horror of death and destruction. Some things people should just not see.

Air disasters strike a particularly emotive note with journalists. When you spend so much time in the air, travelling from story to story the likelihood of running afoul of the odds is high.

There are few more shocking scenes than the horrors encountered at an aircraft crash. I was soon to find out!

In late August 1986, the story literally fell into my lap. It was on one of Los Angeles ubiquitous freeways that I heard a news flash on the radio about a plane crash in the suburban neighbourhood of Cerritos. I was instantly 'on the job', and the office was alerted to send a cameraman.

Normally a 'car park' on most days, the freeway was running smoothly. It was a Sunday and I raced to the scene. It was not hard to find. A huge plume of smoke settled over a good part of suburban Los Angeles and I arrived not long after firemen were unfurling their hoses. The full complement of emergency services had not yet reached the scene, so clutching my press pass I ran towards the fires.

The smell of Avgas and the pungent aroma of death was everywhere. More than a dozen homes in the quiet suburban street had been destroyed, fires raged and plane wreckage littered the area. The tail section of the aircraft was imbedded in the roof of a house not yet consumed by the blaze. The airline's distinctive Aztec design and paint colours identified it as an Aeromexico airliner.

Without a camera, I could do little but try to find eyewitnesses, and line up emergency personnel for interviews later. The confronting sights were overwhelming! Bodies littered the fiery landscape; charred corpses remained strapped to blackened airline seats. The tiny lifeless body of a baby hung grotesquely from the roofline of a shattered home. Fire fighters moved from house to house dousing flames and checking for residents killed on the ground.

My network's affiliation with NBC News allowed me to ask a favour of one their cameramen, and I recorded a quick piece to camera, while waiting for our man, to record interviews and overlay vision later.

When he arrived, I was to learn the full extent of the disaster. One of the great myths of news reporting is the man at the scene is in command of the facts. That is often not the case. The live crosses you see on television happen these days with the invaluable input of producers feeding reporters the latest details through an earpiece. In the 1980s, the job was done without the assistance of mobile phones, internet connection and instantaneous access to the latest information.

I learnt from my cameraman that the Aeromexico DC9 was on final approach to LAX when it collided with a light aircraft shortly before midday.

The small plane, a Piper Cherokee, with three people on board had fallen into a school playground not far from the crash site. As we arrived at that scene, the bodies were being removed from the surprisingly intact aircraft and put into body bags. This shocking scene remains one of my most graphic memories of that day.

I remember, perversely, watching the body, it later emerged, of the 26-year-old daughter of the pilot being pulled from the wreckage. The strapless shoes were still on her feet, and most of her body seemed remarkably unmarked.

I saw many graphic and disturbing images that day, but for some reason the loss of that young woman disturbed me most.

Hours later, the death count was put at sixty-seven in the aircrafts and fifteen killed on the ground.

Decades later, as I watched a reconstruction of the accident on the television program, 'Air Crash Investigation', authorities pointed the finger at both the pilot of the light plane and local aviation authorities. An intrusion into commercial airspace was blamed for the accident, prompting the Federal Aviation Authority to improve anti-collision technology, and clarify air space regulations into the busy international airport.

It was an up-close look at horrific death that I had no wish to see again, but in my line of work, the odds were stacked against that hope.

The year before, a complete coincidence thrust me into the reporting role of an aviation disaster that stunned America. The Channel 7 crew had just finished a weeklong swing through the East Coast of the United States, shooting stories to be aired later.

We were booked to fly via Dallas Fort Worth on the way back to Los Angeles. The flight into the Texan city was bumpy, as thunderstorms swept across the flat plains of the Lone Star State.

The date was August 2nd, 1985. We were about to re-board the flight to Los Angeles, when a public announcement notified passengers of the cancellation of all flights in and out of Dallas.

Delta flight 191 from Fort Lauderdale, a Lockheed TriStar, had minutes earlier crashed on approach into the airport.

Again, the story fell into my lap, 'Johnny on the spot'. Another air disaster, and depressingly, the same heart-wrenching storyline.

Word spread quickly through the airport and tears flowed freely. The sirens of emergency vehicles could be clearly heard, and an intangible sense of panic gripped the airline lounges. I turned to the 7 News Bureau in Los Angeles to find out the latest. Like most unfolding news events, details were slow to emerge.

The plane had gone down near the airport perimeter, I was told. The name of the airline spokesman was passed on. It was up us to chase the story down.

Unlike the disaster in L.A, where I found myself amidst the devastation, emergency services moved quickly to isolate the media and prevent efforts to get close to the wreckage, which would soon be masked in darkness.

The scene developed into a feeding frenzy with frustrated media kept well away from the crash site and drip-fed details.

There were angry scenes, much yelling and cursing of airline officials for not giving the media boys what they wanted. It was shaping up as casebook study on how not to handle the dissemination of facts to the press during a crisis.

Delta Airlines, of course, had its own agenda and responsibility in establishing the fatality count and notifying the next of kin.

It took another 12 hours before cameras were allowed out to film the wreckage of the smoldering jet from behind barriers a considerable distance from the crash site. Again, this didn't sit well with news networks wanting to get a closer look at the carnage.

Emergency services and air crash investigators were swarming over the wreckage. Small red flags could be seen dotting the site, bodies not yet recovered, and once again the overpowering smell of Avgas and the pungent, sickly scent of death.

For our part, the first story had been filed and we were put on standby to await further developments. The crew's energy level was flagging as we had worked non-stop for nine days.

We knew, of course, we would have to wait to find if any Australians were on board the ill-fated aircraft. It was one of the sick, yet predictable realities of television news. A thousand people could be massacred, but if there wasn't an Australian among them, the message was clear.

"No Aussies, come on home!" Maybe a slight exaggeration, but you get the idea. Cynical you think?

Forty-eight hours after the crash, a clearer picture was emerging as to what had brought the big jet down. A microburst caused by thunderstorms in the area was the chief suspect. The aircraft had been literally pushed into the ground by a sudden explosive downdraft that sent it ploughing into a roadway and two water towers short of the runway.

The pilots were powerless to prevent the accident, though the NTSB was later critical of their decision to fly through the thunderstorms in the first place. One hundred and thirty-six people died, plus the driver of a car on the nearby freeway; twenty-seven passengers and crew survived. There were no Australians onboard.

Many years later, I again watched the forensic analysis of the disaster on 'Air Crash Investigation'. It was an eerie experience, rekindling many of the emotions I felt in Dallas on that day, more than twenty years earlier.

The disaster prompted the accelerated development of the onboard Doppler Weather Radar, which can detect wind shear and help prevent similar disasters.

For a reporter used to covering breaking news, I always envied the producers of shows who enjoyed the luxury of revisiting and analysing disasters, catastrophes and assorted historical mayhem.

I was to see another of the stories I covered in America featured on one such show.

It was sensationally pitched to television viewers as, 'Horror in the Skies over Honolulu', and dealt with the incident involving a United Airlines 747 jet.

The year was 1989, and we were scrambled in the L.A. Bureau following reports that a fully laden jumbo jet was in trouble in the skies over the Pacific Ocean, off the coast of Hawaii.

United Airlines Flight 811, with three hundred and thirty-seven passengers onboard had just taken off from Honolulu bound for Auckland and Sydney, when the cargo door blew out causing an explosive decompression.

Minutes after the first news flash hit the screens in Los Angeles, we were headed to LAX to board a plane for Hawaii.

The phones were running hot from producers in Australia. This was why television networks spent many millions of dollars establishing news bureaus in America.

With more than two hundred Aussies and Kiwis on board, interest back home in the endangered aircraft was intense.

By the time we were airborne, the jet had safely returned to Honolulu, but not before a remarkable story of tragedy and bravery unfolded.

Ironically, as we landed on the Hawaiian island, the crippled airliner stood on the tarmac, surrounded by emergency vehicles and investigators.

It was a mad scramble after deplaning to collect the gear and go in search of the story.

For United Airlines, perversely, this was a 'good news' story.

A spokesman was quick to detail the heroics of the captain and crew, and answer questions about what they thought had happened in the sky over the Pacific Ocean. It was a very different scenario to the procedures adopted when a commercial plane crashes, killing all onboard.

It was a chilling tale of how close to death over three hundred people had come, and just how lucky most of them had been. The 59-year-old Captain, David Cronin was at the controls and passing through 22 thousand feet in stormy skies, when a loud thump was heard on the flight deck. He was not to know, but the forward cargo door had blown out, sparking an explosive decompression, and sucking nine business class passengers out into the night skies.

With a huge hole torn in the side of the aircraft, power in two of its engines reduced, and a damaged wing, the crippled jet declared an emergency.

Forced to dump fuel and anticipate what would be a 'hot landing' because of damage to the aircraft, the veteran pilot guided the plane back to earth against the odds.

While it was good news and a lucky escape for most on board, the families of nine passengers, including two Sydney men and a New Zealander, would soon be attending funerals without the bodies of their loved ones. They would never be found. Investigators later announced that traces of human remains were located in one of the engines!

This was not simply a story for the nightly news. Everyone wanted a piece of it. The phone line from Australia was ringing non-stop. The Breakfast show, "can you get us a Sydney survivor?" The daytime shows, the current affairs program; all looking for a different angle on a story that had all the ingredients of an epic tale.

It was an assignment that demanded much of reporter and crew. With so many people on board there was no shortage of eyewitness reaction. The terror of a honeymooning couple who thought they'd be denied a chance to raise children; the lucky escape of a female purser, who clung to the railing of a staircase as passengers nearby disappeared into the dark void; the bravery of passengers who helped a similarly endangered flight attendant. The near miss for a Sydney businessman sitting behind three of those killed, guiltily admitting he had lost his shoes, which had been sucked out the gaping hole.

With the airline forced to put stranded passengers into hotels near the airport to await ongoing flights, the hunt for the angles began.

Media outlets from around the world were competing for the story.

Less than 24 hours after their lucky escape, many of the passengers again lined up for flights to Auckland and Sydney. Nerves were jangling and this event on its own was worthy of a follow up story.

As a reporter long use to covering emotionally charged breaking news, I would find myself inadvertently asking what I would do in similar circumstances. Would I get back on a plane so quickly? It was a pointless question, I concluded, as airline policy expressly forbade drunks on board, and very drunk indeed I would have to be! Near-death experiences affect me that way. Questions are often best left unasked. Emotional detachment crucial if one is to chronicle such events.

The story of United Flight 811 would not go away quickly. I watched in awe the actions of New Zealand couple, Kevin and Susan Campbell, who for years campaigned to find the cause of the accident that killed their son, Lee. They crisscrossed the United States, spending their own money to attend inquiries, gather evidence and form an opinion as to why the aircraft suffered an explosive decompression.

Kevin Campbell, a respected engineer, from Wellington in New Zealand, was convinced an electrical problem and a faulty latching mechanism on the front cargo door was responsible for the accident.

In March of 1992, three years after the disaster, the National Transport Safety Board determined, "The probable cause of the accident was the sudden opening of the cargo door, which was attributed to improper wiring and deficiencies in the door's design".

It was vindication for the heart-broken New Zealand couple, who had lost a son because of an aircraft design fault, and spent many thousands of dollars to fully understand why he was taken from them.

The NTSB finding led to the Boeing Corporation replacing cargo door latching mechanisms with new re-designed locks.

Almost thirty years after covering these gruesome and heart wrenching aviation disasters, I still find myself being asked by friends familiar with my background, "Why do you still fly as much as you do?"

My curt reply, "Drinking helps!"

CHAPTER 11
TOP GUN I'M NOT

The things you do for a story!

After assorted adventures in aircraft, I found myself strapped into one of the most potent jet fighters at the U.S. Navy Fighter Weapons School at Miramar, in San Diego.

I had Hollywood to blame. It was 1986, and Paramount Pictures had just released 'Top Gun', the romantic, military action drama starring Tom Cruise and Kelly McGillis.

The movie became a runaway success, grossing 357 million dollars at the box office. Not a bad return on an investment of only 15 million.

Australia was not immune to the talent and charms of a young Tom Cruise. The movie was a smash hit downunder, and the phones ran hot from show producers wanting stories on the actors and the movie.

The duties of a 'news correspondent' are not limited to just 'news' in overseas bureaus. The expectation is to supply content for the full range of programs shown on the Network in the morning, daytime and evening. It could get very busy.

The word 'angle' is perhaps the most frequently used, and abused in journalism.

"What about going to the air base where the movie was filmed; what about getting into an F-14 Tomcat fighter jet?" The questions came thick and fast and resulted in the U.S. Navy approving our visit to their facility.

The Miramar Naval Air Station is a two-hour drive on Interstate 5 from Los Angeles and is one of the country's most important military installations.

It was, at the time, the workplace of some very cocky and proud aviators, who had seen their jobs unrealistically romanticised on the silver screen. However, it no doubt significantly improved their 'hit rate' on the local female population. These men didn't walk, they strutted.

Met by a Naval Public Relations Officer, we were taken to meet some 'warriors of the sky', and were not surprised to see that none of them was as good looking as Mister Cruise.

Interviewing U.S. military types is a unique experience: "yes sir, no sir, three bags full sir". So used to taking orders from superior officers, they are incapable of breaking the habit of addressing everyone as 'sir'.

I felt very important; no one had ever called me sir, but as good as it made me feel, I had to ask them to stop using the bloody word.

The United States Navy was obviously happy with what the movie had done for its image. So happy, that it had no concern about supplying a multi-million-dollar F-14 jet and a tank full of expensive Avgas to whizz an Aussie journalist around the skies. I was destined to get a feel for what it was like to be Pete 'Maverick' Mitchell.

The young aviator tasked with the job of flying me 'rather fast', succeeded admirably. He didn't crash! I did not vomit, and we were all thrilled. I sat behind him in the spot normally occupied by the Radar Intercept Officer, but I did very little intercepting.

It was another assignment that gave an already overworked 'twitching sphincter' more exercise.

The United States Navy would again feature on my show reel when one of its biggest aircraft carriers, the *'USS Carl Vinson'*, visited Melbourne in the mid-nineties.

The Nimitz class nuclear powered carrier was in town after taking part in 'Exercise Ke Koa' in the Coral Sea, and ceremonies to commemorate the end of World War 2 in the Pacific.

Eager to cement relations with its close ally, the U.S. Navy invited local journalists onboard to report on what life was like for the more than six thousand sailors who called the ship home.

The journalists, from assorted media outlets, were asked to assemble at the Point Cook Air Base, south of Melbourne, for the short flight on a Grumman Greyhound transport plane to the supercarrier, anchored in Port Phillip Bay.

Excitement was running high among the group. How many people, after all, even if they were cynical reporters, got a chance to land on the pitching deck of an aircraft carrier? It would make a good story in the pub later that night.

It was unlike any plane I had experienced; the seats faced backwards, so when the aircraft landed and its tail hook was captured by the arresting gear, it felt like your spinal cord was going to puncture the front of your body.

It was an even more spectacular sensation when the plane was catapulted off the ship. If you had been wearing dentures, you might have found them later in your underpants. It was certainly one of the most unusual sensations I had ever experienced in an aircraft.

Having access to the *'USS Carl Vinson'*, a true monster of the seas, was also a rare and fascinating study into the omnipotent strength of the world's major superpower. Interestingly, the deceased body of Osama Bin Laden was turfed from the deck of this carrier into a watery grave in 2011.

Housing ninety aircraft, the carrier was armed with more firepower than most nations in the world. No wonder the United States was firmly established as the world's international policeman.

Built at a cost of four point five billion dollars, the super carrier was, and still is an impressive bit of military hardware.

Not, however, as head turning as the Space Shuttle in Houston, which I found myself aboard while on assignment in 1988. It was definitively the most noteworthy aircraft I had reported on, and while I was denied a voyage into space, the experience fueled many a 'bullshit' conversation at subsequent dinner tables.

A mock-up of the Space Shuttle was used to train astronauts, and was a handy backdrop for stand-ups by television reporters, for their stories on the space program.

For a number of years, I was a regular visitor to Houston, particularly after the destruction of Space Shuttle *'Challenger'* in 1986, which killed all seven astronauts. There were few stories in the 80s that emotionally affected Americans more than this disaster, which shook the country's proud perception of itself as a world leader in space exploration.

I was getting ready for a day in the office in Los Angeles, and was half listening to the launching sequence on a nearby television, when the shuttle blew up, seventy-three seconds into its mission.

Three hours later, I was on a flight to Cape Canaveral with the camera crew. It would be the start of an exhausting week, but a rewarding professional experience, that gave Channel 7 bragging rights as the first Australian broadcaster to file from NASA's Florida launch point. As chance would have it, none of the Aussie TV networks were on hand to cover the space mission; understandably they had become commonplace in the 80s.

It was a mad scramble to get crews to the scene in the aftermath of the shocking accident. The logistics are always difficult in covering breaking news. Australian broadcasters relied heavily on their American partners in supplying satellite feeds and any other help on the ground. Channel 7 at the time was affiliated with NBC and CNN. Our major competitor, Channel 9, was in bed with CBS and ABC.

As the first Australian crew to arrive at Cape Canaveral, the priority was to find our American affiliate and organize a satellite feed to beat the opposition. We did! But, it later emerged we had used CBS, an action that caused considerable angst to Channel 9 News Director, Ian Cook (for whom I had worked years earlier). A simple error, or a deliberate action? I put it down to confusion, explaining that the crew had been approached by a satellite engineer in the broadcast compound inquiring whether we were the Aussie crew needing a satellite feed. I confirmed we indeed were Aussie and in need of a feed!

Two years later, we returned to NASA's headquarters in Houston with an Australian scientist, whose work had been recognized, and chosen to be one of the onboard experiments on an upcoming shuttle flight.

Sydney scientist, Doctor Leopold Dintenfass, was a world leader in the study of blood flow and its use in the diagnosis and prevention of disease. His space experiments would allow NASA to see how the human blood flow was affected by zero gravity. Why they needed to know this I had no idea, but Leopold certainly looked like an intelligent fellow, who could make a valuable contribution to science.

A small, bald and bespectacled man, likened in looks to actor Peter Lorre, he had carved out an admirable reputation in Australia and was no shrinking violet on the international stage.

His life was a tribute to the resilience of the human spirit. Having lost his family to the Nazis in the Polish ghettos, he made his way to Australia in 1950, speaking no English but armed with chemical engineering degrees from Poland and Ukraine.

To be selected by NASA, and given the opportunity to have his work recognised by the scientific community, was a crowning glory in an already distinguished career.

They are stories that have a common theme; a journalist's unavoidable link to aviation. Whether using an aircraft to get to assignments or penning stories about planes that fly, crash or venture into outer space.

I was to report on another remarkable aviation feat while working in the United States.

The year was 1986, and a group of aviation enthusiasts was tasked with building perhaps the strangest flying machine ever seen in the sky. Its name was '*Voyager*' and it was built for the express purpose of establishing a record for nonstop, non-refueled, circumnavigation of Planet Earth!

I first saw the strange craft in the huge hangar where it was built, in the Californian Mohave Desert, near Edwards Air Force Base, almost 12 months before the historic flight.

The hangar belonged to legendary aircraft designer, Burt Rutan, who had a long track record for building some of the strangest and most innovative aircraft on the U.S. market. He was no stranger to breaking all the rules when it came to concept aircraft, and was clever at pitching them to potential customers and the media.

Inspiration for 'Voyager', had come from a sketch on the back of a napkin during a long lunch with his brother Dick and attractive girlfriend, Jeana Yeager, both pilots and aircraft enthusiasts.

Commenced in 1981, it would be the start of a project that would capture the imagination of the world.

I was shown the gangling, twin-engine machine long before the historic flight. It was a strange craft; a long, cylindrically shaped fuselage with small engines on both ends, attached to two more long cylinders from which sprang massively long wings. It was constructed of fibreglass, carbon fibre and Kevlar, crucially lightweight materials to minimise drag through the air, and make it easier for the tiny engines to work effectively.

Dick Rutan and Jeana Yeager would pilot the aircraft, a hellishly uncomfortable feat, as they would have to virtually lie down to fly the contraption. It was an incredible squeeze, and if things went to plan, an environment they'd have to endure for up to two weeks.

At six feet four inches, Rutan risked severe cramping while his diminutive girlfriend would be a tad more comfortable, but it would be an ambitious quest that would test to the max the endurance of both pilots and plane.

My early interviews with the Rutans established a rapport, and demonstrated that Australia would be one country enthusiastically watching the progress of their adventure.

In July 1986, the first test flight was held, off the coast of California. It saw 'Voyager' fly for a distance of nearly 19 thousand kilometres, but subsequent test flights would be plagued with problems. The team, nonetheless, was pressing ahead with plans to have a crack at the record on December 14th 1986.

The frigid day dawned with an estimated three and half thousand media on standby to capture the start of Voyager's historic flight. We had driven through the night from Los Angeles to reach Edwards Air Force base, and were mustered into a vantage point to set up a camera and wait.

At 8 am, the ungainly looking aircraft rolled out of the hangar for its date with destiny. On board, the pilots would have to put aside all romantic notions for the foreseeable future. As one insider had joked earlier, you'd have to be a contortionist to have 'fun' in the cramped interior. Rumours, meanwhile, suggested the couple's relationship was on the rocks after 5 years of stressful preparations for the record attempt.

With the eyes of thousands of spectators and well-wishers focused on the aircraft, it accelerated slowly down the tarmac. It would need over four kilometres of runway to take off, the reason Edwards Air Force Base had been chosen.

Within seconds it was apparent something was wrong. The tips of the spindly wings, heavily loaded with fuel, were scraping along the runway, potentially causing enough damage to bring a halt to the record attempt.

Chief architect of the mission, Burt Rutan was ensconced in a small control room in the hangar to monitor the flight. Just seconds before lift-off he radioed his brother that the aircraft was within its performance specifications and the flight could continue.

It was a rocky start to the ambitious record attempt that sparked raucous applause and wild cheering from the assembled crowd.

On take-off, it weighed nearly four thousand four hundred kilos. It would encounter severe weather systems on the way, including Typhoon Marge, flying at an average altitude of 11 thousand feet and a speed of just 186 kilometres an hour.

'*Voyager*' confounded the skeptics.

It covered 42,212 kilometres to land in front of a crowd of over 55 thousand at Edwards Air Force Base. It boasted 9 days and 3 minutes in the air, setting the world flight endurance record for circumnavigating the earth without stopping.

Only 48 kilos of fuel remained in its tanks, less than two percent of what was on board when it took off. The two exhausted pilots emerged from '*Voyager*' fulfilling an improbable dream. They had taken millions of people around the world on the adventure with them, including viewers of the 7 Network in Australia.

It was a distinct pleasure to shake their hands on the desert runway after their successful return to earth.

The gangly aircraft now resides in the Smithsonian Institute in Washington DC, a tribute to one of the most daring aviation feats of modern time.

Their bold, imaginative and ultimately successful story will be remembered because of its success, but the U.S. aviation industry is littered with projects that did not 'get off the ground'.

I was to report on one such noteworthy case. It involved a trip to Northern California where a Canadian engineer was creating a buzz with a futuristic concept that could have potentially changed the face of aviation, and the automobile industry as well.

He was designing cars that could fly! His name was Paul Moller. It was a promoter's dream, and back in the 80s looked a little too good to be true. The notional image of airborne cars zipping around the skies high above the congested freeways of California was creating quite a stir.

Our Channel 7 crew was met at the small design facility by a quiet, unassuming man, who was the driving force behind this bold and imaginative concept.

Paul Moller described his early childhood, growing up in the rugged mountains of Canada, and an incident, which saw him free two hummingbirds trapped in a barn to watch them take flight on their release.

It provided the inspiration, he said, for the design of what he called 'aerobots'; craft that could rise and hover vertically, mimicking the flight of the tiny birds. It was a colourful introduction to the presentation that would follow.

Moller launched his engineering career younger than most. Born on a rural farm in Fruitvale, British Columbia, he was constantly at work. He helped build a house when he was eight, a Ferris wheel when he was 11, and his first helicopter at 14.

Soon after our arrival, I was settled into a strange circular vehicle, resembling a flying saucer, powered by seven small rotary engines that could lift the craft off the ground. Moller had flown his 'Skycar', he said, but for no great distance. It had to be tethered to a crane for insurance purposes, not the most convincing demonstration of unfettered access to the big, blue skies.

However, two other prototype aircraft produced for the cameras were impressive. They looked like cars that could fly; sleek and sexy craft that were made of lightweight carbon fibre, with four rotary engines mounted on the front and back. Seating up to four passengers, Moller maintained that the aircraft, similar in size to a family car, could reach speeds of up to 350 kilometres an hour, and when put into mass production would retail for around one hundred thousand dollars.

There was one hitch, however, the Federal Aviation Authority had not yet approved the car's operation in the skies over America, and a conspiracy, he alleged, between oil companies and major automobile makers was impeding finance and regulatory support for the project.

The inventor claimed to have the support of no less an organisation than NASA, producing an interview with a senior spokesman, who said it was feasible that these flying cars could be in operation by the year 2000, only 12 years away!

This may not be a 'pipe dream' after all, I thought. On returning to Los Angeles to prepare the story for airing, I rushed to the archives to track down vision of the television program, 'The Jetsons', showing George and Jane streaking through the skies in futuristic flying cars. It would say it all.

By the start of the new millennium the cars were still notably absent from the skies, suggesting that the inventor's dream was just that.

However, years later, he was still working on the M400 Skycar, a cross between a comic book batmobile and a fighter plane.

"I'm into life extension," he told reporters in 2022, aged 85, "I figure I'll live long enough to make this work.

Those brave words were uttered despite years earlier having to file for bankruptcy.

Moller's vision has been taken up other dreamers determined to see cars that can fly.

CHAPTER 12
SPHINCTER TESTERS OVER AMERICA

The Boeing 727 had just started takeoff, when a maniacal shout resonated through the cabin, and a lone figure came hurtling down the aisle, surfing a large piece of cardboard.

The nose-up attitude of the aircraft afforded him perfect conditions to ride the imaginary wave to the back of the plane, and he was clearly excited by the prospect.

It was a sight not seen on commercial jets, but this was no ordinary flight. It was a special charter, carrying dozens of reporters, camera crews and print journalists, who were covering the 1988 U.S. Presidential election campaign.

After more than six months on the road following the action, or lack of it, the press entourage was bored. A number were tipsy, and up for a bit of fun; grizzled, political veterans who had reported on Presidents all the way back to Eisenhower.

Admittedly, the one doing the 'surfing' was considerably younger and had none of the gravitas of his more senior colleagues, but he appeared happy to lead the charge.

My two Channel 7 colleagues and I were interlopers; novices on the election trail, assigned to the whistle-stop tour from Washington DC across the country to Seattle. Vice President George Bush was 'on the stump' trying to beat the Democratic candidate, Massachusetts Governor, Michael Dukakis. George had his eyes firmly focused on succeeding his boss, Ronald Reagan, who had now served his allowable two terms in office, and was teetering on the brink of senility.

It was a one-off foray into the hurly burly world of American politics, and we had little idea of what to expect on the cross-country flight, though our surfer buddy certainly gave us an idea of what was to come.

The old 727 looked like it had been given a last-minute reprieve from the 'airplane graveyard' in the Mohave Desert, and stood in stark contrast to the

Vice President's pristine aircraft, aptly named Air Force 2. I wondered who had chosen and paid for the press plane; very possibly someone who had no love of the Fourth Estate.

'Whistle stop tour' was an appropriate description – six cities dotting the North American continent, each in a more westerly direction, until we hit the west coast.

The routine was the same in each city. The Vice President's plane would land, and minutes later, we would fly in, allowing him and his entourage time to be loaded into cars, headed for the venue to sell his promises to potential voters.

We in the media would be loaded into buses to follow and record the event, while firing probing questions about the latest round of pork barrelling to a consummate politician who, at the time, was well ahead in the polls.

It was difficult not to be cynical about the process. This was politics, even if it was a world away from the brand with which I was familiar. Australia has none of the complexities of an electoral college, or a hellishly long, circus-like campaign dripping in banners and balloons. Thank God, I thought, I was not a specialist political reporter.

The staged events were colourful affairs. Red, white and blue were on prominent display, along with party hats, ticker-tape and an assembled crowd that behaved like they had been handed drugs and tickets to the circus, just before the speeches. Nowhere in the world had I seen such enthusiastic and 'over the top' behaviour from citizens, who would be asked to perform the relatively simple task of casting a vote. Only in America!

George Herbert Walker Bush, 43rd Vice President of America, had none of the soaring oratorical skills of his boss Ronald Reagan, but the election was his for the losing, and he was firm favourite. One of the most qualified men to seek the top job; he had served as Congressman, Ambassador to the United Nations and Director of the Central Intelligence Agency.

Few knew the inner workings of Washington as well as this true blue-blood of America's East Coast aristocracy. With an investment banker father named Prescott Sheldon Bush, who had served in the U.S. Senate, expectations were always going to run high. Little did George know or expect, his eldest son George Walker Bush would go on to serve his country as the 43rd President of the United States, 12 years later. Second son Jeb, ironically the 43rd Governor of Florida, would also have an unsuccessful tilt at gaining his party's nomination in the 2016 campaign won by Donald Trump.

If nothing else, watching and reporting on these aged, political operatives heightened one's own appreciation of the seemingly inexhaustible energy levels needed to contest a Presidential campaign.

It was hard enough for young media types, who it seemed could only hack the pace with the re-enforcement of copious quantities of alcohol.

With little more than two hours on the ground, the circus was on the road again – democracy American style! Political fixers, lobbyists, and the media, urged onto the aircraft for the next round of pork barrelling in a city 'up the ways a bit'.

Once back on the plane, none of the rules and restrictions of a normal airline applied. Seat belts remained undone, the safety briefing noticeably absent, and there was unfettered movement around the aircraft, even during take-off. Overworked flight attendants were kept busy dispensing alcohol to thirsty and bored members of the media, some of whom also carried their own supplies for the odd tipple.

On board were a number of big names on the U.S. media landscape, long-standing political reporters who had seen it all. Sam Donaldson from ABC News, Bob Schieffer from CBS, network men, were institutions in a business not yet dominated by cable operators and the 24-hour news cycle.

By Chicago, in the mid-west, the circus had touched down three times and the routine had been established.

Reporters were constantly filing to meet deadline for news shows, whereas Channel 7 was doing a longer 'think piece'. It was to be edited later, culminating in a live cross into Australia from Seattle, the final destination.

The style of Candidate Bush changed markedly as we flew into the smaller cities in the mid-west. Gone were the affectations of the Washington insider; on went the baseball cap and the 'down-home routine' of a man looking for votes. Some things never change, I thought. It's no different in Australia, where the Akubra is the favoured headwear of politicians wanting to get 'down and dirty' with the country locals, and show that they're just 'one of the boys'.

Sioux City, Iowa, will be forever remembered on this 'magical mystery tour' for testing the nerves and certain netherly muscles of the hardened, cynical newsmen. The Vice Presidential circus had just delivered its two-hour sales pitch to a hall full of wildly enthusiastic locals, before returning to the plane and taking to the skies.

Minutes later our 727 jet lined up for take-off, but it soon became apparent something was amiss! The old aircraft rolled down the runway and as it reached rotation speed, a loud explosion resonated throughout the cabin.

At the back of the plane, where we were seated, the noise was much more exaggerated and frightening. It sounded like one of the rear-mounted engines, just feet away, had blown up.

The nose of the big jet immediately thumped to the ground, and you could feel the throttle being pulled back.

Seconds later as the aircraft stood still on the tarmac, the pilot's voice came over the intercom. It was a laid-back Texan drawl, which we had become accustomed to in the course of the long flight.

"Well, folks, no need to worry, what you just heard was not an engine blowing up," he informed us with a hint of humour. "We are encountering severe crosswinds, which means the air is not flowing through the engines and like a car, they're backfiring, or if you like, farting. We'll just try that again. Sit back and enjoy."

By the expressions on the faces in the cabin, there was little enjoyment to be derived from this exercise. Nervous glances were exchanged, along with the odd joke and several calls for a recharge of drinks.

Minutes later, we again lined up for take-off. Hands gripped armrests a little too tightly as the plane sped down the runway.

At the point of take-off, the loud bang again violently shook the plane, and the pilot immediately cut throttles and brought the jet to a halt.

This time, worried looks were replaced by the unmistakable glint of terror. It was more than a little unsettling, and most onboard had quickly lost all pretense of humour and bravado.

Again, the relaxed Texan voice, devoid of tension, made a futile attempt to calm nerves in the petrified cabin.

"OK folks, as you can see the damn wind is still blowing a little too strong. I know this is no fun, but we are gonna try one more time, and if it's a 'no go' we'll take you back to the terminal."

This time, you could see the whites of fellow passenger's eyes. Some clutched glasses of alcohol, the lips of others moving in silent prayer. I sat with my eyes closed, trying to block out the whole terrifying episode, but all attention was again focused on that split second before take-off. It came, seemingly louder and more terrifying than the two previous attempts; a bang that shook the aircraft and again resulted in a rapid deceleration. By this time, nerves were well and truly shredded.

As the plane taxied back to the terminal, the rank smell of human body odour, and perhaps something more pungent, had settled throughout the aircraft, and the Captain was once again obliged to report to his disturbed passengers.

"OK folks, I know many of you have got deadlines, but here's where we give you a choice to get off for an overnighter, or wait it out, to see if we can take off a little later."

Before he had finished, there was a discernible movement of bodies as the media men prepared to flee. This was confirmed when the aircraft came to a halt and the question asked, who was on, and who wanted out?

Sam and Bob, the senior Network men were among the first to deplane, along with a good percentage of those who had signed on for the assignment. A quickly convened conference with my two colleagues voted to continue, so that we could be on the ground in Seattle for the live crosses to Australia. It wasn't that we were braver. We were just less experienced, and fiercely protective of our reputations as Aussies. We would not allow ourselves to be scared off by a bit of airplane 'farting'.

An hour later, as the 727 again lined up for take-off, we waited expectantly for the another 'sphincter tester', but it didn't come. We lifted off into gathering storm clouds, never to forget our adventures in Sioux City, the small cowboy town famous for its Indians.

In July 1989, the city would hit the headlines when a United Airlines DC10 jet crashed on landing, killing 112 people. I would report the story from our base in Los Angeles. Graphic news footage showed debris sprinkled around nearby cornfields, where many of the 184 survivors, including the pilot, were found.

It was one of the worst air disasters in U.S. aviation history, and was more than a little unsettling to an Australian news crew who spent a good part of the time flying around the country.

CHAPTER 13
TEGUCIGALPA – HOW DO YOU SPELL THAT?

One flight never to be forgotten was in March 1986, when the threat of war hovered over Honduras in Central America. An escalation in hostilities with neighbour, Nicaragua prompted a decision by Channel 7 to send the Los Angeles crew to report on the potential flashpoint.

Eastern Airlines, which later went into bankruptcy, was the carrier chosen to fly us into the capital city, Tegucigalpa from Miami.

"Tegucigalpa?" I had quizzed our Sydney-based Foreign Editor, "how the bloody hell do you spell it?"

Normally one of the busier airline routes into Central America, the flight was virtually empty.

The threat of war had scared tourists away, leaving only a few, crazy or determined enough to see it as a necessary destination. We were a smattering of businessmen and three television crews, two American networks and we Australians.

Media types, being a naturally ebullient lot, and not hating a drink or three, quickly turned it into a party, while discussing possible scenarios in the deteriorating political standoff. The focus of our coverage would be the joint U.S. and Honduran military exercises on the border, and fears it would spark a reaction from Sandinistas leader, Daniel Ortega.

Earlier in the 80s, the U.S. began supplying military aid to Honduras to fund the Contra guerillas fighting Ortega. They built an airstrip and modern port, to make it easier to launch campaigns into neighbouring countries. It was all part of President Ronald Reagan's commitment to stop the spread of communism in Central America.

The flight went smoothly until minutes from our destination, Toncontin International Airport. It was a pre-landing routine like no other. The aircraft went into a 'free fall' as the Captain announced that we were landing in a few minutes. This was not the gradual descent encountered on most commercial airline routes.

The alarmed look in the eyes of fellow media veterans confirmed this was also a new sensation to them. Conversation stopped, and we found our stomachs move closer to our throats as the unusually steep descent continued. The Boeing 757 was buffeted by turbulence, and the sight of a rugged mountain range not far below was doing little to calm nerves.

The sound of wheels hitting the unusually short runway was greeted with a collective sigh of relief that could have been heard back in Miami. Game faces were quickly reapplied, with mumbled jokes disguising the fact the media contingent was badly rattled by its dramatic entry into the Honduran capital.

The jet shuddered to a halt, and didn't move for what felt like an eternity. Finally, we felt it being towed by a support vehicle. The view out the window confirmed we were about ten metres short of the end of the airstrip, which overlooked a deep valley! It was a sight that prompted more than a few expletives.

A late afternoon dash to the hotel was followed by an even faster move into the bar, to settle tattered nerves severely tested by the landing from hell. Perhaps not surprisingly, we found ourselves staying in the same hotel as our American colleagues. Tegucigalpa was not renowned for an abundance of international class accommodation.

After a couple of hours of steady drinking, one of my new American pals directed my attention to two guys seated at the other end of the bar.

"They're the pilots who flew us in," he told me, "the fat one is the captain, and he's with the first officer."

I took in the impressive girth of the more senior aviator, wondering how he could fit behind the controls in the cramped confines of the cockpit. Thank God I hadn't seen him before the flight, I thought; he was a heart attack waiting happen.

In the end, curiosity got the better of me, and I approached the two to question them about the dramatic landing that had so rattled the media guys.

"Enjoyed it, did you?" the fat one asked, "one of the most dangerous airports in the world," he proclaimed. "Why do you think we're drinking; scared the shit out of us, too!"

I looked at the two of them expecting to hear the statement followed by raucous laughter. There was none, though the hint of a smile momentarily lingered on the lips of the Captain.

"I've never dropped so quickly in an aircraft," I responded.

"Got to," he said, "mountains right up to a tiny runway, followed by a serious drop if you overshoot. It's a tester, alright. Even worse on take-off; restricted military airspace to your right and a valley at the end of the strip. You don't want to have engine failure or you'll either crash or be shot down!"

By this time, I had been joined by my crew and the Americans, who all giggled nervously on hearing the Captain's sombre declaration. Something to look forward to when we're heading home, I thought.

Warming up to the small audience, he went on to recite a long list of fiery crashes that had happened at Toncontin Airport through the 60s and 70s, and a couple of uncomfortably recent ones.

Three years later, a Boeing 727 crashed into the mountainside on approach, killing 132; followed by 10 more crashes before the international airport was relocated to a safer area in 2021.

Just months after that nightmare flight into Honduras, the crew and I were to board another sparsely populated aircraft, to fly to Panama City where military strongman, Manuel Noriega's regime was teetering on the brink of collapse. The small Central American country had fallen out of favour with tourists, while outbound flights were full of Panamanians fleeing his brutal and fast unravelling regime.

Getting onto empty aircraft en route to world trouble spots was becoming a habit.

The country was being racked by protest demonstrations, raising serious concerns that the dictator was getting ready to launch a bloody crackdown on the population, sparking civil war.

For years, he had worked with U.S. intelligence agencies and was the CIA's most valued source in Central America. Noriega was a primary conduit for illicit weapons, military equipment and cash, destined for U.S.-backed counter-insurgency forces throughout the region. He was also hailed as an ally in America's war on drugs, despite the fact he had amassed a personal fortune through drug trafficking operations. Though his intelligence handlers knew of this, it was overlooked, because of his usefulness to the United States.

It was an uncomfortably unstable city, particularly for those of us filming and reporting breaking news. It was Easter, and Panama's large Catholic population was packing churches, while banks and businesses were closing their doors, fearing riots and looting.

For several weeks, the government had been withholding pension cheques, and we found ourselves in the middle of a protest march, organized to highlight the plight of people dependent on government assistance. Hundreds of elderly pensioners chanting anti-Noriega slogans made their way through streets, lined by police and heavily armed soldiers. Tanks and personnel carriers stood menacingly on street corners, a potent reminder that the military strongman was in charge, and would tolerate no public disobedience. Tension was thick in the air and we knew it would take very little for emotions to boil over and violence to erupt.

While the old protestors presented little threat to the Noriega regime, such was the level of anger among the population that potential existed for a much more widespread expression of dissent.

Reporting and filming in such circumstances is never easy, but in a country where very little English is spoken, the prospect for misunderstanding was high, despite the fact we had hired a local driver and translator.

With the authorities struggling to maintain order, the presence of foreign media was an unwelcome intrusion for a government trying desperately to put a cap on negative publicity and hang on to power. Just weeks earlier, an American television crew had been arrested and detained.

To an Aussie outfit, more used to reporting on tame street protests in Sydney and Melbourne, where one never saw guns and tanks, the coup-prone regimes of Central America were quite something else.

But, we were here to report and report we would, despite the odd twitching sphincter and mildly disturbing thought of a grizzly death or incarceration in a jail full of rapists and drug dealing criminals.

Well, if you didn't want a bit of adventure, why get into journalism!

Moments after that fleeting philosophical thought, the first sounds of trouble resonated through the crowded streets. We heard the loud popping of tear gas canisters being discharged and witnessed the resultant mayhem, as protestors started running in all directions. Thick clouds of the acrid gas swirled around the rush of bodies, while megaphones carried the harsh Spanish instructions of the police and military.

We, of course, had been warned that this was a standard ploy, and likely course of action in breaking up civil unrest, but unfortunately our gas masks were in the van, along with the driver and translator, who would stand by and witness the action.

They were dramatic scenes, as the heavy hand of Noriega's military regime fell on a bunch of old folks, whose civil disobedience had been sparked by empty bellies and social misery.

The pandemonium and turmoil was a heady aphrodisiac to cameraman, Maurice Roper. He was in his element. He would later go on to a distinguished career with NBC, as a 'shooter' in war zones around the world. Soundman and editor Tim Rodd, however, was more used to the comfortable surroundings of an editing suite, and the chaotic street scenes were clearly not 'what he had signed on for'. The whites of his eyes were a dead giveaway. He, also, would not return to Australia after his American posting and remained in LA as a highly skilled editor.

My role, amidst the chaos, was to direct the crew to the most fertile pockets of action, as I was unimpeded by a heavy camera. It was attached to the sound equipment by a two-metre long lead that threatened to disconnect, as one person ran more quickly towards the action.

It was all quite surreal. With eyes watering and burning, adrenaline pumping, events started to move in slow motion. Terror tends to induce this rare condition.

All about me were the frightened faces of demonstrators running from baton-wielding policemen, while the military appeared to be holding their ground, observing the crowd to see if they should bring in the big guns.

When it happened, I was ill-prepared. A burning sensation sliced across my throat and the back of my neck and I was pulled sideways, almost falling to the ground. I did, however, catch a glimpse of the culprit running away, clutching the gold chain he had just ripped from my neck.

You bloody idiot, I thought, wearing valuable jewellery to a riot!

In the middle of all the mayhem, I took chase after the young kid. Again, everything seemed to move in slow motion. He ran from the main road, packed with policemen, soldiers and protestors and headed for the back streets, glancing back every few seconds, to see if I was still in pursuit. With each twist and turn, it seemed he was slowing down. In seconds I was to find out why, as I rounded the corner into a narrow, darkened laneway. What I saw instantly brought me to a standstill. Not ten feet away stood the young thief, a smile on his face and my gold chain dangling from his fingers. However, it was what surrounded him that gave me reason for pause; about a dozen young locals, also sporting broad smiles, and the odd knife! All thoughts of my gold keepsake were immediately forgotten, as I backpedalled and ran, thankfully not to be followed.

Footage of the Panama protest featured on Australian television that night. It would be the beginning of the end for the Panamanian dictator. In 1989, the United States invaded the small Central American country and Noriega was jailed for 40 years in the United States on racketeering, drug smuggling and money laundering charges.

More adventure was to be encountered in the skies over the world's biggest democracy. The American population's proclivity for the consumption of alcohol and a high incidence of mental health issues would guarantee a steady flow of incidents to be reported for television news services, and many that did not make the headlines.

The least likely place on an aircraft to encounter bad behaviour, one would think, was at the pointy end, in first class, but it was there I was to have a memorable run-in with a fellow passenger.

It must first be stated it was not standard practice for Channel 7 to fly its team first class, but an exception was made on 'redeye' flights across the country, when the crew was expected hit the ground running in New York.

The larger seats would hypothetically afford an opportunity for sleep, but on one flight this was an impossible prospect, due to the actions of a 'gentleman', who appeared to be right at home in the first-class environment.

The year was 1987, about 12 months before United States government introduced an aircraft smoking ban, which took several years to be adopted by airlines across the country.

Not long after take-off from LAX, a cloud of thick cigar smoke rose from the seat in front, well and truly invading my space and making sleep a virtual impossibility. I called the flight attendant and explained the problem. This was not a wisp of cigarette smoke, but a thick continuous pall, probably a pungent Havana. She responded by talking to the smoker, before wandering off to attend to other passengers.

A few minutes later the puffy cloud again came my way, prompting me out of my seat to have a word with the guy, who clearly wasn't worried about the comfort of those around him. He was a large, bearded lump, who bore an uncanny resemblance to movie director, Francis Ford Coppola.

"Excuse me," I said politely, "I understand you've been asked to stop smoking. I can't sleep – would you mind?"

The morbidly obese 'gentleman' squinted in my general direction through beady, rat-like eyes, before nodding and shrugging, without making eye contact. He had the unmistakable aura of a guy used to getting his own way, and not caring a damn about what anyone thought. Mafia, I wondered?

I returned to my seat to attempt to snatch some sleep, only to have the thick pall of smoke waft over the seat several minutes later.

You're joking, I thought! The flight attendant arrived to find me standing in the aisle, staring daggers at the selfish lump of humanity, happily chugging on what looked like an expensive, newly lit, cigar.

"Sir, would you mind not smoking – this gentleman is trying to sleep," she instructed, while I stood next her, my arms folded and glaring menacingly. He showed absolutely no sign of being cowered by my threatening presence.

"Ok, Ok," he mumbled, unapologetically, but again there was no attempt to make eye contact.

Thinking that was the end of it, I returned to my seat, only to watch smoke rise and dance in the illuminated glare of the overhead light five minutes later.

Right, I thought, bounding out of my seat, to confront the man who was apparently enjoying the game. I grabbed the cigar from his mouth, tore it up and deposited it in his lap, waiting for a reaction and perhaps a small fire!

There was none – reaction or fire, save for a 'shit eating grin' that said it all. The skirmish attracted a couple of flight attendants who moved to defuse the incident, and usher me back to my seat, while instructing the smoker to behave himself, or else he would be reported to the Captain.

It was a warning he finally obeyed, but it didn't help me sleep for the rest of the flight. I sat patiently waiting for the fat fool to light up again, so I could make a response worthy of a mention on the nightly news. He did not!

CHAPTER 14
MEDICAL MYSTERIES

For a journalist, few stories are more difficult or emotionally taxing than those involving terminally ill children, and families facing their imminent loss.

In cynical journalistic parlance, they're called 'tear jerkers' and I was assigned many over the years, particularly when stationed in Los Angeles. We were striking distance from Disneyland, which had established itself as an iconic kiddie tourist attraction.

The home of Mickey Mouse was a favourite destination for terminally ill Australian children granted a 'last request' by the remarkable 'Make a Wish Foundation'. It had sponsored dozens of kids over the years.

Those of us who worked in network bureaus came to dread calls from producers in Australia, requesting coverage of a family's visit. One became invested in the stories, and rode the emotional roller coaster with parents forced to watch their children endure unimaginable pain over their short lifetimes. The flight to the United States was often the last shared adventure, and an opportunity to enjoy some fun times together.

As a father, I was particularly sensitive to the suffering and despair of these kids and their families, and it was a rare privilege watching them being given a brief respite from the heartbreak of an inevitable prognosis.

Why them, I would often think as I witnessed enormous courage in the face of tragedy. Life was indeed a 'lucky dip'.

As emotionally draining as it was spending time with the families, it was also a welcome break from the world of American politics, general mayhem and Hollywood celebrity stories that were our daily staple.

The case of one little girl from country New South Wales stands out as perhaps one of the saddest and most tragic stories that I was asked to cover during my time in America.

I received a call from Australia giving me the heads up on the arrival of Becky

Coss, who was suffering from the rare aging disease, progeria. Along with her parents, she was coming to the United States to meet another victim of the disease, which affected a very small number of children around the world.

Robin and Neville Coss, from Bingara, in northern New South Wales, had lived for years with the question, "is there anyone else like me?" Research showed there were nineteen known cases in the world, including Jason Allison, from Boise, Idaho.

They contacted the Allisons, who invited them to fly over to meet Jason, and show Becky that she was not alone in her battle against the rare genetic disorder.

At the time, there had been little publicity about progeria and it remained a largely unknown and unresearched condition. Years later, it would spark the Hollywood movie, The Curious Case of Benjamin Button, starring Brad Pitt.

As a reporter, simply reading about the rare disease left me unprepared for what I would see when we greeted the Coss family at Boise airport, after their long journey from Australia.

Becky, not yet in her teens, had the wizened facial features of an old lady. A blonde wig disguised the fact that her hair had fallen out, and it was obvious her tiny body was racked by severe arthritic pain, as she walked awkwardly towards the young man with whom she shared the shocking affliction.

All eyes were on the two prematurely aging victims, as they made their way through the terminal to the waiting car. At 14 years of age, Jason was one of the oldest Progeria sufferers still living. Doctors had told his mother, Kathy that her child would be lucky to survive past the age of five.

As an overseas correspondent, one gets to report on a broad range of subjects from war and politics, to sport and entertainment, but having to tell the story of a terminally ill child, and the emotional turmoil of a family dealing with the prognosis, is perhaps the most difficult assignment of all.

In the 1980s, very little was known about progeria; research material was sparse and treatments non-existent. For the Coss family, a trip to America to speak to another affected family promised a new level of understanding. The Allisons had pioneered an online website, which had discovered about a dozen progeria cases across the United States.

Unlike the young victims of cancer and leukemia whose lives would almost certainly be cut tragically short, children diagnosed with progeria faced a more uncertain future, because so little was known, apart from the fact that few seemed to survive past their teens.

The Coss family would spend a week with their American hosts, and it was agreed that our cameras could record the interaction for two days.

The awkwardness of introductions was soon forgotten, as the two families got to know each other. Fathers, George and Neville quickly fell into conversation over a beer, and mothers, Robin and Kathy effortlessly found common ground, while Jason showed Becky photos of a recent get-together of more than a dozen progeria kids. It was the question she had asked for years. Yes, there were other children going through what she was.

Perhaps the most sensitive issue when speaking to families that agree to open their lives to the intrusion of television cameras, is just what they feel comfortable making public. A heavy responsibility lies with the reporter, to try to make the experience as easy and least confronting as possible. I tried to do so.

The local high school was chosen for one photo opportunity and it couldn't have been better for graphically illustrating the toll the disease takes on its young victims. Becky was invited to sit in Jason's science classroom, filled with healthy young teenagers. The contrast could not have been more dramatic.

Physically small, the two were dwarfed by their peers, who for years had watched Jason grow old before their eyes. At three years of age, he had lost all his hair. A year later, he was forced to wear glasses. Before his ninth birthday, he was suffering hardening of the arteries, and as he reached his teens his body was racked with painful arthritis. The disease had not impaired his intellectual capacity, but the frailty of his fast-ageing body kept him off the sports field.

Filming in the classroom could not disguise Becky or Jason's body language, which showed they were very used to being on the receiving end of strange looks. Outdoors, however, all that changed. The Allisons suggested a drive into the nearby snowcapped mountains, where they often took Jason and his brother to ride toboggans on the snowy mountainside.

It was the first time Becky had seen snow. Her new friend, an expert on the slopes, took control and their peals of laughter could be heard as the sled raced down the hillside.

For mother, Robin it was a magic moment. She tearfully related what life had been like watching her daughter cope with progeria and the toll it had taken on the family. Neville let his wife do the talking, explaining he could not speak about his daughter's battle without breaking down. It was a frank admission that underscored the enormous courage required to keep his small family together. Witnessing the raw emotion of that moment was humbling, depressing and yet, oddly inspiring.

The Coss family returned to Australia believing the trip had been worthwhile. Their daughter knew she was not alone in her battle. Becky died at the age of 18, just months short of her High School graduation.

In 2003, fourteen years after I interviewed Becky, a news conference was held in Washington DC to announce the discovery of the Progeria gene. Extensive research has since identified a drug, which extends survival in children who suffer from the genetic disorder.

CHAPTER 15
HEART TO HEART

In the course of a career as a foreign correspondent an assignment will stand-out for different reasons; the interview of a world leader, a natural disaster that kills thousands, or a medical breakthrough that saves lives.

In 1989, I came across a story that was both inspiring and uplifting and would make, I thought, a great human-interest story for audiences in Australia. It concerned a heart transplant recipient, who just months after undergoing the operation decided to compete in a triathlon.

Gary Clarke, a 46-year-old insurance executive from Tucson, Arizona, was diagnosed with viral cardiomyopathy, a condition that attacked his heart, leaving it to function well below normal capacity.

He was told that unless an acceptable donor heart was found, an artificial, mechanical heart would have to be inserted, otherwise, he would die within days. It was a daunting prospect, but just hours before the scheduled procedure, a compatible organ, recovered from a motor cycle accident victim was delivered to the hospital.

The operation was a success; so successful in fact, that 4 months later, doctors were unprepared for a request from their grateful patient. He wanted to compete in a grueling 52-kilometre triathlon.

The man who performed the complicated 7-hour operation, Doctor Jack Copeland, from Tucson University Hospital, cautioned Clark against competing in the event, warning it could kill him.

He subsequently ignored the advice and, under the watchful eyes of three nurses, finished the event and remarkably, in the following ten months ran, cycled and swam in another six triathlons.

Clarke's remarkable feat attracted the attention of local newspapers and TV stations, but had gone unnoticed by the national media. The clock was ticking.

A phone call to the man who performed the operation, confirmed the fact that his patient had received the heart of a 19-year-old, whose identity was protected by the hospital's privacy policy. He did, however, get permission to give me his star patient's phone number.

I quickly established that Gary Clarke was more than happy to talk about his life-saving operation. He spoke with 'born again' enthusiasm, leaving no doubt he considered himself the luckiest guy alive.

"I was a slob; a three-piece business suit slob", he confessed, adding that he'd changed, now that he had a second chance at life.

Though he knew the donated heart came from an accident victim he had no idea of the identity of the donor. The passion with which the company executive spoke confirmed he was great talent and would have no difficulties sharing his story on camera. He was articulate, confident and charismatic, qualities sure to excite television viewers. Gary Clarke agreed to be interviewed and feature in a story for Australian television, but before a date was set, I wanted to try to find the identity of the heart donor.

The only clue lay in one line of the hospital's press release about the transplant operation. It confirmed the donated heart came from a young man killed in Phoenix, the capital of Arizona and a three-hour drive from Tucson.

Subsequent calls to the Phoenix Police Department and local newspapers, established the date of the accident and name of Robert Tweed, killed in the accident. Could it be that other journalists had tracked down the parents of this boy, only to be told they had no interest in sharing their grief or being interviewed about the loss of their son?

I needed to know if Gary Clarke wanted to meet the family of the young man whose heart now beat in his chest. He jumped at the suggestion, but insisted that the meeting would only take place if the family was comfortable.

It is never easy talking to people who have suffered the loss of a loved one, and the media landscape is littered with stories of ambitious, insensitive journalists intruding into the lives of grieving families. I would soon find out that I was actually doing my interview subjects a favour.

While Gary Clarke didn't know the name of his donor, the hospital had told the Tweeds the identity of the recipient. Could I persuade the family to agree to an interview by telling them Clarke wanted to thank them personally for the great gift he had received?

In a phone call to Robert's father, Herb, I emphasized the story would only be aired in Australia, which I hoped would allay any fears about privacy. I should not have worried.

His reaction was overwhelmingly positive. Yes, he'd read reports about the heart recipient, and the family most certainly wanted to meet this remarkable man.

The 'go ahead' given, planning started on how best to cover the story. Interviews were set up with the heart transplant surgeon, Jack Copeland and Gary Clarke at University Hospital, where twelve months earlier, the operation had taken place.

Much of Arizona is desert; flat, hot roads, fringed by giant cacti and windblown tumbleweed intruding into the odd, sparsely populated and irrigated community. Driving through the state is notoriously boring, but the morning we picked Gary Clarke up for the drive to Phoenix there was little chance of anyone nodding off. He was driving as we filmed and interviewed him about the upcoming meeting.

He looked fit and healthy and bore an uncanny resemblance to country singer Kenny Rogers. To say he was highly nervous would be an understatement, but there could be no doubting his enthusiasm and need to express gratitude to the family who had lost a son and saved his life.

I had no idea of the circumstances of the Tweed family as I had only spoken by phone to Herb Tweed. After filming a sequence on the road, the crew, who were following in a second car, drove on to the address so that they could set up and be ready to film our arrival.

Spontaneity was always going to be the key to capturing the emotions of the moment. The Tweeds did not live in one of the many affluent suburbs of Phoenix. They called home, a small, neat trailer in a modest park, which tellingly spoke of their economic circumstances.

After hearing so much about the man who now carried their son's heart, it was a long-awaited meeting, and seeing him in the flesh proved too much. The tears flowed freely.

Embracing his donor's mother, Brenda, he explained how doctors had told him he only had only hours to live, if a heart was not found.

Doctors were preparing to transplant the mechanical heart when news reached them that a donor had been located in nearby Phoenix, and tests had shown the heart was compatible.

I will remember the story of Gary Clark and his 19-year-old heart for many reasons, not least for the tears I saw in the eyes of my colleagues and the ones I felt burning in my own eyes as we watched the emotion charged meeting.

CHAPTER 16
A DAY AT THE OFFICE

The occupational pursuits of most people are predictable affairs, well structured, and for the most part unremarkable. From the time they get out of bed until they pull up the sheets at night, there are generally few surprises in store, in the course of a day in the office.

That was certainly not the case in my working life. Journalists are not like 'most people'. No surprises there, you say, they're all ratbags! While some days in a newsroom are predictable, the nature of the business – News – means just that. Something 'new' is in the offing, and that means one may end the day in another city, county or country, a common occurrence in the course of an overseas posting.

It's what makes the career so enticing, and a lot more exciting than that of 'most people'!

That's not to say that on many days, nothing significant happens and it is more difficult to work out what story should lead the nightly news. On other occasions, it is more than obvious and the task is to make our coverage more insightful and interesting than our competitors.

Even scheduled interviews and activities don't always go to plan, a la Clint Eastwood. It was set up correctly, but failed in the communication department. However, many other days stand out for more interesting outcomes, like having dinner with Michael Douglas in New York after our interview ended. He obviously needed a drink and being one of the last in line to learn about his latest movie, 'Fatal Attraction', I was invited to join him in the libation that led to dinner. I don't know whether my line of questioning impressed him, but it was a memorable outcome, with a few 'off the record' stories.

An encounter in Melbourne with the Dali Lama was another noteworthy experience. The man exuded a very special aura, easily picked up by the eager media scrum whose job it was to shine a light on this deeply spiritual man.

Years earlier, I had been assigned to follow Pope John Paul into the highlands of New Guinea. The sight of him, surrounded by scantily clad natives with bones through their noses and spears in their hands, is a colourful memory few get to see.

Not all the supposedly religious figures who've crossed my path have been as benevolent, as I found out when I spent 3 days covering the Davidian siege in Waco, Texas in 1993. The flames sparked by an FBI raid on the religious compound resulted in the deaths of 76 cult members, including 28 children and the sect's leader David Koresh.

Visits to high security jails also proved to be a venture into the dark side. From the unsuccessful parole hearing of Charles Manson in San Francisco, to an encounter with serial rapist and murderer, Alan Baker in an Australian jail, both men occupy a notorious status in the respective country's criminal histories. They shared 'crazy eyes' and I remember staring into Baker's in the woodwork room of Grafton High Security Gaol several years after he and Kevin Crump were convicted of the murder of Ian Lamb and pregnant Virginia Morse. The NSW Minister for Corrective Services was leading journalists through a tour of the facility when his press secretary spotted Baker, a diminutive figure, and asked him why he had committed the brutal rape and murder of Morse. It was a reply I'll never forget, as I was standing next to him when he answered. "It was my defense at the trial that I suffered headaches, which resulted in blackouts and loss of memory. In fact, I feel one coming on now."

It prompted a swift end to the conversation, and the media men moved quickly on with the tour. The encounter brought new meaning to the phrase, "looking into the face of evil." Manson, unsurprisingly, would never be released, and died in a jail hospital in 2017.

Interviewing famous entertainers was much easier, less threatening and a pleasure for the most part. Singer, Roberta Flack turned out to be a little more pleasure than I expected.

What I realized is that all these so-called 'stars' are just human beings, dealing with the reality of being put on pedestals, and expected to be role models for the 'great unwashed'. They are just lucky to have become household names, with the glamour and often, financial rewards of that status.

I recall Tina Turner responding to the question "what do you think of being called the Queen of Rock and Roll?" She said she wasn't into 'tags', and that, as she hadn't given herself that title, it meant little to her. Sadly, she passed away, aged 83, while this book was being written.

Interviewing the 'rich and famous' also can have a downside, especially when managers or partners interfere, and try too hard to make a point. In the 1980s, I recall a New York interview with Elle McPherson, who at the time was one of Australia's most recognizable figures. She was at the top of her game both as a model and owner of a successful fashion business. That status apparently gave her older, French photographer husband reason to hover around and interject, until Elle told him to 'piss off' in no uncertain terms.

Working in an overseas bureau guarantees a diverse list of interview subjects and so it was in my case when I came across such sporting greats as Carl Lewis, John McEnroe, Rod Laver, Greg Norman and Mike Tyson.

The 'daily grind' also included attending the annual Oscars and filing stories on such luminaries as Harrison Ford, Madonna, Mel Gibson, Michael York, Olivia Newton-John, Paul Hogan and Tom Cruise. One memorable interview was recorded with Hogan's wife and co-star in Crocodile Dundee, Linda Kozlowski, at the couple's Malibu mansion. I had been contacted by producers in Australia urging me to follow up on magazine articles detailing Linda's struggle with cellulite on her shapely legs.

I was less than thrilled with the request, and had a fair idea she had no wish to discuss the tabloid trash, but it was obvious that one of the current affairs shows was planning a story to run off the back of the media headlines.

I waited until the very last question in the interview, which had been going well, to ask her to comment on the 'cellulite allegations'. Predictably, she was none too pleased, and any goodwill I'd banked earlier in the interview was shredded. Despite my apologies, it was a frosty exit from the Hogan beachside home.

Even after hours, when the cameras were switched off, it was usual to spend time in the hangouts of the big names, especially in Los Angeles. However, it was back in Sydney when I realized what a handsome rooster I must have been; at least Elton John seemed to think so when he gave me 'the wink' at the bar of the Sebel Townhouse. Even though I'd accepted April Ashley's invitation for a peek-a-boo, I did not fancy the experience with Elton!

Some interviewees are memorable for the generosity of their time and their innate goodwill, such as American President Ronald Reagan, who wielded enormous charm, and had the knack of putting journalists and those on both sides of the political fence at ease. It was perhaps the reason he made the easy transition from actor to politician.

In sharp contrast, Malaysian Prime Minister, Dr. Mahathir, not only kept us waiting for hours, but was abrupt and downright rude. I later found out that the Australian authorities had not accepted his medical degree, and he harboured a lasting dislike of all things Aussie. Luckily, he was the exception, rather than the rule.

Most people we interviewed wanted to be there, and were often promoting a new movie, book or career. They needed something from us, and we needed content to fill up TV programs of all descriptions. It was a very symbiotic relationship, which worked well most of the time.

I relished being in a business where you didn't know what you'd be doing for much of the time, and had no idea where you might end up at the end of the day. Covering the siege at Waco, or on a chopper filming an erupting volcano couldn't have been anticipated, but when it happened, what a buzz!

CHAPTER 17
TAIWAN TRAVAILS

The sight of the Eva Airways jumbo jet sitting on the tarmac of Sydney's Kingsford Smith International Airport provoked a nervousness I had seldom felt.

This was not another overseas assignment, like so many I'd taken in a broadcasting career spanning 25 years.

It was a life-changing decision, which involved 'pulling up stumps' and moving to Taiwan with my family, to an uncertain future, and without the comfort of a secure salary.

By any measure, it made little sense, but for someone used to living on the edge and in need of a challenge, the move was not totally unexpected. For a number of years, I had lived with the expectation that my employer, Channel 7 would send me to Asia to set up a network news bureau.

It had been discussed during my time as a reporter and newsreader in Melbourne and Sydney, in the years after returning from America.

When it became increasingly unlikely it would happen, due to industry-wide cost cutting, and, after an unfulfilling time working for the network's current affairs show, Today Tonight, I was ready for a change.

I had always been fascinated with Asia. My parents had married in Singapore, and as a child I had spent time there. In 1979, I married Kathy Wu, a Taiwanese who had migrated to Australia in the early 70s. Subsequent trips to the small island, regarded as a renegade province by the mainland Chinese, confirmed my liking of the country and its people.

I felt an instant affinity, which led to the boast, usually under the influence of alcohol, that in my previous life I must have been born Chinese.

Language barriers and cultural differences meant little to me, so comfortable did I feel, and confident in my abilities to make a new life far away from my native Australia.

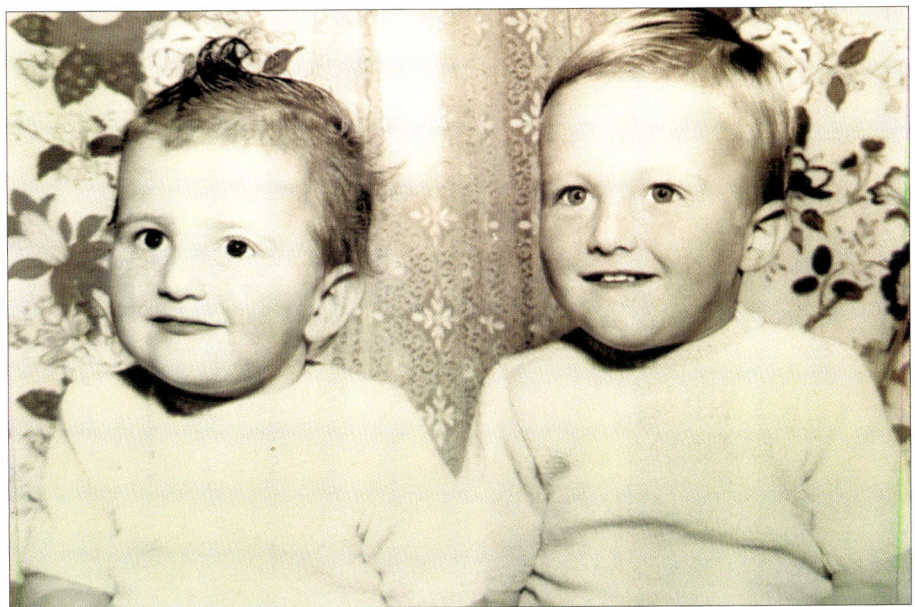

1. Wedding Bells in Singapore for Eileen (Lyn) Hodder and Gordon Hyslop on 26 March, 1949
2. The Twins - Ian Phillip and Diane Elizabeth

3. Lyn relaxing into island life on Cocos
4. Life in Paradise – Lyn and Gordon with the twins on Cocos Islands in 1955
5. Gordon fishing for the family dinner

6. Lyn (4th from left) 'treading the boards' with the girls in Cocos Islands
7. Qantas 'Connie' arriving in Cocos Islands in mid 1950s
8. Lazy days on the beach in Cocos Islands with all the kids – but where are the crabs!

9. French President, General Charles de Gaulle drops into Cocos for a visit in 1956
10. Gordon escorting a very 'dubious bride' in 'Queen of the May' production on Cocos Island
11. Lyn's childhood home: 'The Oaks' in Abersychan, viewed from the oak tree.

12. The Twins meet Santa
13. The Hodder Family home in Hanbury Road, Abersychan, South Wales
14. The Hodder Family Clan in 1963

NOT SO SLOPPY

15. Di and Ian feeding the pigeons in Trafalgar Square, London with Nanny Hodder – 1963
16. ABC cadet journalist, Ian Hyslop in 1973

NOT SO SLOPPY

17. Reporting for Channel 9 outside NSW Parliament House with Geoff Carroll and Gilbert Farkas
18. The photographer said 'look serious' and I did. Channel 10 in 1981
19. On the road in Africa with Producer, Nick Farrow and Cameraman, Scott Barnett

20. First News Reading gig in Sydney, 1981
21. Cameraman, Maurice Roper gets the best vantage point at the 1988 Republican National Convention in New Orleans
22. Interviewing Great Train Robber, Ronald Biggs in Rio de Janeiro in 1988, with Maurice Roper filming

23. Raymond Burr (AKA Perry Mason) after being interviewed by Foreign Correspondent, Hyslop. With Channel 7 Legend and Office Manager, Zane Bair.

24. On Royal Australian Navy frigate, *HMAS Darwin*

25. The crew getting to know the locals in Kenya, with Wayne McKelvey and Scott Barnett

26. With cameraman, Maurice Roper, flying with U.S. forces into Honduras in 1988
27. Our Los Angeles home in 1988, with Daniel and Kathy
28. Reporting politics when Reagan was President

NOT SO SLOPPY

29. Thirsty work, this reporting and filming caper. With cameraman, Maurice Roper, enjoying a well earned libation!
30. Exchanging Vows with Rhonda on the *'Silver Wind'* off the coast of Madeira, April 2004. Best Man, Colin Seale from Barbados in attendance

31. The fruit of my loins, Daniel Lee and Morgan Dee
32. A new start with Rhonda, AKA Lady Barnett – March 2005

NOT SO SLOPPY

33. The Hyslop/Edmonds/Coulson Clans gather at Christmas in Belrose, Sydney in 2010. *Rear L-R:* Roger Coulson, Mark Edmonds, Daniel Hyslop, Ian Hyslop. *Middle L-R:* Morgan Hyslop, Brooke Rosconi (Coulson), Rebecca Killalea (Coulson), Stephanie Rogers (Edmonds), Rhonda Barnett. *Front L-R:* Di Coulson (Hyslop), Lyn Hyslop (Hodder), Janine Edmonds (Hyslop).
34. My old boss and Best Man, Mike Worner joins the Wedding Party, along with bridesmaid/niece Stephanie Edmonds

35. 'Dressed to the Nines' on *'Silver Cloud'* off the coast of Africa in 2017
36. Proud Mum, Lyn with her brood – Ian, Diane and Janine - Christmas 2010
37. Another 'My Life My Legacy' documentary production, for the Szekely family in 2019

NOT SO SLOPPY

38. Exploring Antarctica in style on *Seabourn Quest*, December 2016
39. Three generations of Hyslop men – Ian, Daniel and Jude: June 2017

40. The eternal 'publicity shot'

My wife's family connections in Taipei helped us settle in, providing a cushion from the loneliness commonly experienced in a move to a foreign country.

In hindsight, I should perhaps have examined more thoroughly whether Kathy had any interest in returning to the country of her birth. I would find that out later.

My single-minded determination to start a new business as a freelance journalist was an unashamedly selfish act, driven by the belief that the region would soon become a hotbed of action.

I would be well placed to cover developments. Our arrival in Taipei in 1997 coincided with the Asian financial crisis, where most currencies in the region had been devalued by around 30 percent. Taiwan's economy remained the strongest and most resilient in Asia, but politically there was a new tide of unrest brewing.

The Nationalist Party or Kuomintang had ruled Taiwan continuously since the founding of the ROC in 1949. Leaders, Sun Yat-sen and Chiang Kai-shek had fled the mainland at the end of a bloody civil war, which saw Mao Zedong take power and the communist party replace the pro-western government.

Under the Nationalists, the small island, formerly known as Formosa, became an Asian economic tiger, growing enormously through the 1970s, 80s and 90s; a phenomenon I witnessed on my numerous visits.

Chiang Ching-kuo, the son of the ROC founder Chiang Kai-shek, was in power, ruthlessly driving economic expansion and building up the island's military defense capabilities. The policies and strategy were modelled on Japan's rise from the ashes of WW2, and were proving to be very effective.

However, rapid expansion came at a cost, with most of the big cities shrouded in thick pollution, a by-product of heavy industrialization. In the 15 years since my first visit and my arrival in 1997, much had changed. The population generally enjoyed a high standard of living and bank balances had swollen.

But, the dynamic capitalist economy, that was driven largely by industrial manufacturing and exports of electronics, machinery, and petrochemicals, exposed the economy to fluctuations in global demand. When the recession hit in 1998, the country's gross domestic product plunged.

Uncertain times and an increasingly sophisticated population started questioning political leadership, which remained firmly in the hands of the Kuomintang. A pro-democracy movement was gaining traction, and the fledgling opposition party, the DPP, attracting more supporters.

The writing was on the wall, and President Lee Teng-Hui, a Cornell University-educated economist, was tasked with guiding Taiwan's transition to a democratic era.

I would interview the President not long after receiving my media credentials. It was an important meeting and served as an introduction to government officials, as one of the only resident western reporters in the country.

I soon found my status as a freelancer was not going to turn too many heads, so I started looking for regular assignments with international news organizations. After 25 years of working for Australian television networks, I felt distinctly naked without affiliated news credentials to flash. This freelance caper was not easy!

After taking on several stories for Hong Kong-based CNBC News, I was rewarded with a letter confirming me as their man on the ground in Taiwan. That, however, was not going to pay all the bills, including Daniel's private school fees back in Sydney.

From news reporting, I diversified into producing two documentaries for the Discovery Channel, which would importantly connect me to the man who would become my partner and good friend to this day.

Jonathan Chan ran a production company in Taipei, and had many business interests in mainland China. Most of his family had migrated to America, where they ran the biggest Chinese language book publishing business in the country.

He would provide the camera crews and editing facilities and importantly, was well connected to all the broadcasters in the city. It was a relationship that was invaluable in developing a major story I was to break in 1998.

I had been living in Taipei for almost 12 months, when I received a phone call from a Melbourne woman, who asked for my help in tracking down her daughter's birth mother.

My contact details had been given to Nola Wunderle by a former colleague at Channel 7, who knew I was now living and working in the Taiwanese capital.

She told me a remarkable story of her daughter Kartya, who was adopted from Taiwan in the 1980s; one of more than 60 babies sold to western parents in an illegal, baby-selling racket.

We ended the phone conversation with my promise to look into the story and a request that she send me further details. Minutes later an email arrived with Kartya's story; a compellingly, sad account of her troubled teenage years.

It was a graphic story of her difficulty coming to terms with her life in a country where she looked and acted differently to those around her, including her family. Her often violent response included drug use and short stays in various foster homes. She really was the 'little girl lost' and felt that she desperately needed to find out where she came from and why she was 'given away'.

Nola sent more adoption details, which allowed me, through local interpreters, to track down the principals of the defunct adoption agency, and the woman whose name appeared on documents as Kartya's birth mother.

I found her living on the outskirts of Taipei; a 53-year-old woman who told me she had been paid 10,000 NT dollars in 1981 for listing herself as the girl's mother. With tears streaming down her face, she said she believed she was helping the baby find a better home. "I am sorry for causing so much pain. I was poor and did not know my actions were breaking the law," she confessed.

She had served 10 months in jail after a Taiwan court found her guilty of conspiracy in a 'baby trading ring' organized by a 32-year-old law clerk, Julie Chu, who was also jailed. There had been over 30 arrests and 60 illegal adoptions.

More than 15 years after being released from jail, Julie Chu was living with her husband in the mountains near Taipei. They had put the past behind them, and moved on to a more lucrative and legal business career. During my meeting, she agreed to help to find the real identity of Kartya's biological mother.

The scene was now set for a possible reunion, but many details needed to be ironed out before the troubled young woman could meet her Taiwanese family.

It was an amazing story with international appeal, but I first needed to know if Kartya had overcome her drug addiction, and if she would be capable of fronting an aggressive Taiwanese media pack, that made western journalists look timid. Nola assured me her daughter had beaten her habit, and was eager to make the trip.

I may have had an exclusive story, but as a freelancer, chances of getting international coverage were limited. I decided to share the story with Taiwan's biggest circulation daily newspaper, a move that would assure maximum coverage in a country with a population of 23 million people. I flew to Melbourne with Taiwanese news journalist, George Gao, to meet and interview the Wunderle family for the documentary I planned to produce and the article he was writing.

The trip left me in no doubts that Kartya was serious, and capable of handling what was certain to be a media feeding frenzy in seeking a meeting with her biological mother.

When the story broke in Taipei, I was thrust into the spotlight as the foreign reporter who uncovered the story, and the newfound notoriety allowed me to approach airlines and hotels, to sponsor the Wunderles' trip to Taiwan. They had limited resources to travel.

Few countries in the world are serviced by such a large contingent of print and television reporters. It is an insanely competitive media sector that epitomizes and surpasses the 'dog eat dog' culture of its western counterparts.

They didn't much like the idea that an Australian journalist had so much control over the story, which had caused a sensation when it first appeared in the country's biggest circulation newspaper. Other media outlets were clamoring to catch up.

Their chance came when Kartya and Nola flew into Taiwan in June, 1998, for the much anticipated reunion.

The Intercontinental Hotel, which had agreed to sponsor the Wunderles' stay, made its grand ballroom available to host the press conference, an event that was telecast live around the country. Virtually every major media outlet was present to report on the baby smuggling story, which had stained Taiwan's reputation and captured the rapt attention of a nation.

Kartya told her heartfelt story to the assembled press, and two weeks later the birth mother came forward, having recognized a distinct birth mark and one oddly shaped ear! Police confirmed that DNA testing had identified the true biological mother.

A meeting took place behind closed doors at Police headquarters, where Kartya was introduced to her mother, who was wracked by guilt and apologized for not being able to raise her. She discovered that her birth father had sold her to the illegal adoption agency and he had since passed away.

At a subsequent press conference, tears flowed and the raw emotion of the moment provided rich fodder for an eager media scrum, whose job it was to report details of the controversial reunion.

Kartya would remain in Taiwan for more than three months, learning about her new family, and gaining an insight into the culture of a country she left as a baby.

As a freelance journalist I felt no small amount of pride in helping break the story, and letting the Wunderles solve the mystery that for so long had torn the family apart.

I pitched the story to Sixty Minutes, for a sum that helped pay my son's hefty school fees in Sydney. The story appeared on Australian television screens several months later.

CHAPTER 18
THE MOTHER FINDER

The baby-selling story took on a life of its own.

No sooner had Taiwanese headlines carried the story of Kartya's reunion than a local woman came forward, hoping to be reunited with the daughter she had put up for adoption.

Yen Kan gave birth to a baby girl out of wedlock in 1980, and was paid 285 US dollars by the same fake adoption agency. She had been moved to come forward after seeing the heartwarming reunion of the Australian teenager and her Taiwanese mother.

The adoption agency assured her at the time, that her child would be given to a Chinese family, but she then discovered her daughter was about to be taken overseas by a foreign couple.

The young woman told Taipei police she went to a hotel, where the couple from Australia was waiting for documentation to be completed. She wanted the baby back, but it was too late.

I learned of the case from a journalist at the United Daily Newspaper, who wanted to find the couple, and proposed a joint investigation, bringing the daughter and parents back to Taiwan from Australia.

The identity of the couple was quickly established. Ian and Sue Butler, from Adelaide in South Australia, like dozens of couples around the world, had no idea their adoption had been illegally processed and the documents forged.

A phone call to the Butlers, and 18-year-old Aimee revealed a happy and well-adjusted teenager, who told me she had no real desire to meet her birth mother.

Her story could not have been more different to Kartya's. Aimee had won a scholarship to one of Adelaide's most prestigious colleges and was a gifted musician, playing both piano and violin.

Not knowing her birth mother had caused her no pain. She had grown up in a happy household with loving parents, and two adopted siblings from South Korea.

The odds of persuading her to come to Taipei were not high, but Aimee agreed to be interviewed in Adelaide for my documentary and a newspaper article by journalist, George Gao.

We arrived to find the family residing in a leafy Adelaide suburb. I had come armed with an emotional video recording of Aimee's birth mother, Yen Kan, appealing for a face-to-face meeting. It clearly struck a nerve, with both parents and Aimee in tears, viewing the emotional plea that had been translated into English.

I explained how the Taiwanese people had reacted to the baby selling racket and the resultant outpouring of emotion around the country.

The story had attracted sponsors who were willing to pay the costs incurred in getting the family to Taipei. We spent the day filming interviews before receiving an assurance from Ian and Sue that they would consider coming to Taiwan. However, it all depended on whether Aimee was prepared to expose herself to all the publicity. She was a shy girl, so it would not be easy.

We returned to Taiwan with little confidence that we would see them again, but less than a week later, I received a phone call. They would make the trip. It was on!

George Gao's article, published on his return to Taipei, served to provoke interest in Aimee's story and once again stirred up the huge local media contingent.

I found myself part promoter, part journalist, as I once again started organizing details to make the Butlers' visit as painless as possible. I had warned them to expect huge media interest, which could be daunting.

It was left to me to write a press release, translated by my Chinese business partner, for distribution to all media organizations. A concert hall was hired for the press conference and audiovisual presentation of Aimee playing the piano.

It turned out Kartya was still in town and was happy to make a short introductory speech, which I wrote.

She said:

Good morning everyone,

It is almost three months now since I stood before many of you and asked for help in finding my birth mother.

At that time, it seemed an almost impossible task. But as you all know my dream came true and my mother and I were reunited after 17 long years. I will, forever, be grateful to the media and the people of Taiwan for their assistance in

bringing us together.
I come before you today to welcome Aimee and tell her I understand what she and her birth mother are going through.
It is not easy. It takes courage on both sides to come forward and reveal your story to the public.
Aimee has lived and loved her adoptive parents and family since she arrived in Australia as a three-month-old baby.
I know it was my story that moved Aimee's birth mother, Yen Kan to come forward. She has always wanted to know what happened to the baby girl she gave up in 1980. Now she can see what a beautiful, talented girl Aimee has grown up to be.
At last, Aimee can find out why she was given up for adoption, she can see where she came from. These are important questions for all human beings to know.
There were dozens of Taiwanese babies illegally sold to overseas parents in the 1980s. I'm sure not all of them want to find their birth mothers, but for those families who do – this is a wonderful experience.
Thank you again for helping make my dream come true and I wish Aimee and her birth mother, Yen Kan, all the best for the future."

There could be no mistaking the tears of joy on the face of the painfully thin Taiwanese woman, who had never married, and lived a frugal life in a tiny, city apartment. Yen Kan walked self-consciously onto the stage of the Taipei Concert Hall to meet her daughter and adoptive parents.

With the arc lights illuminating her gaunt features, and dozens of television cameras rolling, she threw herself to the floor, hands raised in prayer, in front of Ian and Sue Butler, a dramatic gesture of gratitude to the couple who had raised her daughter for 18 years.

It was an emotion charged moment, made even more so when Aimee ran to her mother's prostrate body and pulled her into an embrace.

Through an interpreter, Yen Kan explained her overwhelming sorrow at having to give up her baby, born out of wedlock. She felt she had no alternative and had no idea the adoption was illegally processed. She was grateful to the Butlers for giving her daughter a wonderful life, and simply wanted to explain the circumstances of her actions.

A clearly nervous Sue Butler was asked to speak and outlined the life Aimee had lived in her adopted country, and the love she had brought to the family.

She spoke glowingly of Aimee's academic achievements and her passion for playing the piano and violin.

The audience was clearly moved, as both birth and adoptive mothers sat beside each other holding hands, as they watched and listened to Aimee's musical talents.

To a nation that places so much importance on the education of its children, and emphasis on musical training, the story resonated in a completely different way to the troubled tale of Kartya, that had dominated headlines a few months earlier.

For the talented young lady who told me, before coming to Taiwan, she had no real interest in meeting her birth mother, the experience had been overwhelmingly positive.

"I'd always wondered where my looks came from and who my birth mother was, but I was never driven to find out. Now I have, I am so happy. She is a lovely woman and I will keep in contact with her."

The Butlers flew home to their quiet life in Adelaide and after 6 months of throwing my energy into adoption stories, I could get back to building the freelance business I had come to Taiwan to establish.

A good part of my savings, channelled into developing the documentary, had evaporated, and the priority now was to generate income to support my family. How I missed the security of that big salary back in Sydney.

Around this time, I found I had picked up a 'nickname' given to me by members of the Taiwanese media. Translated into English it meant, 'Mother Finder,' though I'm sure many would have used the ruder tag with the same initials! Not everyone appreciated my efforts in developing the story that had attracted widespread interest around the island. I was seeing the reverse side of the racism, that Australians had been accused of by migrants over the years.

As our second Christmas in Taiwan approached, I received an email that would again thrust me back into the role of 'Mother Finder'.

It was written by a Swedish university student, Hanna Andersson, who told me she had seen the stories on the internet, and was moved to tears by their respective reunions. Like the Australian girls, she had been sold to her Swedish parents in the same illegal racket in 1978.

She appealed for my help in finding her biological mother, but on learning the details, I cautioned her prospects for success were not good as the birth mother did not come from the island's largest city, Taipei.

Hanna, 22 years old, a university economics student near Stockholm, believed her mother was a 16-year-old student who became pregnant out of wedlock in the southern Taiwan city of Tainan. These were the scant details revealed to her by her adoptive parents.

I turned to the Swedish Trade Commissioner in Taipei, Carsten Svensson, to be the face of an appeal to the media for help in finding Hanna's mother.

But first, I booked a flight to Sweden to meet and interview the family, before organizing an airline seat for Hanna, who would come back on her own.

I arrived at Arlanda Airport in Stockholm, as a record snowfall was dumped on the city, making transportation extremely difficult, and temperatures almost unbearable to someone whose blood had been thinned by the heat of Asia.

The Anderssons' small suburban home was a welcome sight after a long drive through, at times virtually impassable roads. It provided a warm refuge and the offer of a glass of the traditional Swedish Christmas wine, Glogg, an even warmer welcome.

Hanna spoke perfect English, her oriental origins unmistakable as she introduced her parents, who exuded a quiet, defensive manner that left little doubt they were unsure about their daughter's need to track down her birth mother.

This was confirmed in the interview, as they expressed concern that a trip may threaten the security of their relationship with Hanna.

On hearing this, their daughter interrupted the interview and embraced her mother, whispering assurances in Swedish that nothing could alter her love for her parents. It was a highly emotional moment caught on camera.

My questions to Hanna established that she'd grown up in a loving family, and her need to seek out her mother should not be interpreted as implied criticism or rejection of the parents, who had given her a good life.

I flew back to Taipei two days later, comfortable that the family now fully understood the need to resolve Hanna's question. That would not, however, make it any easier, given the limited facts we had to start a search.

Hanna arrived in Taipei in early December, aboard a British Airways flight from London. Dozens of reporters and cameras were waiting to tell her story to a nation, which had been exposed to the baby-selling stories for more than 6 months.

My business partner, Jonathan's relationship with a leading PR firm allowed me to step back from organizing sponsorship of flights and accommodation, and concentrate on finding the birth mother.

The Taipei police department was again enlisted to conduct DNA testing of those who came forward in the course of the investigation.

As was the case in the two previous searches, documents were found that showed Hanna's mother, but again it transpired to be just a woman paid to put her name to the birth records.

When Hanna flew into the small southern city of Tainan to make a public appeal for help in finding her birth mother, interest was overwhelming. People had been watching the national press coverage in Taipei for months. Now it was their chance to join the search, and help the young Swedish student.

Several women came forward and agreed to be tested, but all were found to be negative matches. As I feared, the chances of success were limited. Twenty years had passed since Hanna had been adopted out of the country.

Hanna Andersson would never find her birth mother. She left Taipei just days before Christmas Eve, in time to fly home and spend the holiday season with the people she had called mother and father for 22 years.

She had tried, but failed to answer the pivotal question in her young life!

CHAPTER 19
TEARS BEFORE BEDTIME

The tears in the eyes of my 9-year-old daughter, Morgan, were clear evidence of the massive upheaval she'd endured at the hands of a father, who had taken her a long way from family and friends in Australia.

It had become a morning ritual, the short walk to a school she clearly hated. "I can't understand them, Daddy" she would tearfully tell me, squeezing my hand with the strength of someone much older.

"Don't worry Sweetheart, you'll learn quickly," I reassured her, trying to keep the emotion from my voice, and the tears from my eyes.

She was a fast learner, and within six months had become a popular little girl in a classroom full of kids, who had never before met anyone from Australia.

It was perhaps the greatest relief of my new life in this hectic Asian city that offered private English education, at a cost I simply could not afford.

That indulgence had been previously afforded for Daniel who was enrolled at Knox Grammar, and living with his grandparents on Sydney's North Shore. It had made sense to enrol him when I had the benefit of a large corporate salary at Channel 7.

Thrift had become a new word in my lexicon, as I no longer enjoyed the inflated expatriate package I had received in America, or the handsome Australian salary paid into my bank account every month.

We were living like locals, shopping in the small neighborhood markets, eating at noodle stalls and residing away from the expensive enclaves reserved for foreign nationals employed by the major corporations.

Within weeks of my arrival, I was doing battle on Taipei's frenetic, congested road system. The teeming city was home to the largest number of motorcycles in the world, which prompted an article I wrote for a local English tourist magazine.

HOW TO SURVIVE DRIVING IN TAIWAN

So, you've arrived in Taiwan and now face the age-old problem of getting about town.

If you hail from a western background where road rules and regulations are followed and strictly enforced, then the bright lights of Taipei may hold a rude shock.

If, on the other hand, you come from the back blocks of Panama City or Rio de Janeiro, where many a Formula 1 driver has cut his teeth – relax!

The first rule for all newcomers…there are NO rules!

That's not to suggest that the relevant authorities have not laid out a long list of do's and don'ts for the local populace to follow. It's just that very few of them appear to observe any laws.

First lesson for the intrepid traveller, Do Not approach Taiwan with the assumption that driving here is not all that much different to hitting the roads back home.

The first thing to look out for, and they're hard to ignore, are the millions of screaming motorcycles, that buzz around town in the same manic style as a swarm of drunken mosquitoes.

They make living in the crowded city dangerous, and while there are no exact figures, it's generally accepted Taiwan boasts the highest number in the world.

Why so many of them?

Well, try getting around town in a car!

Yes, folks, there are simply too many of them for the hopelessly congested roadways. Economic boom times have brought the tiny island an embarrassment of riches, and the car has, for many come to symbolize wealth: hence the disproportionate number of Mercedes Benz and BMWs.

However, for those who have missed the economic gravy train and are none too happy about it, they can ride their bikes and exact revenge by scratching and denting high-priced paint jobs without fear of apprehension.

It's a common sight on any downtown road, the speeding, weaving form of a motorcyclist handling his pulsating machine with reckless abandon, as he throws it in and out of gridlocked stationary cars.

To the unwary driver, the rear vision mirror offers no assistance in detecting these speedsters, who often end up imprinted on the heavy metal panel work of a four-wheel opponent.

To the driver, there's the equally unsettling sight of entire families sitting astride tiny motorcycles, not an uncommon or ridiculous sight to the blasé local. But to the newcomer, it's a frightening reminder that a mistake could result in a tragic death, certain to spoil a holiday or working visit.

Yes, it is very different!

And then, there are the more pleasant distractions, as beautiful, young women plunge through city traffic, astride their throbbing Yamahas and Kymcos.

They are distractions, which keep many foreigners off the roads and firmly committed to travelling the city's reliable public transport system.

But, if the visitor is determined to take to the roads on either a two or four-wheel conveyance there are a number of rules that should be strictly observed.

Rule No 1. *Never hesitate! Push and plunge into traffic. Match the aggression of locals. Blend in by wearing a full-face helmet, giving no hint of your foreign origins, or risk the assumption that you're fair game. Timidity or indecisiveness can result in death. When you encounter an over-aggressive local driver (and there are plenty of them), roll down your window, smile, and match his or her aggression. They usually back off.*

Rule No 2. *Watch out for buses. Bus drivers receive incentive payments for the number of times they complete a run on a given shift. This explains the maniacal look on their faces, and the numerous accidents involving the cities privately owned, aging bus fleet.*

Rule No 3. *Beware of 'bing lang' (betel nut) chewing truck drivers. They are perhaps the most dangerous road user you're likely to encounter on the island's teeming motorways. Massive insurance payouts by truck company owners have prompted a little publicized edict along the lines that "if you get involved in an accident make sure it's a fatal". The payout is nowhere near as much!*

Rule No 4. *Always understand that taxi drivers have right of way!*

Rule No 5. *Never get on the back of a motorcycle with a local female aged between 18 and 30, no matter how attractive she is. The 'woman driver' factor is a shocking reality.*

Rule No 6. *Avoid, at all costs, aging motorcyclists wearing 'coke bottle' thick spectacles. They have the disconcerting habit of ignoring stoplights, pedestrian crossings, and the terrified cursing of western visitors.*

Rule No 7. *Never drive between the hours of 2 am and 5 am in the major cities, particularly Taipei. These are the witching hours, which claim the lives of thousands of innocent victims, mown down or crushed in spectacular high-speed accidents caused by drunken drivers.*

Rule No 8. *Avoid large black luxury cars, usually the latest model Benz or BMW. They invariably speed; the occupant often seen through tinted windows clutching a mobile phone in one hand and the leg of a woman in the other.*

Rule No 9. *Watch out for the opening of drivers' side doors. The occupant often spits out voluminous quantities of the blood-red betel nut juice, certain to ruin the day of a visiting western motorcyclist. Don't be intimidated by all* the apparent puddles of blood smearing city streets. The blood actually gets cleaned up!

Rule No 10. *Always be on guard for small blanket-wrapped bundles falling from speeding motorcycles. Mum may have lost one of her three kids, who are forced to cling to her as she makes her way around town.*

Rule No 11. *Avoid the thousands of mobile noodle cart vendors who dodge in and out of traffic escaping the attentions of an over-zealous police force. There's nothing more ridiculous than having to wear your dinner.*

Rule No 12. *Be careful of the myriad of small, brightly-coloured private language school buses. They let off their tiny charges with little warning. Having a bunch of kids laughing at you as they peel you off the back bumper bar is no fun!*

Rule No 13. *Don't get irate or upset when the rearview mirror is ripped from the side of your car by a speeding motorcycle.*

Rule No 14. *Pay attention to ridiculously unsafe speeding ambulances that hurtle around town on bald tyres, while the head of the critically ill, unsecured occupant stains the windows red.*

Rule No 15. *Particularly watch out for pedestrians, a battle weary lot, who've seen every type of road carnage and do not care anymore. They leap from the sidewalk in what appears to be strange acts of mass suicide. Hitting one is no fun! Try calming down a mob, when your Chinese language skills are non-existent.*

Rule No 16. *Never drive a car younger than ten years old – they think you care!*

Rule No 17. *Perhaps the most important tip to the adventurous visitor intent on giving the roads a go: beware of English language road signs. It's not uncommon to grapple with a dozen different spellings of the same street, suburb, and town.*

Rule No 18. *Always understand that speed signs mean nothing!*
And that, folks, is your guide to surviving Taiwan's road system.
Happy driving and good luck!

Whether it was on a motorcycle or driving the car gifted to me by a brother-in-law who moved to Shanghai, I took to the roads enthusiastically. I obtained a local Taiwanese license, and embarked on a campaign to terrorize the locals.

My numerous visits to the capital city had armed me with a smattering of Mandarin Chinese, a language spoken by a wife, who had assiduously avoided teaching it to our two children.

If I was to do business and work in the city, I knew I would have to try to learn it, but had no illusions about mastering the frustratingly complicated language. I would sit at night with my daughter listening to mandarin tapes, in our race to see who could become more proficient.

She won the contest 'hands down', leaving me to seek language exchange lessons with anyone keen to learn English. I wasn't going to fall into the trap, like so many American 'gweilos' of speaking English, and refusing to learn Chinese, a form of cultural arrogance I could not abide.

There are certain sounds a mouth is not naturally designed to make. In the case of Asians speaking English, words with L, R or TH and for Westerners, sounds that require the tongue to be virtually stuck to the roof of the mouth, a position rarely adopted by a gweilo. It is a real challenge.

As we closed in on the new millennium, the political scene started to hot up, with the Mayor of Taipei, Chen Shui-bian, entering the Presidential race, as head of the Democratic Progressive Party. It would be the first time the Kuomintang's 50 years of continuous rule would be challenged. Nightly news bulletins showed politicians brawling in the Legislative Yuan, providing rich fodder for overseas broadcasters and their coverage of 'Democracy Taiwan Style.'

In the 1980s and 90s, the tiny island state was pumping billions of dollars into strengthening its military, aimed at discouraging aggression from mainland China. War games were staged every year, and I was to report on them for a number of international news outlets.

'Cross-strait' negotiations between the mainland and Taiwan were also a hot topic and a story CNBC News was eager to air. I organized interviews with government officials and academics, and reported on any shifts in the position of either side. Neither seemed prepared to give ground and the standoff continued.

The mainland's contention that Taiwan was a renegade province flew in the face of the island's proud perception of itself as an independent country that had built a remarkable economy; one of the strongest and most dynamic in the world.

There was no shortage of stories to develop for international consumption, but it was the natural disasters, a constant threat to the island, that was a guaranteed income source for a struggling freelance journalist.

Between July and September most years, typhoons sweep in from the Pacific Ocean and bring assorted death and destruction. Derived from the Mandarin term, Taifeng, meaning 'supreme wind', they wreak havoc, displacing thousands of people and causing massive damage.

My family was to experience the awesome power of one not long after moving to Taipei, when gale-force winds and torrential rain relentlessly battered the city for three days. We could not move from our fourth floor apartment, as floodwaters engulfed the first two levels of the building.

I watched on powerlessly as the raging torrent inundated my car, which was parked on the front street. It would not survive the savage assault and we would have to rely on public transport for several months.

However, it was much worse in other parts of the island, where 'Typhoon Winnie' caused enormous devastation and claimed dozens of lives. I would write about this destructive power:

WINNIE STRIKES TAIWAN
There is no stronger or more powerful climate agent in nature's formidable repertoire than wind. For when it blows, the potential for massive death and destruction climbs significantly with each small measure of speed.

The people of the Pacific and South East Asia call them typhoons and around July to October each year, they smash into these countries, with scant regard for life and property, killing, maiming and leaving misery in their wake.

Like their climatic cousins, hurricanes and cyclones, the typhoon displays the same behavioral aberrations. Spawned by a combination of warm oceans and unique atmospheric conditions, they start their death missions as ominous circular swirls on a weather map. At the end of the murderous trail of destruction, all that remains is a death toll, a statistic that conveys none of the horror felt when they fall victim to the 'big wind'.

Typhoons are always watched and anticipated, but no amount of preparation can divert them from their destructive path.

Its name was 'Winnie' and in mid-August 1997, she cut a trail of destruction through the Eastern Pacific, first sweeping over southern Japan before building up speed and strength to move onto the small enclave of Okinawa.

So far, there was nothing to overly disturb Taiwanese typhoon veterans lying in her path to the southeast.

Ever since the 16th century, when Portuguese explorers named her Formosa or "Beautiful Island", Taiwan has experienced the awesome force of the wind they call the "tai fon ".

This time there was no great concern. State of the art weather forecasting facilities on the island had painstakingly tracked this monster from the first minute she whipped up whitecaps in the Marshall Islands. The official bureau bulletin described her as a medium strength typhoon, with winds gusting to 180 kilometers an hour.

Nothing Taiwan hadn't seen before, and couldn't bear again.

And so, the first seeds of contempt for Winnie were sown; guards were dropped from Kaohsiung to Taipei. Residents went to sleep with little fear in their hearts.

Charles Lin, his wife and two young children prepared for their first typhoon in a new 5-million-dollar apartment in the suburb of Hsichih, perched in the hills overlooking Taipei.

Lincoln Mansions was the grand name given to this newly built, up-market development; another luxury offering to the capital's increasingly expanding upper middle class.

Like everyone else, Charles Lin was not overly concerned about 'Winnie'.

A 42-year-old advertising agency executive, his early family life had been spent in the south of the Island, and he grew up seeing plenty of these 'big winds'.

However, Charles Lin was not to know that just hours after tucking his two children into bed, Lincoln Mansions would shudder and slip off its foundations, pushed by a mountain of mud loosened by torrential rain.

The multi-million-dollar tower toppled over like Lego blocks into the structure next door. The ground floor and basement were pummelled into the sodden mud. Twisted concrete entombed the bodies of more than thirty residents, including the Lin family, whose ground floor apartment was hardest hit.

It took seventeen hours for rescuers to recover the bodies. First to be pulled from the tangled mess was 3-year-old Jensu, her tiny body shattered by the concrete slab that doubled as her small bedroom's ceiling and the floor of the apartment above. There was little doubt this child suffered less than her 6-year-old sister, Chin Chin. The older girl's body was found wedged in the corner of the room where conceivably the first few hours of her hellish entombment were spent in an air pocket, sucking desperately for those last remaining gasps of oxygen. Hers was a comparatively slow death.

The Lins were among 46 people in Taiwan killed by 'Winnie', and damage was estimated at ten million dollars. For Taiwan's 23 million residents 'Winnie' started off as just another typhoon, but the fact that she killed this many, would reserve for her a special place in the collective memory of a nation.

While typhoons are certain to attract media attention, far more frightening and potentially life-threatening are the earthquakes that hit the island regularly. Located on the Pacific Ring of Fire, and at the edge of the Philippine Plate, Taiwan is in one of the world's most seismically active zones.

No stranger to earthquakes after living in California for years, my family was experienced in 'riding them out', but that made them no less terrifying!

In September 1999, the island was hit by a 7.7 magnitude earthquake that killed over 2,400 people and injured more than eleven thousand.

The epicenter in Jiji was 150 kilometres south of the capital, but it was violently felt in Taipei, and we were thrown out of beds shortly before 2 am.

Thousands of houses collapsed in the central part of the island and more than one hundred thousand people were left homeless. Just two kilometers from our apartment building, a ten-storey hotel collapsed, killing and trapping dozens of people and sparking a major rescue operation.

With aftershocks rolling through the darkened city, I made my way to the scene, ready to report on the disaster that had traumatized a nation. Hours later as the sun illuminated the chaotic scene, I crossed live by satellite to the ITV Morning show in London and later flew by helicopter to the worst hit areas. The rescue operation would go on for almost a week, sniffer dogs helping to locate dozens of people buried deep in the rubble of townships around the country.

It was the sad reality of a freelance journalist's life; death, destruction and natural disasters meant money in the bank and food on the table.

CHAPTER 20
BEER MONEY

The phone call came 'out of the blue', a far away, detached voice of undeniably Australian provenance.

"G'day mate, how would you like to make a little beer money?"

I was sitting in my apartment in Taipei, coincidentally thinking about the same subject, and the suggestion was more than a little appealing. He had my attention.

Michael Worner was my former Editor at Channel 7 in Melbourne, where we had worked together for 3 years, after my U.S. network posting.

We were good mates. I supported him through the trauma of a messy divorce, while he became Daniel and Morgan's favorite babysitter.

He was a tall, awkward man, sporting an obvious toupee, which sat upon his head much like a cowpat sits in a grassy paddock. Once a champion athlete with a colorful history as a 'lady's man', he was a highly respected, award-winning journalist, who had worked in print as well as television. It was good to hear his voice.

"I've left 7 and moved to Sydney," he told me, "I'm now General Manager of AsiaNet, a division of Australian Associated Press. Got a proposition for you," he offered.

For the next 20 minutes, he explained how AsiaNet handled the business news of American and Australian companies wanting to send press releases to publications in Asia.

"We are leading a consortium of government news agencies in the region," he told me. "They include Kyodo in Japan, Antara in Indonesia, Bernama in Malaysia, Yonhap in Korea, and also Xinhua in China."

"Problem is, we need someone in Taiwan, where there's huge business activity. We can't send the releases to China, because the Taiwanese hate them and the translations are no good, and if we give the work to the Central News Agency, in Taipei, Xinhua will pull out of the consortium".

"What do you think? You'd be the circuit breaker. Will you do it? We'll pay you for each release you translate and distribute to the newspapers and trade magazines. It might give you a little beer money."

It was an opportunity I was not about to turn down. My mind was racing; who would do the translations; how would I compile the distribution lists?

It would be a marriage made in heaven and the start of a business relationship that would last long after I left Taiwan, and provide more than a little beer money. 'Hyasia' would become the eighth member of the consortium, a one-man news agency, in name only.

The bulk of AsiaNet's business came from PRNewswire in New York. They wanted organizations on the ground in Asia, to disseminate the huge number of targeted press releases, generated by American companies doing business there.

The timely offer changed the dynamic of my small, struggling business. No longer did I have to rely on news reporting as the only source of income. A relationship with one of the biggest PR companies in the world, and a string of national news agencies gave me instant credibility and a business card that allowed entry into Taiwan's major corporations.

Along with my partner, Jonathan, who helped organize translators and media lists, Hyasia was up and running, and I was investigating how we could use this new business to gain entry into the corporate video market.

Many large Taiwanese companies were also clients of PRNewswire, sending press releases out of the country to American and European publications.

A little-known fact about Taiwan is that it has one of the biggest and most competitive media markets in the world; hundreds of trade magazines, spawned by a hi-tech industrial base, and dozens of newspapers and TV channels.

Flushed with success back in the 1960s and 70s, many Taiwanese executives sent their children overseas, to be educated at some of the finest universities in the world. They came back, speaking English and ready to launch themselves into careers that would contribute to Taiwan's amazing economic growth.

I was now in a position to interview them; Stan Shih from the computer giant, Acer; Jeffrey Koo, the banking billionaire; men who were influencing the direction of international commerce from their base in Taipei.

Things were looking up, but my journalistic curiosity remained dedicated to filing stories on the quirky, human-interest angles that could be found in abundance in the hectic city.

The Tea and Beer Wars were two aired on CNBC in Hong Kong, timed to coincide with the opening of Starbucks, Taipei and the marketing of beer by overseas brewers.

Predictions that coffee shops would fail in a country famous for tea or cha consumption, sparked the story. It aroused spirited debate among locals, prepared to bet that Starbucks outlets would never outnumber the teahouses that thrived in the crowded city. Years later, they would lose that bet.

It was equally disturbing for locals to think that the award-winning Taiwan beer could be replaced by foreign brews as the most popular amber fluid. Things were changing fast, as international companies flocked to the island, eagerly chasing the population's huge reserves of disposable income.

Taiwan may have been recognized as a world leader in the area of technology and computer science, but it remained faithful to an ancient culture that embraced religion and superstition at its core. As the Asian currency crisis hit countries around the region, locals could be seen burning fake money at temples and outside businesses, a sight that prompted another story filed for CNBC.

After years of being assigned stories and working in specialized areas of journalism, I was now furiously pitching ideas to producers that would not always be accepted.

In one memorable email exchange, I apologized to a Hong Kong editor for missing a story that could very possibly have led their bulletin.

It concerned an overnight police operation in Taiwan that I had seen reported on the domestic news wire. The headline was a jaw-dropper. 'Man has sex with goose – blames alcohol.'

The body of the text went on to read:
"A man who raped a goose early yesterday in Changhua County was taken into custody, but later released as police said he could not be charged with any violation of law."

The incident took place shortly after midnight in the Toucheng Township.

Police said that two officers in a patrol car spotted the naked 33-year-old, lying face down in a van. To the officer's surprise, they found a goose lying under his body when they knocked on the vehicle's window.

He claimed he had too much wine, and could not help having sex with the bird.

After reading the report, I couldn't help but amend the last paragraph in the email I sent to Hong Kong.

"Hsiao claimed he had too much wine and could not help having sex with the unfortunate creature, which he described as "a very good-looking bird".

Not surprisingly, the email produced a laugh, but little regret that it had not been included in the nightly news bulletin.

The necessity of writing stories for a living was one thing, but I constantly found myself penning observations of the Taiwanese people and culture that I found fascinating. It was vibrant, hectic and oddly contradictory; on one hand fighting to lead the world in technological innovation, and yet passionately respecting its ancient history and culture.

On early morning walks into the hills, looking down on the awakening city, I would find out just how unusual my presence was in the city. I would be greeted by startled looks on the faces of early risers, not accustomed to seeing a large 'waiguoren' (foreign devil) walking the mist-shrouded mountain trails. However, initial shock would soon give way to shy smiles and a willingness to test my basic Mandarin language skills. They are a warm and friendly people; something I could not always say about their mainland Chinese neighbours.

The early dawn hours were reserved for retirees, who would pack the huge forecourts of SunYat-sen and Chiang Kai-shek Memorials to exercise and practice the ancient art of Tai Chi. Their sons and daughters were too busy getting ready for the exhausting daily work regimes forced upon them.

While the pace of life is hectic, it is much more relaxed in country areas. The damage done by decades of runaway industrialization has left ugly scars in major cities, but there are stunningly beautiful vistas in the mountains, that form a rugged spine down the middle of the island.

With 268 peaks above 9,800 feet or 3,000 metres, the central part of Taiwan is home to the island's aborigines, a group of 16 tribes that makes up about 2.5 percent of the population. These people have inhabited 'Isla Formosa' for over 10 thousand years, long before the Han Chinese colonists arrived in the 17th century.

They are gentle folk, disinclined to engage in the hurly burly of commercial life, and happy not to be defined by economic success. I gained a special insight into their culture, through a brother-in-law, who became a good friend and surrogate teacher. We would take long walks into the mountains around Taipei and taste the remarkable oolong teas for which the area is renowned. The fine Taiwanese beer was also sampled, a reward for the long hours of walking, that I found more challenging than my aboriginal in-law.

His kindness will be forever remembered, but his advice was not always welcome. After a particularly arduous walk of more than 6 hours, I found my inner thighs badly chafed and bleeding. He pulled a brightly coloured tube from his backpack and told me to apply it to the affected area.

Within seconds I was up and running, excruciating pain coursing through my body. He had given me 'Tiger Balm' a fiery ointment used by Asians for virtually anything that ails you. Years later the sight of the stuff brings back vividly painful memories of that infamous day on the walking trails of Taiwan.

His poor English and my limited Chinese were irrelevant to a relationship that grew strong, as I grappled with life in a foreign culture.

We would drive down to the middle of the island often, taking our wives and kids to visit their parents and grandparents. They were farmers in the small town of Puli, near Taichung, about a 4-hour drive from Taipei; a world away from the fast pace of the big city. My father-in-law was mayor of the small town and I would join him and a stream of visitors in the daily ritual of drinking oolong tea. As he spoke Taiwanese, not Mandarin, I had absolutely no idea what they were talking about, but I would sit quietly, sipping tea and smiling. I was a fine advertisement for the assiduously polite foreigner. I was also a novelty to a local population that rarely saw 'gweilos'. My first visit in 1982 was a revelation. As I walked through the food markets of the town, children would run up and touch me, laughing and yelling out the word 'ah-dok-ah'. Quite charming I thought, until it was explained to me, the Taiwanese term meant 'big nose.'

They hadn't seen too many 'big noses' and I revelled in my newfound role of token 'waiguoren', or foreign devil with a big nose.

To the surprise of the family, I became great mates with one of my father-in-law's best friends, an old fish farmer and an aboriginal, whose ancestors had lived in the area for generations.

With family members translating, I would organize to meet at his farm where we would sit on the edge of one of the huge ponds and drink beer. He would use his substantial expertise to pull prawns, fish and oysters from the water and fry them on a small fire. There was no awkwardness or concern about not being able to speak each other's language. We laughed and smiled, and communicated through hand signals and eye contact. I have very fond memories of time spent with my old Taiwanese mate.

With the gamble of coming to Taiwan now looking like it would pay off, I started to find an inner peace, and actually enjoy the anonymity of being a westerner in an overwhelmingly foreign environment. Gone was the need to conform; I felt a rare sense of freedom, that only increased my need to prove I could succeed in making a good living in a country far away from home.

It was a particularly fertile period, getting Hyasia up and running, and meeting editors to pitch the press releases from the AsiaNet consortium.

News reporting would also figure heavily, as the island was being swept by a new wave of political activism. The appetite for change was growing, especially in the south of the island.

China was watching the contest, fearing a DPP win would increase the push for independence, a move it vehemently opposed, and one that was increasing regional tension.

I would follow the election campaign closely, and file for a number of broadcasters including CNBC. Restricted to a one party system since foundation in 1949, Taiwan's population was increasingly excited by the prospect of democratic change.

That came in at the start of the new millennium, when the DPP swept the Kuomintang from office, ending 50 years of uninterrupted rule. There were wild scenes around the island, as the people celebrated their newfound democratic status.

Little did I know that change was also about to come into my life, resulting in a marriage breakdown and a new start.

CHAPTER 21
A NEW START

Conducting a post-mortem on the breakdown of a marriage is perhaps not the most productive exercise to undertake, but when indulging in deep reflection, in the course of writing a memoir, it is unavoidable.

There was not one incident or obvious reason that led to the end of our 20-year relationship, and when it came, there were no angry words or nasty histrionics.

As a couple we had lived in countries around the world, enduring the usual ups and downs of married life, but it had been a largely easy time, fueled and funded by a healthy wage, a nanny to look after the kids and a lifestyle most would envy.

So, when Kathy was asked to return to the country of her birth after being away for almost 30 years, the lifestyle change was dramatic. She found herself in the role of dutiful 'tai tai', following a husband to realize an ambition he had always harboured.

Working as a foreign correspondent for 7 years of our life together included a hellishly busy travel schedule, and weeks away from home. The self-absorbed nature of the job was not always conducive to paying close attention to family life.

There was no doubt my decision to pack up and bring the family to Taiwan was a somewhat selfish act, based on a need to prove something to myself and former employers.

Equally, my wife's decision to return to Australia, in my eyes, was an equally selfish act, that failed to take into account the amount of work that I had put into building the business in Taiwan.

She wanted to return because of concern, she said, about our daughter's education, but there was little doubt there were other factors at play, not least her difficulty in coping with a culture she had left behind.

I was committed to stay. After years of working hard to build the business and now seeing the first hopeful signs of success, returning to Australia was not an option.

I had made my own bed in Taipei and would have to lie in it – alone. It was a considerably more lonely space now, but that would soon change when I convinced my son, Daniel to come to Taipei to learn Mandarin for a year before returning to start an Economics degree at Sydney University. He had been living with my parents, younger sister, Janine and her husband, Mark at the family home, while finishing his private school education.

He brought with him a good mate, Lewis and together we settled into blissful co-existence. The two boys vigorously threw themselves into life in Taipei, while studying, trying out the local bars and playing rugby with the expatriate team, the Taipei Baboons.

The experience would lead to another epistle penned by a father, happily forced to watch the weekly contests and join post-match celebrations.

RUGBY – TAIWAN STYLE
What do rugby players and large monkeys have in common?

Quite a bit, some wits contend, but the question has special significance when asked in Taipei, the frenetic capital of Taiwan, in which a small band of foreign workers and students take considerable pride in calling themselves Baboons.

"It started twelve years ago," says Baboon Club President, Peter Burns.

"We were sitting in a Taipei pub discussing the alternatives when it was pointed out that several of our players bore an uncanny resemblance to the large apes that populate the world's jungles. It just seemed right at the time", he offered, with the hint of a wry smile creasing his beer-foamed lips.

"Besides, the sight of a raging pack of hairy baboons charging an opposition team was sure to give us a psychological edge".

Jokes about the name aside, one would be making a grave error of judgement to think that this eclectic bunch of foreigners was less than serious about the game played in heaven.

Most Saturdays, over an inordinately long season that stretched from October to May, they would be seen pulling on the red and black striped colours of the club jersey.

The weekend ritual takes place at Bailing Rugby Field, near the Tamsui River, a body of water that has a disconcerting habit of flooding the playing surface with frightening regularity.

The jerseys slip easily onto the skinny, white torsos of some, while the durable fabric battles the bulges of the beefy forwards, whose job it is to pack down into a scrum and thrust their heads up each other's arses.

"To many local people not familiar with the rules of the game, that's what it looks like we're doing", says 18-year-old prop forward Lewis Jones.

"I mean, I really don't like getting that close to another bloke's private parts, but when all is said and done there really is a wonderful feeling of bonding and camaraderie".

The 195-centimetre, 112-kilogram prop forward, came to Taiwan from Sydney to study the Mandarin language with Daniel. The youngest player on the team, he says homesickness has been held at bay by his huge extended family of footy friends.

In a sport where age is an all-important consideration, there is no 'use by' date in this team.

"So, a few of us won't see the other side of forty again", says Peter C, who abbreviated his long Polish surname, not long after his arrival from America in the early eighties.

Club captain and English teacher, Ben Walker, took over the top job at the beginning of the 2000 season. A hard-charging, 'never say die' type, the 27-year-old Canuck's legend has steadily grown on the back of inspirational half time pep talks, described by former Wallaby coach, Rod Macqueen as 'fucking great'.

A noted naturalist and former President of the Alberta Nudist Club, Walker had been highly critical of the Taiwan Rugby Association for rejecting his proposal for the introduction of a nude rugby competition.

This brand of innovative thinking is rife in a team, which draws men from the four corners of the earth; a melting pot of races, ideologies, and football philosophies.

"We have players from seven countries", says Peter Burns. "English, American, Australian, South African, Canadian, Solomon Islanders, New Zealanders – they're all represented."

"It's bloody great", contends former Australian Rules player turned rugby star, Dwight Johnson.

"You've got all types; pommies, poofters, yanks, frogs, black fellas, kiwis, kafers, pisspots, wowsers, wives, kids, hangers on and plenty of sheilas and footy groupies too. You'd swear you'd died and gone to heaven".

Contracted to come to Taiwan after a rash of major airline disasters, the Tasmanian-born aircraft engine consultant, was unequivocal when asked about the merits of Rugby over the game he played as a boy.

"No bloody contest mate! Aussie Rules is a game for fairies. Rugby's a thinking man's game and the wives love it too".

Airline professionals, teachers, computer experts, businessmen, diplomats, salesmen, students, architects; the Baboons boast a wealth of talent from a range of diverse backgrounds.

Their common passion – the game of Rugby!
Brisbane native, Max Murphy, reputedly the biggest side stepper in Taiwan rugby history, sums it up this way.

"When you pull on a Baboons jersey, a jolt of electricity courses through your body, and the realisation that so many great players have worn the colours, it really is a humbling experience."

Murphy, a fluent Chinese speaker, points to the social benefits of being a Rugby player. "After a game there's nothing better than getting a raffle going and pulling a couple of chicks! I guess you can say they just love a good Baboon."

For so long a game played by westerners in western countries, how then has rugby been accepted by Taiwan players and spectators?

South African second row forward, 'Brucie the Loosey', puts it this way; "Well, they go down like a sack of shit when you hit them, but they can also dish it out. Get them off that rice and put a bit of meat into them, and they'd be as frisky as a springbok on the veldt."

Solomon Islander and Trade representative to Taiwan, John Washi, agrees.

"I don't think they're used to seeing a large black man approaching them at speed – I notice that, before mowing them down. It's in the whites of their eyes".

Washi, who, legend suggests, eats a whole suckling pig and 16 pounds of taro before each game, believes the ethnic diversity and mixed background of the Baboons makes the experience of playing together truly rewarding.

English fly-half Ben Boyden, a computer expert, brushes the team's sometimes poor performances aside. "We Englishmen are used to losing, but that's not really the point. It's about socialising with like-minded human beings who enjoy a good piss-up".

To expatriate spectators, a trip to a Baboons match is an enlightening experience.

Young children playing on the sideline can be heard asking mothers why dad keeps making loud gasping noises when tackled by opposition players.

Mothers have been heard castigating youngsters over the use of foul language, only to be told that Dad uses those words too.

Girlfriends have complained that yet another injury will prevent mates from fulfilling after-hours duties.

It's a complaint often repeated on witnessing the post-game beer-drinking sessions at the Tavern Pub, the Baboon's long time watering hole.

Continually on the lookout for new recruits, the aging English President, cautions that while fresh players are always welcome, not all meet the stringent club requirements.

"I suppose the toughest one is the IQ level. It has to be measured at below 90, says Burns.

"To date this has not presented a problem, particularly among Australian starters".

And then, there are the drinking rules.

"We understand player's tastes in alcohol will vary, but the club cannot be swayed from the demand that participants consume no less than 14 pints of beer over a four-hour period on match day".

Other rules include:

No farting in the scrums.

Homosexual acts sanctioned only in the case of consenting forwards.

Married players banned from having sex with wives for 24 hours before game time (48 hours with mistresses).

Children of players required to refrain from shouting obscene remarks at struggling fathers.

Wives, likewise, asked not to call husbands "fat bastards" from the sidelines.

Girlfriends asked not to congratulate or in any manner approach opposition players with warm words after watching Baboons humbled.

Players over forty years of age required to wear testicle restraints, so as to avoid the unseemly display of hairy gonads.

Similarly, Baboons are asked to wear suitably baggy shorts so as not to intimidate opposition players.

In addition, coloured team members are asked to desist from in any way touching or brushing their genital areas with the possible outcome of arousal.

New Zealand players are warned that under no circumstances are they allowed to perform the Haka, for fear of frightening the shit out of opposition players and spectators.

Solomon Island players are also asked not to pull shockingly fierce facial expressions aimed again at frightening all and sundry. This is a family event and it's just not on.

Australian players are required to sign an undertaking that they'll be responsible for the cost of all damage incurred at public places on the way to and from matches.

American newcomers have been warned of severe fines, should they catch the ball on kick-off and run the wrong way.

South African team members are cautioned that firearms are banned in Taiwan, and local law enforcement officers take a dim view of shooting animals from car windows.

Girlfriends of players are asked to dress sensibly and be aware that most footballers are sex-crazed losers, who are easily distracted by the hint of breast flesh.

Wives too, are asked not to make suggestive remarks to hubby's team mates as this can be a source of potential unrest and unneeded sexual tension in the camp.

French team members are asked to desist from making wild claims about being the world's most accomplished lovers when American, English, Australian, South African, New Zealand, Canadian, and Solomon Islanders know it's a bloody lie.

And finally, players are asked to refrain from peeing in the shallow end of Tony's pool after the game, as the rapid colour change is a dead giveaway.

Club Treasurer, Jamie Hall, concedes the rules are tough, but defends them as necessary, so as to maintain the standard, which has made the Baboons the most admired expatriate rugby team in Asia.

"It's these rules that have prevented us from slipping to the piss poor level of other teams characterized by drunken, loutish behaviour that has brought disrepute to the wonderful game of rugby union".

My socialization with the expatriate rugby players introduced a new element to life in Taipei. For over 2 years I had been immersed in trying to make a living. Now, with a wife and daughter back in Sydney, the temptation of losing focus was strong. I found myself drinking more, and becoming resentful about losing her support in efforts to carve out a future in Taiwan. It was the start of the marriage breakdown and my acceptance that it was over.

While my efforts were divided between filing news stories and building the Hyasia business during daylight hours, night times were becoming a problem. I was increasingly finding myself frequenting an area called the 'Combat Zone', named during the 1960s and 70s by American servicemen, who flocked to the area to enjoy the profusion of bars and female company. Twenty years later, it had largely lost the 'red light' reputation, but it was still a meeting place for the small expatriate population looking for social contact.

My little group included mainly older Americans, who had come to Taiwan during its transformation from a third world economy to a world leader. They had ridden the wave of success, and now found themselves either marooned or willing residents in a city they had come to love. We would meet in the Front Page Bar of the InterContinental Hotel and move on to watering holes reflecting the nationality of their owners; the Waltzing Matilda, and the Malibu, two of our favourites.

The eclectic group included an English language magazine editor, an old CIA spook, teachers, academics and businessmen, who all found solace in each other's company.

There was huge demand for English teachers in the city at the time and it was to this noble endeavour I would turn. I had taught some classes while waiting to get media accreditation when we first arrived on the island.

I bought my way into a small school that taught children during the day and at night offered 'one on one' lessons to a broad range of adult professionals looking to improve their language skills.

It was around this time Daniel and Lewis returned to Australia to start their university courses. I was again flying solo, and determined to fill the evenings with a more productive activity than bending the elbow.

It was a wise decision. I found I enjoyed teaching, particularly to older professionals, who needed to learn English. Daytime was devoted to business, while at night I took on a selected number of achievers. The Taiwanese and Chinese, in general, have a much greater respect for teachers than their western contemporaries. Hourly pay rates were high and the older student mix interesting.

I formed a strong relationship with a number of students, and stay in contact to this day. One was a China Airline pilot and former squadron leader in the Taiwanese Air Force, Iwen Chang. We would have spirited discussions about cockpit culture in Asia, with me suggesting the military background of many pilots resulted in too much saluting and not enough questioning of the captain in the left hand seat. After a number of years, he begrudgingly admitted that I had a point. My standing in his eyes rose significantly when I agreed to teach his 16-year-old son, Jefferson, resulting in impressively high results in an English Speech competition.

Another student, who would remain a good friend, was a middle-aged Taiwanese woman, Nico Hsu, whose family owned and ran one of the world's biggest BBQ manufacturing businesses, with factories in China.

I would teach her and her daughters for two years, and enjoyed their hospitality on my many business trips back to Taiwan over the next decade.

The success of Taiwanese businesses and the strong trade numbers with the U.S. meant that many American corporations were sending press releases to media outlets in Taiwan. The number was steadily growing, and Hyasia was becoming a more important member of the AsiaNet consortium.

My former colleague, and now boss, Michael Worner's gamble of contacting an old mate was paying off, and allowed AsiaNet to navigate its way through the tricky diplomatic and political minefield of cross straight relations.

Over the next decade, I would attend meetings around the region and watch my friend work hard to get his Asian colleagues to build their businesses. It was not easy. Many seemed happy to distribute press releases, but demonstrated little enthusiasm in getting local corporations to spread corporate news through AsiaNet and PRNewswire.

Still, every year he would rally the troops, and we would meet for the familiar pep talk. It was a popular junket for the men from Seoul, Beijing, Tokyo and other Asian agencies, who struggled in the course of meetings to stay awake, but miraculously came to life in the evening, when food and drink were plentiful.

On one visit to Bangkok, seminar delegates were caught in the middle of a military coup, not unusual in the Thai capital. It proved to be quite a distraction, as many of the delegates had journalist backgrounds and were asked by their agencies to provide some form of coverage.

Bali, Langkawi, Tokyo, Taipei, Sydney and Beijing all got their chance to host an AsiaNet seminar that I attended.

They were colourful affairs, but one in particular, held at Bandung in the Indonesian mountains, stood out for all the wrong reasons. An epistle I penned summed up the frustrations faced by Michael Worner, Esq.

JIVING IN JAVA

The furrowed brow, nervous tic and pronounced look of horror on the face of AsiaNet General Manager, Mike Worner said it all; another disaster on the road, this time at the hands of the Indonesians!

Not new to a state of perpetual angst, the aging journalist displayed all the signs of a man under pressure, and close to an ugly attack of hysteria.

This is how we found him in the lead-up to Christmas. It was in the Indonesian city of Bandung, preparing to host the Forum, an important event for AsiaNet consortium members. It had been planned for almost 12 months. Instructions had been clear; book a four or five-star venue for the event held in the Asia Pacific region every two years.

"Yes," said the Indonesians, "we've got just the right place."

And so, as Christmas decorations were going up in households around the western world, consortium members headed for the fifth largest city in Indonesia. Nestled in the lush mountains about two hundred and fifty kilometers from Jakarta, it's a popular getaway for well-healed locals, desperate to escape the sweltering chaos of the nation's capital. Bandung had been agreed upon only after an overwhelming number of delegates rejected Yogyakarta, when told it could only be reached by an internal flight on Garuda. The country's national airline had a less than stellar safety record, reinforced by a recent disaster, which claimed the lives of 21 foreign nationals. The subsequent crash inquiry painted the disconcerting picture of a captain ignoring the protestations of his first officer, while landing the aircraft at twice the recommended speed.

Emails went out to consortium members detailing plans to pick them up at Jakarta International Airport and shuttle them to Bandung by bus.

Three hours into the allegedly two-and-a-half-hour journey, Hyasia Director, Ian Hyslop found himself in a Kentucky Fried Chicken outlet on a freeway exit, chewing on a piece of the outlet's soggy product. Little did he know he was only halfway through the bus trip, which would arrive shortly before 2 am, (almost as long as it took him to fly to Jakarta).

"It really wasn't that bad," said Hyslop, "though things got a little hairy when the bus driver started playing chicken with a car in rainy conditions about midnight. I felt compelled to lean across and squeeze his arm while shaking my head vigorously, and wishing I could swear in Bahasa Indonesian."

Meanwhile, at the hotel, perched high in the mountains on a road barely reachable by four-wheel drive, delegates were settling in for a short night's sleep on the eve of the Forum. It was also, it turned out, a national Muslim holiday weekend, celebrated by most of the country's 231 million faithful.

Australian Associated Press CEO, Clive Marshall later claimed he found himself on the floor of his room, after being blown out of bed by high-pitched screams around 4 am.

"It sounded like a maniac in my bathroom using a megaphone," said Marshall, who at first light, discovered a mosque located about fifty meters below the scenic cliff face, on which his room was perched.

Next morning, Marshall said he bore no malice toward the mosque's Imam. However, he was overheard in heated discussion with underling, Mike Worner, arguing the suitability of holding an event in a location where one was likely to blown out of bed by a "call to prayer".

In another hotel room, that appeared to be in the later stages of completion, Canadanews delegate, Tim Mountie, was grateful he was traveling with wife Wanda, after an ugly incident in which she helped extract a small hose from his rectal cavity after it became stuck during a routine ablution.

"How was I to know, the place didn't have toilet paper", Tim later told fellow delegates. "First time I'd ever used a frigging' hose," he lamented.

Also grappling with local conditions, AAP National Sales Manager, Tom Enright, awoke to find a large cockroach exploring the nooks and crannies of his face.

"Bloody scared the shit out me," Enright said! "As a British migrant to Australia I had to get used to creepy crawlies, now to find a bloody big roach a short crawl to the inner sanctum of my slumbering brain was no fun, I can tell you!"

The problems continued for another delegate who inquired about the location of her air conditioning switch, only to be told it did not exist. It was not needed, she was informed, as Bandung was in the mountains, where it was much cooler.

The stories swapped over breakfast on the first day of the Forum prompted a steady flow of nervous laughter; not least the reaction to New Zealand delegate, Simon Randall, who regaled everyone with the story of him coming to terms with the unique design features of his room.

"There I was," he said, "finished with the obligatory shit, shower, and had lathered up for the shave when, much to my consternation, I couldn't find a mirror, so there was nothing else to do but sit on the toilet and finish the job by looking at my reflection in the highly buffed floor tiles. Where there's a will there's a way," he shrugged philosophically.

Tatsuya Nagasaki from Japanese News Agency, Kyodo, stunned delegates when he appeared for breakfast looking disheveled, his graying whiskers evidence of uncharacteristic slovenliness.

"I apologise for my appearance," he told delegates with the hint of barely concealed anger, "I didn't bring my toilet bag, as I was under the impression it was a five-star hotel and the essentials would be supplied."

It was an emotion shared by colleague and Forum Joint Chairman, Masa Kikuta, whose normally well-coiffured hair sat in a crinkled mess upon his head.

"They told me there were only two hairdryers in the hotel and I understand that an Australian delegate has one of them hidden under his bed," he said, careful not to look directly at the offender who sat smiling, not a hair out of place.

But worse was yet to come, when late in the day, Mike Worner, found out the hotel was 'dry'! It was an astonishing discovery that threatened to sabotage the all-important icebreaker session, where delegates had been instructed to wear silly hats.

"How can they be asked to look that stupid without a drink," he told colleagues. The call went out, and two hours later hotel staff returned from a local store with warm beer and Australian red wine, which they immediately put on ice!

But wait, there's more. It came in the form of a panicked conversation between Operations Manager Marcello Rossi and General Manager Worner.

"I'm telling you Mike, how am I supposed to showcase our latest website developments, when the bloody hotel is on 'dial-up' and I can't retrieve my email in less than an hour?"

Well, you can only speculate on the response from the man not renowned for his coolness under fire.

A New Start

The fact that the three-day Forum was ultimately hailed by all as a success is testament to the indomitable spirit of the human species.

"There's just one shadow hanging over the event," lamented Worner. "We are still waiting for the test results, but fingers crossed he'll be alright".

Pressed on the nature of the medical emergency, Worner was uncharacteristically reticent. "Suffice to say, sitting in a hotel hot tub full of chemicals can leave lingering doubts, but at least management has agreed in future to translate the poolside warning sign into English."

My connection to the AsiaNet consortium and PR Newswire lasted for more than 10 years, well after leaving Taiwan and returning to Australia, to a new life and lover.

The business would continue to operate under the stewardship of my Chinese friend and partner, Jonathan and press release traffic would grow, spurred on by increased business activity on the island.

I would fly to Taiwan regularly, to meet magazine and newspaper editors, and be the public face of Hyasia, which was fulfilling its role of placating the Xinhua News Agency in Beijing.

My attachment to the small island, through marriage, then journalism and business is a strong one, and I watched on with much interest as the people and the government came to terms with the complicated concept of democracy.

It was because of the possibility of looming confrontation that I made the move to Taipei in 1997. Could I have been ahead of my time or just plain wrong? Time will tell, but more than a few international analysts believe the region, particularly after Russia's invasion of Ukraine, will be the world's next conflict zone.

CHAPTER 22
LADY BARNETT

Rhonda Margaret Rose Stewart Barnett was born in Melbourne on 25th March, 1955, a year before the eyes of the world focused on the city to witness the Games of the XVI Olympiad.

This noteworthy occasion, in no way influenced or inspired her to concerted athletic endeavour of any description.

Truth is, the sight of her 'breaking a sweat' is very rare indeed, particularly on the sporting field, but it was in other areas she would make her mark.

I first met Rhonda back in the early 80s, the friend of younger sister, Janine, and a newcomer to the harbour city. She was an unapologetically assertive young woman, who had already started vigorously pounding on the 'glass ceiling' in an effort to force her way into the male dominated Sydney business world. She had no doubt about what she wanted, and assiduously avoided playing the coquettish, coy seductress as a way of getting it, though I dare say she had more than the odd dalliance along the way.

She made the move from Melbourne in 1979, around the time I first committed myself to the institution of holy matrimony. Little did I know that years later I would repeat the nuptials with her. Back then, she scared the hell out of me, as I'm sure she did most blokes, comfortable with the notion that as 'hunters and gatherers' they deserved the upper hand in a relationship. How things have changed!

Through the 80s and 90s, we laboured hard in our respective fields, both achieving success. My job as a journalist resulted in a nomadic existence with stints around Australia, America and Asia. She concentrated on building a resume in Sydney, where she would join the exclusive Jewish boys club, after being hired by Westfield boss, Frank Lowy. The diminutive Czech immigrant had an eye for recruiting talent to help him build what would become the biggest shopping centre group in the world.

A gentile of English, Scottish, Swedish, Irish and Welsh heritage, she was the first female executive to join Westfield's Leasing Department, and quickly went about establishing her credentials. Oblivious to the so-called 'rules of the game' played at a high level by boys with testicles, Rhonda took to the field, happy she could compete without being weighed down by such an onerous burden. No amount of locker room humour, dirty jokes, heavy drinking or misogynistic behavior could phase or embarrass the girl from Melbourne. If they thought they could shock her, they were dreaming. She had already developed a joke repertoire capable of bringing colour to the cheeks of hardened wharfies, not to talk about a prodigious tolerance to alcohol, but it came at a cost.

The simple fact was that she intimidated most men, who were not used to assertive women with an IQ of 150. Her ability to negotiate deals and place retailers into the fast growing portfolio of Westfield Shopping Centres was soon recognized, and my future wife was on her way to a very successful career.

I knew little of her trials and tribulations, successes and romantic entanglements for the best part of our respective professional careers. Those details would come out in pillow talk years later, but I would hear snippets from family members who she stayed in close touch with over the years. My Mother was one.

A 'Rhonda Story' that reached me while living in America only served to reinforce her fearsome reputation as a 'tough cookie' who took no prisoners, as one ex-lover was to find out.

An Officer in the Merchant Navy, of Irish/Indian heritage, he asked Rhonda to marry him. The fact that he was not an Australian citizen was remedied by her move to sponsor him, on the basis that they planned to become man and wife.

However, that knot would never be tied after Rhonda discovered evidence of his infidelity. The immigration authorities were notified, sponsorship withdrawn, and he was duly invited to go back to whence he came! Rhonda settled back to life as a single, until the man of her dreams came into her life years later.

While blissfully ignorant of what the future held for us, we both worked at a ferocious pace in our respective fields, and our paths crossed on one notable occasion in the intervening years.

Word reached me that Rhonda was headed to Los Angeles on the way to an International Real Estate Congress in Chicago. Because of the close family ties, an invitation was duly proffered and she stayed with us in the Westwood family home for two days.

It was a benign encounter with no spark or hint of romance. She was soon on her way and we both resumed life in the fast lane, me as a foreign correspondent, married man and father; she as a footloose and free single businesswoman, holding down a high-powered position.

And so it remained, until the start of the new millennium. She was still working for Westfield, but I had left mainstream television and moved to Taiwan.

I would return to Sydney periodically to see Daniel and the family, and take a short break from the relentless pace of life in Taipei. It was during one such trip that I saw Rhonda again, at a family get together.

The contact would lead to the beginning of emails between the two of us when I returned to Taiwan. It was a welcome diversion for me in my new life on my own, and an attempt by Rhonda, I speculated, to scope out whether my marriage was over and I was back on the market.

The prospect of getting involved, particularly while building the business was not at all appealing, to be honest. The events of the past few months had already taken a bruising emotional toll, and it was a distraction I probably did not need. Rhonda was a family friend that I had known for more than twenty years. The hint of romance had never reared its head in that time, and her strong personality, willful character and long-term single status scared me just a little. I was no shrinking violet either; I spoke my mind, and the prospect of getting together was daunting.

That, however, was not likely to happen, I reasoned. I was committed to building the business. She had her own career in Sydney, and Taiwan was a long way away.

The emails meantime, continued to flow and it was during this process an astounding thing happened. Well, not that astounding, but interesting, at least for the two of us. We found we got on extremely well. Her writing was quirky, funny and grammatically correct, and did little to hide the keen intelligence and no nonsense attitude that had propelled her to a successful career and a reputation as one tough lady.

Emails graduated to phone calls and frighteningly, they were taking on a more serious and personal nature. Now I was scared!

I was soon given reason to be even more wary, when news reached me that Rhonda and my Mother had been chatting, not that unusual as they had been friends for years. But now, a trip to Taiwan had been suggested by the Welsh Witch!

"What did I think," I was asked.

To say I was a little apprehensive was an understatement. Assuming I had some say in the matter, I proposed that we meet in Saigon for a few days, then fly back to Taipei. If our first meaningful encounter didn't turn out well then 'nothing ventured, nothing gained'.

The details were left in her very capable hands. She had recently played chief organizer and travel agent for friends wanting tickets and accommodation during the Sydney Olympics and had a long history of planning overseas adventures. I threw myself back into work and waited for the details of our highly anticipated Vietnam/Taiwan encounter.

When the day arrived in late October 2000, I was unprepared for the shocking humidity that engulfed the teeming crowds at Tan Son Nhut airport in Saigon.

I stood waiting for her aircraft to land, bathed in sweat brought on in equal measure by the climate and nervousness about the impending assignation; a 47-year-old man sweating like a callow youth on his first date.

If it was any consolation, I quickly detected Rhonda's nervousness in the taxi on the way to the Rex Hotel; one of Saigon's oldest and grandest. It had been used as the headquarters of the U.S. army during the Vietnam War and was famous among news correspondents, who drank and chased stories there. I had stayed at the hotel before and dined in the famous French rooftop restaurant, which served frogs legs soaked in garlic, my favourite.

At the front desk of the fine establishment, we were presented with the key to a 2-bedroom suite, with a central living area. Not surprising, I thought, given the fact that we barely knew each other; at least not in the biblical sense. My travelling companion was not going to make the assumption that intimacy was a 'slam dunk'.

Here we were in an exotic foreign city, not my first rodeo, accompanied by Rhonda, the 'vestal virgin', pussyfooting around the prospect of sharing a bed. It was really quite charming, in a quaint old fashioned way.

'Nudge, nudge, wink, wink' I thought, not daring to look at the organiser for fear of dissolving into uncontrollable laughter.

The first night was spent in our respective bedrooms, after a great dinner, good conversation in our 'living area' and a positive feeling that the ice had been broken in an aboveboard, decent way.

On the second night, however our collective consumption of alcohol combined with a strong sense of expectancy, rendered one of the bedrooms redundant. It was a shared initiative. Suffice to say the combined 'physical history' of two healthy, mature, well-travelled veterans made for a good time. We both came out of the gate after a spell and proved to be in fine fettle!!

Our exertions were followed next morning by a barrage of overseas phone calls from international broadcasters, not, I stress, due to our recent earth shattering 'horizontal folk dancing'.

There had been a Singapore Airlines 747 crash at Chiang Kai-shek Airport in Taipei and they all wanted live coverage. My suggested Vietnamese adventure with Rhonda would end up costing a lot of money. A big story missed!

That quickly put aside, our discovery of Saigon commenced at a riverside restaurant, which boasted perhaps one of the funniest menus either of us had encountered in the course of our worldwide travels. The "chinglish" was hilarious, made more so by the vigorous consumption of local beer, which we blamed on the sweltering conditions. The perusal of each new dish prompted peels of raucous laughter, which had local heads turning to inspect the noisy offenders.

The reason we found ourselves in stitches? Offerings like 'Delicious Roasted Husband', 'Fat Cock', 'Boil Half a Child', 'Fuck the Duck til Exploded', 'Steamed Crab Discharge 6 Children' and 'Fried Crap Stick'. One suspects that the restaurant owners had some English-speaking pals with a warped sense of humour!

Each dish was accompanied by a colour photo, so on viewing one described to us as 'beef testicles' the temptation was too much to resist. Truth is, it did not look at all like a set of balls, and our curious minds were intent on savoring this oriental delicacy. I suspect Rhonda had an ulterior motive, thinking it may well improve sexual performance.

As a child I swore I would never again consume testicles. I had been served sheep balls on a trip to Wales, but here I was again, about to tuck into the genitals of another unfortunate animal.

If we were food critics, the dish would have rated barely two out of ten, but for entertainment value, our lunch on the Mekong River in November 2000 remains unsurpassed.

It was a good start to our much anticipated Saigon rendezvous, and reinforced the clichéd saying, 'laughter is the best medicine'. The tour continued at a furious pace, with me playing guide to fascinating food markets in Cholon, war museums, restaurants and a short road trip to the coastal resort town of Vung Tau.

It was Rhonda's first visit to Vietnam, and I felt a proprietorial interest in showing her around the country. I had reported here for over a decade, firstly on the U.S. trade embargo, which had held back the country since the war. Several subsequent assignments, including a trip to mark the 25th anniversary of the end of the conflict, had only increased my regard for a people who had endured so much.

The whirlwind holiday continued with kisses and smiles, and a comforting knowledge that we really did like each other. Rhonda no longer scared me (well maybe a little bit), and I had discovered, despite unkind allegations by male colleagues, that she did not have testicles. What a relief!

However, we still had several days to spend together in Taipei, a city she wanted to see, given my plan to develop business there.

I will never forget the look of disdain on her face as she entered my modest three-bedroom apartment in the Songshan district of Taipei. Perhaps it was the rat droppings, cockroaches and ants she discovered in the tiny kitchen, or maybe the state of the bathroom that doubled as a wet room that had initially horrified her. She appeared unmoved by the charming Japanese tearoom and rooftop garden, a rarity in the crowded city. It was an old building, but I actually enjoyed its location on the top floor, even if it didn't have a lift. It was a long way from the high rent districts that housed the small expatriate population, who seemed to resist any form of social intercourse with the locals.

They say there is a pivotal moment in any new relationship where a new partner cements him or herself forever in the heart of their lover.

That moment came for me when I returned home to the apartment, to find Rhonda on all fours at the base of the toilet cutting out plastic tiles to cover the bathroom floor. This woman of action was not going to tolerate wet feet while performing the simple task of having a pee.

A short walk to the newly cleaned kitchen also revealed a whole fish simmering on the stove, the result of a visit to the local street market, where she had gone shopping alone, with minimal knowledge of the local language.

Is there anything this woman could not do?

Rhonda could not have had a better guide to show her the place first named 'Beautiful Island'. We set out by car, after she had spent the best part of two days cleaning the apartment, and eradicating all signs of assorted vermin.

My planned itinerary would take us through the magnificent mountains down the centre of the island, and along the eastern seaboard, often battered by typhoons. A check of weather conditions for the upcoming week forecast no problem, and bright sunshine augured well for our long drive. First stop was Hualien City and nearby Taroko Gorge, one of the most scenic and beautiful spots on the island, but also one of the most dangerous. Narrow treacherous roads overlooking deep ravines, accommodated long lines of tourist buses and a never-ending stream of motorcycles that buzzed around sharp bends.

The 'not so leisurely' drive was punctuated by Rhonda's sharp intake of breath and muted screams, confirming earlier warnings that driving in Taiwan was not for the feint hearted. I'd like to think my confident command of the car and icy nerve finally settled her down, and the sparkling conversation offered a distraction. It was all good. I was accustomed to the chaotic traffic, and aware that many locals chewed betel nut, a mild narcotic responsible for some strange behavior behind the wheel.

After an overnight stop, the road trip took us through Taitung and Puli. Along the way, we'd pulled up at roadside stalls and markets and colourful temples, but the highlight for Rhonda was prawn fishing. It was a popular pastime for locals who would crowd around small concrete ponds filled with the delicacy, and patiently troll for their dinner. It was something she had not, understandably, done in Australia. On a later trip to the island, she would witness the extraordinarily generous nature of the locals. On that occasion, our efforts were proving unproductive, as we dangled wooden poles and baited lines that seemed stubbornly resistant to any prawn's attention. An old gentleman sitting opposite was meantime reeling them in at a furious rate, and would wave periodically, clearly urging us not to abandon our futile efforts. Thankfully, our consumption of beer was blunting the disappointment we felt, but that soon changed when the old man walked up and handed us a large bag filled with the delicious crustaceans. Our offer to pay him fell on deaf ears, and he wandered off, to no doubt tell family members about the foreign couple's miserable efforts at the prawn pond. He missed the sight of us throwing the 'prawns on the barbie' and partaking of a feast that tasted all the better for the generosity of our Taiwanese friend.

There is no better way to explore a holiday destination than by car and certainly no better way to get to know the personality of the individual accompanying you on the journey. Long hours on the road visiting every conceivable topic of conversation, is a guaranteed relationship maker or breaker.

And so it was with us; that road trip, more than 20 years ago established that co-habitation was not an impossible proposition. To a cynical journalist the word love is one not to be used easily or frequently. Certainly it wasn't used then, but after dozens of road trips, sea voyages and flights with the woman I now call Lady Barnett the word love does come easily and frequently.

CHAPTER 23
WHAT TO DO NOW?

It is often said timing is everything in life.

You would get no argument from the two of us. Getting together in our younger days would almost certainly have been doomed.

Demanding jobs and driven personalities would have made co-habitation a dicey proposition, but here we were in our mid to late 40s thinking of doing just that.

The most unlikely things happen 'out of the blue', and so it was with us, but some major lifestyle changes were needed to make it work.

The Westfield Group had employed Rhonda for almost 20 years. She had done extremely well, hanging onto every share option to build an impressive portfolio, and in the process acquired investment properties in the expensive Sydney real estate market.

Still relatively young, she was in the comfortable position of walking away from full time employment.

My situation was nowhere near as settled. I faced some difficult decisions. Hyasia was doing well distributing press releases around the country, while my freelance journalism work made me one of the few Western reporters on the island. I was loath to give it up, but knew the demands of a new relationship would be significant.

I should not have been concerned. Lady Barnett was not dizzy or love-struck. Nor was she any longer the ambitious 'man eater' some colleagues had characterized her as, in the world of retail leasing.

We were older, wiser, and less driven to prove something in our professional careers, and thus more capable of making a relationship work.

Two quick trips to Taiwan introduced her to my professional world and the potential upside of maintaining a presence. She was soon to get a close up look at the business, when she accompanied me to Langkawi, in Malaysia for an AsiaNet conference, which saw consortium members fly in from around Asia.

PRNewswire executives came from New York, to rally the troops and hear what the newest member of the consortium, Hyasia was planning for the future growth of business.

It had been a busy 12 months organizing distribution lists and a translation service, to send the news releases to hundreds of trade magazines, television stations and newspapers in the growing market. Rapid economic growth had propelled the small island to a leadership role in the high-tech, computer chip industry and made Taiwan famous as a business destination; any wonder international corporations were keen to exchange a flow of information.

Much of the work to put the lists together had been done, with little distraction, but it soon became apparent that Rhonda and I would be spending a lot more time together. Meeting up in Taipei, Sydney and various Asian cities had a certain romantic appeal, but it was not the perfect formula for the long-term survival of a relationship.

Her decision to retire from Westfield in December, 2001 forced my hand to look at how best to proceed. There was no way Rhonda was going to move to Taipei, so the challenge for me was to keep the business going while 'testing the waters' in Sydney.

As it turned out, that would prove to be no problem either, in the short or long term. I had been running the business from my apartment, but that would change. My Chinese partner, Jonathan's production studio would become the new home of Hyasia.

With PRNewswire in New York pushing to introduce video news releases in Asia, operating from a facility with camera and editing capabilities made perfect sense, and held promising prospects for future development. In addition to the AsiaNet business, we had collaborated on the production of two documentaries for the Discovery Channel and numerous corporate video projects. I had in Jonathan, a reliable partner invested in the future, and a man who had become a good friend. Rhonda's well-honed business instincts also confirmed that he was a man to be trusted.

I would come to appreciate and rely on those instincts, as we looked at business opportunities in the future. In the meantime, I was getting used to the idea of travelling to Asia periodically, while moving back to Sydney.

Rhonda had for all intents 'hung up the boots' and retired from Westfield, but she was still in demand as a retail consultant. This allowed her to pick the occasional project, rather than be at the beck and call of a full-time employer.

Little did I know, she was also getting ready to use both our talents in setting up a new company, 'My Life My Legacy', which continues to operate to this day.

Long interested in family history, she believed there was a market for people with 'deep pockets and a strong sense of family' wanting to tell their stories. Who better, she argued, to interview these folks than a journalist with many years in the business and an impressive resume. It was not a new concept to me. I had come across it in America in my years as a foreign correspondent, but private family commissions did not light the same fire as broadcast journalism. However, like all old journos who have left the stage, so to speak, the question was invariably, 'what now'?

I still had freelance work in Asia and the press release distribution business, but the prospect of working with Lady Barnett was both interesting and daunting.

I didn't have long to wait before she had our first 'My Life My Legacy' commission. Her good friend, Judi's husband Doug was interested in the concept. A doctor, he was acutely aware of his father's medical condition, which threatened to take him from the large extended family in the not too distant future. He wanted his father's incredible life story documented as a lasting legacy.

Winter Hor was indeed a remarkable man, who left his home in Canton, China at the tender age of 12. He travelled alone to Hong Kong, and ultimately immigrated to Australia with only a few dollars in his pocket.

He worked hard in the early years, opening the first Chinese restaurant on Sydney's North Shore, 'Chopsticks', and built a sizeable property portfolio. In the process, he fathered four high achieving sons. It had all the ingredients of an inspiring 'rags to riches' migrant story. However, it would not be a story for public consumption; a pity, I thought.

In the course of researching it, I was able to source old black and white vision of Hong Kong at the time a young Winter Hor was employed as a restaurant worker. I was to later find out how valuable the vision was when a clearly delighted father told his sons the restaurant was the same one he worked in, pointing to a number of waiters on the film that he knew (keep in mind this was a 70-year-old film clip). You can sometimes be lucky!

A treasure trove of old movie vision of the boys growing up and photos of the family's progress through the years brought the colourful story to life, but it was one segment that clearly delighted the old man.

In the course of the interview, Winter told me that one of his regular customers at 'Chopsticks' was none other than the Prime Minister of Australia, John Howard.

A call was made to the PM's Canberra office, explaining that a video was being produced of the old restaurateur's life, and would he be interested in contributing.

"No problem," a senior staffer replied, no doubt aware of the importance of keeping Sydney's influential Chinese community happy. Eventually, a tape arrived of John Howard paying fulsome praise to the man who had often fed his family at the famous Crows Nest restaurant. To a close Chinese family, proud of their achievements, this was the ultimate compliment and a worthy tribute to the patriarch. We also recorded the many tributes of family members who would later gather to watch the completed 'My Life My Legacy' documentary. It is safe to say there was not a dry eye in the house, including Winter!

That first project proved the power of the concept, and while it was not an easily marketable product, word of mouth and a professional website would draw clients over the years. The retired leasing executive was now marketing manager of MLML and had many noteworthy achievements in the role.

Her old school friend, Clive was now the private pilot for one of Australia's richest property tycoons. His 93 year old father would be the subject of the next documentary.

In producing these documentaries, I would use only professional cameramen and editors, who I knew from my days in television. If I was putting my name to the product, I wanted only a top quality outcome.

Over the years, we have filmed a number of diverse documentaries on the lives of everyday Australians; each one unique and interesting. We have recorded stories for surprise birthday presents, family reunions, and the life journeys of many happy and thankful immigrants to Australia. However, the filming hasn't been confined to just Australia.

We were tasked with putting together the life story of an Irish couple who had long passed away, but their grateful family wanted to celebrate the 100th anniversary of the day they arrived in Australia. We located a cameraman in Dublin and spent some memorable times filming the ancestral home and the cemetery where many of the family were buried. Rhonda had the idea to re-enact the wedding ceremony in the Dublin cathedral where they were married. The sight of her profile, under a lace curtain from the local school, nodding away while the priest performed the old marriage service, was classic!

These family stories have allowed me to continue using my experience as an interviewer and writer, with the added benefit of scheduling them in between trips to Asia.

However, an extra dimension would come into play after Rhonda and I 'shacked up' in Sydney in late 2001. In her single days, she had taken a number of cruises and wanted me to 'dip my toe in the water'.

"Cruising," I blustered, "that's for old farts waiting to die!" (remember that line). Little did I know that this activity would allow me to use my love of writing to pen epistles, while travelling around the world; the adventures of Lady Barnett and her hapless offsider.

For one initially resistant to the idea of cruising the world's oceans, I soon found myself walking regularly up the gangplank of numerous small, prestigious ships claiming 6-star status.

None of the rich and exotic passengers on these seafaring excursions could escape my eagle eye, as I sat using my sometimes drunken wit to record our various interactions during these voyages of conspicuous consumption.

Some of the observations will feature in the chapters that follow; a segue, if you like, to the latest phase in the career of an old journalist reflecting on his life and times.

CHAPTER 24
HERE COMES THE BRIDE

The year was 2004, and Lady Barnett and I had been living blissfully 'in sin' for 3 years.

In that time, she had been extolling the virtues of taking a cruise on the high seas, a pastime she thoroughly enjoyed and assumed I would too.

"I've found a great deal, she told me, "across the Atlantic on a 6-star ship, you'll love it!"

The very thought of the ocean immediately conjured up images of the bottom of a toilet bowl and I felt the first beads of sweat spring from my furrowed brow. I once again repeated my mantra, "Cruising is for old farts about to die," a statement aimed at hosing down her suggestion, but she somehow interpreted that to mean 'not no' and off she went to book and pack.

It was not long before we found ourselves flying off to Antigua in the Caribbean, and my first cruise aboard one of the world's most exclusive cruise ships, the '*Silver Wind*'.

We were the only Australians onboard, and were poised to shove our snouts into the trough, to savour a lifestyle reserved for a small percentage of the world's population. A privileged few, who, through hard work or crooked dealings, were putting their bodies and bellies on the line for a taste of the good life.

It didn't take long for a colourful cast of characters to reveal themselves in the busy bars and restaurants. Top of the list was a ridiculously flamboyant older couple, who looked like court jesters or members of the on-board show. The senior gentleman sported one white shoe, and one red one, and was topped off by a gold lame jacket. Upon his head sat a stunning toupee designed to take years off his fast-advancing age. His wife was similarly outrageously attired. It turned out that they were German doctors, who had a penchant for dressing 'on the wild side'. Georg was a retired cardiologist, who had returned to his first love of organ music and did recitals all over Europe. Barbara was still working as a GP, and both volunteered each week to patch up motorists who'd 'come a cropper' on the (no speed limit) German autobahns.

Our 'partners in crime' came in all shapes and sizes and hailed from the four corners of the earth, all with one thing is common. They were generally older, and highly successful in their chosen fields. There was Charles, the New Yorker or 'Longa Islanda', an irreverent partner in crime whose piercing, nasal, destruction of the English language created much mirth. "Hellooo, who says New Yorkers are rude" and "oh reeally, whattaya saying, ya smuck?"

He was a man who had worked in textiles for much of his life, and was very capable of spinning a good yarn! Much of his acid-tongued vitriol was heaped upon his Asian business associates – one country in particular: "those goddamned kimchi-eaters, worst place in the goddamned world!"

To state the obvious, when you put an Australian and a New Yorker together you're going to get a load of fun. But, throw into the mix a Barbadian, whose favourite drink is White Lightning Rum and you've got the potential for a real party.

Using a good deal of journalistic license, I soon had the ship recognising and respecting this stylish, unassuming man of Caribbean colour. "I'd like you to meet Colin Seale, the Prime Minister of Barbados" I intoned with a straight face, on more than a few occasions.

The fact that he was accompanied by his stunningly attractive wife, Faith, a barrister, confirmed in the eyes of passengers he had to be a politician, taking a much-needed break from the weighty pressures of office (and maybe his real wife).

The 'Prime Minister's' conspicuous consumption of White Lightning made my puny efforts of sipping Bombay Gin positively un-Australian.

However, after many hours of quiet, measured discussion at the Pool Bar, watching over our roasting fellow travellers, a strong bond of comradeship and mutual respect developed. The regard for each other's considerable intellects grew proportionally to the amount of hard liquor consumed!

He confided that if he really were the Prime Minister, he would have no hesitation in appointing me to a key role within his cabinet, such did he regard my enlightened counsel!

Ship life, however, is not all about drinking. A full schedule of sports and leisure activities are available to divert attention from the fact that all the booze aboard is free, thus heading off the embarrassing prospect of multiple cases of alcohol poisoning.

It was against this backdrop and with the view to preserving our reputations that the 'PM' and I sought out an activity that would afford us exercise, and a prominent position on deck where fellow travellers could witness the fact that we sometimes took a break from the 'grog'. And so it was, we turned to the ubiquitous game of table tennis or ping-pong.

Now, if you've ever tried to play ping-pong on the pitching, rolling deck of a ship in the middle of the Atlantic, while being 'three sheets to the wind' and a tad seasick, you'll know it is no easy feat. Add to this all the obstructions; steel pillars, deck chairs, and toasting bodies, that one is likely to run into while trying to hit the tiny ball, and it is indeed a challenging game.

While I tried hard, I never could best my older and more experienced opponent but, on reflection, I had no doubt it was the White Lightning that gave him the edge. When I wearied of dodging ping-pong balls, I went below deck (a nautical expression for going downstairs).

It was on Deck 5 on the vast carpeted foyer area that I was able to indulge another passion – putting.

Now, to the uninitiated, the sight of a gaggle of mainly older chaps with a smattering of women, including Rhonda, standing around clutching putters may seem a tad ridiculous. However, I can assure you the rush of adrenaline one attains by stroking the ball into a putting machine ten meters away is arguably more satisfying than certain horizontal pursuits. What appears to be a simple straight run to the imaginary hole is complicated by each pitch of the ship, and the effort takes on the awesome task of holing a snaking, evil putt on the 12th at Augusta. Of course, the effort wouldn't have been so much fun had alcohol not featured in the equation. Many of the competitors had lingered over lunch, depleting the ship's wine cellar before striding to the 'green'.

When the heavy regime of sporting activities proved too physically exhausting, we turned to the more cerebral pastime of Trivia Competition. Now, here's an activity, I said to myself, at which Rhonda and I should excel, being a couple of smart arses. I remember the first day we strode into the lounge to size up the opposition. An assorted bunch of mostly mature faces reflecting the sage-like wisdom of time. It was an unsettling feeling and one that was soon translated into a humiliating loss.

However, on the occasions we threatened to win these tussles, the American sister duo of Marcia and Mary made significant contributions for the team and the quiet presence of Petrus, the South African, produced the odd surprise. Johnny, our Madeiran dentist mate, came up with a notable winner when he correctly answered (much to the relief, I'm sure, of his patients) that there were four canine teeth in a human mouth.

And so it was after these mentally bruising contests that Rhonda and I would return to our sumptuous stateroom to ready ourselves for the busy, evening social whirl.

Now, these affairs allow all aboard to transform themselves from near naked, informal slouches, to elegant visions, clad in designer gowns and well-padded monkey suits. Days before leaving Australia, I had been persuaded to purchase one of these stylish outfits to make sure I caused no embarrassment to my darling who, unlike myself, was a veteran of the cruising circuit.

With Captain, officers and striking shipboard hostesses forming a human 'greeting chain', we filed into the Panorama Lounge, much like a parade of roosters and peacocks into the hen house.

It was in this environment that I came across Alan, an English north countryman, whose ancestors, for a reason that never became clear, had escaped transportation to the Antipodes. A delightfully direct gentleman, his career in industry had taken him from humble beginnings to a comfortable position as Chairman of the Board. His opening line could have been spoken by half of Sydney's male population, "lot of poofters aboard!"

As this was spoken quite loudly and within earshot of a group of elegant gays, I thought, "now's here's a man who speaks his mind!"

An engineer by background, he immediately put me at ease, and re-assured me that the ship was in safe hands, as he had brought along his GPS. He was plotting our position just to make sure the Italian Captain got it right! His encyclopedic knowledge of the ship's mechanical functions, and position of every lifeboat vindicated my decisions to stick close to him for the remainder of the cruise.

But that was not the only reason for remaining on good terms. He accompanied a wife of rare charm and beauty. A sophisticated, yet down to earth girl, whose warmth radiated like a coal fire in a London townhouse. Totally without pretension, and quite obviously one of the sharpest knives in the draw, Annette brought to every dinner table and cocktail bar a touch of class.

It was during these cocktail sessions that some of the funniest sights were witnessed, begging the question, 'what is about ships that make people do strange things?'

Take the actions of Washington State resident, Kent Beech, a social butterfly, and a man with a wicked sense of humour. Not content with the luxurious bed in his spacious stateroom he took to sleeping on a banana lounge on his balcony. It was on the second night out of port that he was woken from a fitful, drunken sleep, after being swamped by a small part of the Atlantic Ocean.

"I like to hear the sound of crashing waves," he informed everyone. But it was later in the cruise that his proclivity for 'sleeping rough' came home to bite him. Returning in a drunken state to his banana lounge shortly before 4 am, he noted there was a distinct absence of crashing waves. He sprang to the phone and asked to be patched through to the bridge.

"What's going on?" he slurred. "We've slowed from sixteen to seven knots, sir", he was told.

"Well that's not good enough", Kent shot back. "I spent big bucks to hear crashing waves. Pick it up"!

The story spread like wildfire through the ship and every time the *Silver Wind* subsequently slowed down an irreverent bunch of us would yell "pick it up, we paid big bucks to hear crashing waves!"

And while on the subject people doing weird things on ships, I cite my own perverse actions. For a man who has assiduously avoided dancing for most of his life, I found myself thrusting assorted women towards the dance floor. What followed, I'm told, defied description. 'A hamster on heat' was the one particularly unkind description, meted out by Rhonda.

But it was another action that, I believe, brings into focus serious questions about the strange hypnotic effect of the sea on the behavioural patterns of human beings.

My proposal of marriage to Rhonda Margaret Rose Stewart Barnett came, as they say, 'out of the blue'. She was quite literally stunned.

After days of staring at the clear blue and incredibly calm Atlantic Ocean from a bar stool, the notion struck me that a little marriage ceremony might be a good idea.

To get the ball rolling I went to the Captain, a delightfully passionate Italian by the name of Ignazio Tatulli, and asked the big question, "can you do it?"

"Wella, my friend, I canna do it, but itta ain't gonna be legal" came the answer.

"You bloody beauty," I immediately fired back. Romance without accountability!

"We canna do it tomorrow night at sunset on the Bridge" he told me, emotion making his voice waver and his eyes water.

I quickly accepted the offer, trying hard to disguise my lack of disappointment at the illegal status of the proposed union, and traipsed off to see if Rhonda would be in it!

She, of course, had no idea that I was carrying a diamond engagement ring with me, hand-crafted by our good mate, Bill O'Loughlin, a top Sydney design jeweller.

Our cruise was nearing its final destination in the Canary Islands, and Lady Barnett was thinking of booking at the 'Relais et Chateaux' Restaurant for a special dinner together.

"Well" I said, "we can go there, or the main dining room, or we can get married!" That stopped her in her tracks, and the lipstick she was applying shot up the side of her face.

A romantic dinner may have been on her radar, but an actual marriage ceremony, I'm positive, did not figure in her expectations. "Don't worry" I assured her, "it won't be a legal marriage, just an exchange of vows."

The good 'Capitan' had explained that marriages at sea do not meet the legal requirements necessary to satisfy registration. We were Australians on an Italian ship, based in America, registered in the Bahamas, and sailing off the coast of Madeira (Spain).

Having never married before, Rhonda was quite happy that the arrangements were more symbolic than legal. She was up for it!

All our newest 'best friends' were delighted to be invited up to the ship's bridge for the special event, and I asked Colin (the 'PM of Barbados') to be my 'Best Man'. It was 'formal night', so everyone was in their 'Sunday Best'.

Georg Kaiser, the German doctor, who bore a stunning resemblance to Liberace in both wardrobe and mannerisms, provided organ musical accompaniment, and was playing 'Land of Hope and Glory' with what suspiciously looked like a tear in his eye, when the bride arrived on the Bridge!

It was an emotional ceremony, conducted as a stunning sunset stained the ocean red. We made the appropriate vows, and then headed down to the bar, while the Captain announced our nuptials over the ship's intercom system. There were congratulations all round!

Our respective parents were phoned from the ship and informed we were now 'illegally married', which prompted equal measures of happiness and confusion.

When we returned to Sydney, plans started to make the union legal, but my 'blushing bride' wanted a year to get in shape.

Eleven months later, we hosted 130 of our nearest and dearest to our wedding at 'Mandalay' in Lane Cove. Several of our newest friends from the previous year's cruise flew in from London and New York. Other friends came from Germany, Taiwan, San Diego and all around Australia.

We were lucky, at our ages, that both sets of parents were there to witness the happy occasion.

It was all timed to coincide with Rhonda's 50th birthday – she couldn't be accused of rushing it!!!!

CHAPTER 25
HONEYMOON HANGOVER

It was Rhonda's standard line.

"We're from Australia, and we're on our seven-week honeymoon!"

She smilingly delivered it to everyone during our epic post wedding gallivant spanning the globe. It was a proud declaration, commonly received with a furrowing of the brow and a quick, appraising movement of startled eyes over the recently betrothed couple. We blatantly contradicted the tired stereotype of a blushing young bride and a gloating groom.

"Oh, congratulations!" came an overwhelming number of replies, sincerity not quite matching surprise, I often thought, as I stood awkwardly, smiling dumbly, and nodding my head in mute confirmation of my wife's proud declaration.

Now don't get me wrong! I had been excited and thrilled to offer the proposal of marriage to my cherished Rhonda, the woman responsible for introducing order into my chaotic life, direction to my rudderless boat and love to the 'old fart' I'd become.

But why couldn't she just say we were on holiday!

I know. It's been pointed out more than a few times. It's her first. Of course, she is going to publicise the big event!

It was just that I wasn't prepared for all the bloody fuss the statement inevitably caused. `

That fact was never more graphically illustrated than at the Pool Bar on the 6-star '*Silver Shadow*', with cocktail hour looming. Equipped with a Bloody Mary and facing an ancient couple oozing the cheery disposition of American retirees, Rhonda opened up with, "Hi, I'm Rhonda, this is Ian, and we're on our honeymoon from Australia".

Well, you'd swear she'd just told the old couple they'd won the twenty million dollar Arkansas state lottery.

"Oh my God!" the old girl shrieked, almost knocking her dapper old mate off his bar stool.

"Married and Australian, well honey, congratulations to you and this fine looking man. I'm Betty from North Carolina and this is my hubby, Harley. We did it fifty-six years ago!"

I looked at Betty sideways wondering what it was she and Harley had done fifty-six years ago, but wasn't about to explore the issue as he was busy fiddling with his hearing aid, no doubt turning it down after Betty's deck-shaking exclamation.

"Well congratulations, son, you don't know what you're in for," Harley intoned, in the syrupy southern twang of a long-suffering mate. His sad eyes drooped like, Beau, the aging bloodhound, I imagined was waiting for him back home in the Carolinas.

Nodding and pressing a gin and tonic to my lips, I thought to myself that compared to old Harley and Betty, we were just kids and Rhonda had wisely picked her mark to discuss the marriage. Then I looked on in horror as Betty lifted her ample bulk from the bar stool and yelled to group of fellow Americans standing nearby.

"Hey folks, come and meet the newlyweds!"

The oohs, aahs and goddamns continued through several gin and tonics. My hand was sore, my back well slapped and I'd developed a permanent tic in my right eye from returning the winks of all the well-wishers.

The experience was exhausting. The muscles around my mouth cramped from the sickly, fixed smile and my head would not stop nodding. I resembled one of those toy dogs placed in the rear car windows of the ethnic suburbs of Australia.

If Rhonda thought I could meet my conjugal duties after such an experience, she was dreaming.

But, while her insistence on telling all and sundry about the happy event unnerved me, there was 'method to her madness'. Her cheery, but also shrewd, honeymoon declaration often succeeded in encouraging hotel and airline staff to offer a free bottle of something, along with heartfelt congratulations. However, it was on the second day of the honeymoon, just outside Dublin, that she most decidedly struck gold.

Checking into the Portmarnock Hotel and Golf Links for a two-night stay, she dealt the honeymoon card, after being taken to a small, pleasant room, tantalisingly close to the Irish Sea, but with only a limited view of the windswept 18th hole.

"It's quite nice," she said to the young concierge, "but we were really hoping for something with a view of the sea".

Now, keep in mind she'd already got the best price imaginable for a standard double room in the swank golfing resort, through a discount site on the internet.

"Sorry Madam, the entire top floor is occupied by the Irish Rugby team who are staying with us and they've got the views."

Christ, I thought, there's a group of boys who'd really appreciate a view!

"But look," he added, "there may be a room overlooking the first hole."

During our walk to the alternative room it emerged that the young man had just returned from a 12-month working holiday in Australia, a country he described as 'paradise' or something along those lines.

Upon opening the door with a flourish, however, his face fell as he watched the lines of disappointment, clearly etched upon Rhonda's face.

"Oh," she said, "It's okay, but very small. We've been travelling for 32 hours and it's our honeymoon and I was just hoping for something a little, well nicer."

"I see," he said, clearly embarrassed and not quite sure how to handle the charming, pushy woman from the land he'd recently fallen in love with.

"Look – wait here and I'll go and see what I can do!"

Watching him disappear, I collapsed onto the biggest piece of our luggage and rolled my eyes, trying desperately to convey my feelings to the darling girl engaged in delicate negotiations.

Minutes later Ronan returned, and my new bride was soon to savour the sweet taste of success, as the young man led us to the magnificent honeymoon suite. The huge oval room boasted a massive four-poster bed and a bathroom bigger than the two rooms we'd rejected.

"I hope this is alright," Ronan said, a twinkle in his eye threatening to set the room afire!

I glanced over at Rhonda, who wore a radiant smile on her face which left me in no doubt I'd have to try harder in bed if I was to see anything that would match it in the future.

On the wall close to the writing desk, hung a portrait of a tall, distinguished looking gentleman sucking on a pipe and clad in fine Irish tweed. Ronan followed my eyes.

"The head of the Jameson Whisky empire," he informed us. "This is his ancestral home and this was the main bedroom. Now it's our celebrity suite. Bill Clinton stays here when he plays golf in Dublin, and Michael Douglas and Catherine Zeta Jones were here recently."

I looked across at the gigantic bed sitting in the middle of the room and entertained for a fleeting second Catherine's beautiful naked body, under the ornate, bright blue canopy.

I tried hard to eliminate the imagery of my own sweating, heavily padded torso sharing the experience with Michael's wife. After all, he was a man I'd interviewed, liked and had dinner with in New York. 'It just wouldn't be right to have impure thoughts – particularly on one's honeymoon.

So there we were, in Ireland, staying in a EU1000 a night room for which we paid a fraction of that price. Life was good! The epic voyage had gotten off to a good start. Rhonda was my hero, or is that heroine, even if she wouldn't stop telling everyone we were on our honeymoon!

But, like so many things in life, highs are often followed by lows. After a wonderful week in Ireland taking in the lush, verdant scenery, and being hosted by our friends, Stan and Lucy to copious quantities of Guinness and Bushmills whiskey, the moment had come to leave the Emerald Isle. Time again to try Rhonda's skills in the high stakes game of eliciting advantage in exchange for her 'honeymoon declaration.'

The next test came at Dublin's International Airport, at the check in counter of Ryanair, the low cost airline, well known for its inflexible policies regarding just about everything. We had been warned, of course, but Rhonda clung to the naïve belief that honeymooning Australians were entitled to travel with more baggage than anyone else.

It's a conversation worth relating.

"Good morning," a beaming Rhonda opened up looking unusually large and formidable. This was, no doubt due to the seventeen layers of heavy clothing wrapped around her tiny body.

"So what if I look like the Michelin man," she'd earlier protested. "This is just in case we do have to pay some excess."

"Good morning," the unusually sombre young woman replied. "How many pieces of luggage?"

Now this was really a moot point, as she'd watched us approaching, buried under a bloody mountain of baggage, while everyone else in line carried, approximately, a clean pair of knickers and a toothbrush.

"Three pieces," Rhonda offered, "A little heavy, I'm afraid. We're on our honeymoon from Australia, and we're away for seven weeks."

The news was greeted with a curt nod. This was a woman in charge of her emotions. There was not even the hint of a smile, or a look of sympathy after hearing Rhonda's poignant honeymoon declaration.

As I stood behind my battling bride, listening to the encounter and trying desperately to disguise the four other items of heavy hand luggage, I could sense clearly where this was heading.

"I'm afraid your bags are 27 kilos overweight. That'll be 189 euros," she pronounced, her face showing no involvement whatsoever. That was more than we paid for the two plane tickets!

Looking at the back of my wife's head, I waited for the fireworks. Her already heavily clothed body swelled up like a giant puffer fish!

My embarrassment over the scene, which was surely to follow, was only slightly overshadowed by the pride I felt in the feisty combativeness, of my new wife, who was about to dispute the ridiculously rigid policy of this pissant Irish airline.

"I'd like to speak to your Supervisor," Rhonda declared, a slight imperiousness creeping into an ever so calm manner.

The gloves were about to come off!

"Come this way please," the woman answered, leaving the thirty or so people lining up to check in their baggage unattended, while she stood by Rhonda across the other side of the terminal, to listen to the ensuing argument.

One could not escape the conclusion that the young miss was protecting a commission she would surely get, once the Australians were put in their place and sent on their way.

This happened minutes later. However, it wasn't the end of the story.

Ryanair was going to treat us to a day from hell! Still seething and shaken from the excess baggage episode, we listened as the airline announced a short time later that there would be a flight delay, with no reason given. Six hours later, having missed our connection in London for the ongoing flight to Limoges in France, we demanded our baggage be returned, and booked an Air Lingus direct flight to Paris.

Standing at the Irish national carrier's check-in counter, Rhonda repeated that now famous phrase,

"Hi, we're from Australia and are on a seven-week honeymoon. And, I'd like to travel on a proper airline!!"

"Well isn't that lovely, congratulations!" was the smiling reply.

And yes, there was NO excess baggage charge and we took off to begin the next 6 weeks of an action packed honeymoon.

CHAPTER 26
HIJINKS ON THE HIGH SEAS

"All you can eat and drink!"

What is it about the innocuous catchphrase that sucks us in and demands an investigation of its veracity?

It's a well-worn marketing ploy, designed to appeal to our most basic instincts, a fact evidenced by examples of shocking behavior in restaurants that boast a plentiful and constantly replenished buffet.

They're easy to spot.

Usually grossly overweight, they stand in line in eager anticipation, their hands sweatily grasping two plates, their eyes hungrily following the actions of those ahead, their mouths salivating at the prospect of the feast that lies just seconds away.

It's all too obvious to a trained eye, especially one in the same queue balancing the same number of plates and facing the same baffling dilemma of choice.

Now, don't go jumping to conclusions!

I wasn't referring to myself, or the bride, though it has to be conceded she is no slouch in the buffet queue.

No, there's another dimension to the psychological implications of the catchphrase and it has to do with thrift.

That's right, thrift!

By definition, a thrifty person is preoccupied with the concept of 'value for money.'

And in that department, it must be said, my wife, Rhonda Margaret Rose Stewart Barnett, is High Priestess and Grand Poobah all rolled into one!

No surprise to those who know her well. In the competitive world of retail leasing her negotiating skills are legendary; her nose has been seen metaphorically twitching in search of a deal, akin to a Frenchman coveting a smelly piece of cheese. She is relentless in her single-minded pursuit of a 'good deal!'

And so it was, we found ourselves on a ten day Mediterranean cruise, which would threaten numerous records in the Guinness Book of Records for 'conspicuous consumption.'

Where better to conspicuously consume than on a six-star ship with the crème de la crème of the International jet set and lots of rich 'old folks'!

In fairness, though, it's not all about food and beverages. The 'deal maker' in Rhonda came to the fore, and once again she turned to the internet and waited for the last minute rate before pouncing on the tickets, in much the same way as a famished cat goes after a rat.

It paid off in spades! My devilishly clever better half could hardly conceal her joy when in conversation with an elderly passenger, she discovered the old girl paid approximately five times more than we shelled out for the same luxury stateroom.

The look of triumph was something to behold!

For those of you who have never had the great good fortune of finding themselves comfortably ensconced in the luxurious bosom of 6 stars, it really is something else.

When I was introduced to this rare pleasure for the first time, so overwhelmed by the delicious experience, I conspicuously consumed a goodly amount of fluid and then, asked Rhonda for her hand in marriage.

Understandably, when a cruise was mentioned in pre-honeymoon discussions I was not fiercely opposed to the idea.

We settled on a jaunt from Venice to Rome via the Croatian coast, Sicily and Malta; a circumnavigation of the 'Italian boot.' As neither of us had experienced the Adriatic coast before, it made sense and helped us in our never-ending quest to leave no place on earth untouched by our eagle eyes.

At the starting point, Venice opened its heart and skies to us. With the amount of rain we experienced, there was every chance of the city fulfilling forecasts and sinking! Gondoliers could be seen furiously bailing out their crafts, as bedraggled passengers hid under plastic raincoats, looking anything but enchanted by the charm of this magnificent, but currently soggy city.

St Mark's Square was as crowded as ever with thousands of pigeons diving bombing and pooing on the seemingly never-ending stream of dripping tourists.

Arriving by train, we discovered within seconds the stark truth about this renowned city. There are no roads, no taxis and no hope of avoiding the crowded waterways. My travelling companion's two previous visits to

Venice had failed to equip her with a strategy to move the 50-odd kilos of baggage with which we'd saddled ourselves. Despite spirited exhortations and a 'small whip' she kept concealed in her handbag, the load proved too much.

I sat exhausted and dispirited atop one of the largest bags, forcing the new bride to go off in search of a solution. It came in the form of two muscular, young men, the proud operators of a 25-foot motor launch that offered salvation.

Fifty euros and a rain soaked ten-minute ride later, the huge bow of the '*Silver Shadow*' loomed into view, heralding the start of ten days of excess and debauchery, the likes of which is hard to comprehend.

It started with the obligatory champagne on arrival. No surprises there! Also, the crew's solicitous bowing and scraping, slightly embarrassing, but nonetheless comforting. After all you've spent big bucks, and a bit of pampering doesn't go astray.

However, it was during the long walk to our stateroom that a level of discomfort set in.

We were forced to pass through a virtual honour guard of maids and butlers whose nodding heads and beaming smiles assured us 'no stone would go unturned' to make our voyage as pleasurable as possible.

The cruise line's eye for detail was immediately obvious. Within seconds of settling in, a loud knock was answered and through the door stampeded a young, heavily built lass, dressed in a black and a white maid's uniform, a colour scheme she was born to wear.

"G'day!" she greeted us, "My name's Renee, and I'm from New Zealand. Where in Oz are yer from?"

I looked at the delightfully blunt young woman thinking if she wore a pair of football boots and an 'All Black' jersey she would bear an uncanny resemblance to the present Maori hooker in the fearsome New Zealand Rugby team.

"G'day, how yer going" I comfortably responded, slipping back into my native Australian tongue with all the relish of a goanna with a gold tooth!

Whether or not she had any appreciation of the game played in heaven, Renee's efficiency and easy charm soon became apparent.

"What can I get for yer?" she enquired, her eyes darting from me to the person most likely to give her an quick, straightforward answer.

Rhonda didn't miss a beat; an experienced Silversea traveller, she replied with not a hint of embarrassment, "a bottle of Chivas, Bombay Sapphire, Drambuie and, of course, champagne, Aussie shiraz and chardonnay."

Renee gave no indication of any shock at the request. Her response left me wondering just how many other drunks were on board.

The alcohol was designed for a little pre-dinner tipple, before hitting the restaurants and bars each evening.

And so, well provisioned with booze, we comfortably settled into shipboard life.

A helpful tip to first time Silversea cruisers is – don't rush in – stand back and observe the passengers, before blundering headlong into conversation. This can save painfully boring sessions trapped at restaurant tables in the company of folks you'd rather be an ocean away from.

It's very much like a visit to a large city park where one can observe the behaviour of dogs. Rules of engagement differ widely, from the brash, direct approach that involves a cacophony of barking, followed by a quick dash and sniff to the more subtle introduction. This results in eye contact, feigned indifference, followed by sexual relations.

Not only can one point to canine behaviour as a handy guide to shipboard life, but it's hard to escape the conclusion that many onboard closely resembled certain dog breeds.

Take one American gentleman; I'll call him Ed, a small, grizzled individual, short in stature but wide in girth. He went nowhere on the ship without a huge cigar protruding from his mouth. It produced a pungent pall of smoke that enveloped his head, no doubt killing off what little hair remained on his freckled dome. He was a New Yorker, as was his travelling companion, a young, handsome man in his thirties, who spent most of his time lazing by the pool while Ed power-walked the deck. He had apparently been a 'big wig' with a major American movie studio. But to me he looked like a bulldog and was to be avoided at all costs.

Then there was Harley from North Carolina. He had large ears and big, sad eyes that dominated a long head attached to a tall, wiry, frame. Harley was over eighty years old and quite delightful. I only wish I had had the courage to ask him what sort of dog waited for him back home, because I would have bet it was an aging bloodhound. One indisputable fact, though, Harley's sniffing days were most definitely over; a fact I learned as we sat by the Pool Bar one sunny afternoon.

Ever the provocateur, I asked Harley if he was concerned about becoming sexually aroused sitting next to the pool for so many hours, with the half-naked assortment of femininity nearby.

He looked at me stonily and said, "Shit son, ain't a woman on this ship could move that goddam thing!"

Sniffing, however, was definitely the speciality of two aging Brazilian beauties. They had left husbands back in Sao Paulo and by day they resembled coquettish, 'hard to get' poodles. However, at night, on darkened dance floors, they turned into a couple of highly sexed hyenas prowling in anticipation of a kill.

There was of course an abundance of stylish, birdlike, bejeweled older women who resembled shih tzus or maltese terriers, and one particular yappy and almost permanently pickled American lady who was a 'dead ringer' for a chihuahua.

As a bounding young labrador, I took it all in, and instructed my partner, the whippet, to remain downwind of the others and sit on the deck if anyone came a 'sniffing'. It seemed to work!

One highlight of six-star cruising is the formal evenings. Passengers are encouraged to dress 'to the nines' and try to outshine each other by the extent of expensive jewellery and designer fashion sported. In the case of the gentlemen, it's the ease with which they're able to disguise their corpulent bellies with the help of a fine tailor.

I have no doubt the majority of my fellow male passengers were not short of a dollar, and proudly sported their huge guts as an unashamed badge of honour. A number proudly exposed them to the sun, and one particularly ingenious Frenchman used his as a table upon which to sit his and his wife's cocktails.

Needless to say, the odd skinny Latino or Italian among the passengers walked with an affected swagger, that didn't go unnoticed by the girls and the perceptive, overweight, men aboard.

With wealth, of course, usually comes age and it was obvious from the start that many of our fellow cruisers were in their twilight years. A conservative estimate put the average somewhere in the late-seventies, a fact that calls easily to mind that famous Australian War Veterans lament, 'age shall not weary them, or the years condemn.'

Unfortunately, in the case of one elderly gentleman that was not to be the case. During the course of the evening meal he was sharing with his 92-year-old girlfriend, who was also wheelchair bound, he collapsed, which triggered a full-scale medical emergency.

Horrified diners watched on, as stretcher-bearers and the doctor worked furiously to revive him. We were later to find out that he was dead before he hit the floor! It was a grim reminder of one's own mortality. Later, in bars around the ship, a common theme emerged in hushed conversations concerning the old chap's good fortune of 'falling off the perch doing something most people would die to do!'

The incident also served to bring to light an obscure fact that would otherwise have remained undiscovered. Somewhere in the bowels of the '*Silver Shadow*' are 12 coffins and a very large refrigerator, used exclusively to house the bodies of the dearly departed.

Now if that ain't good planning I don't know what is!

CHAPTER 27
BIG SEAS, BIG FEARS

"What about another Transatlantic cruise?"

She asked the question, with thinly disguised excitement, no doubt thinking that I, a relatively new convert to the joys of cruising, would enthusiastically embrace the idea. Forget the simple fact that the huge, hostile pond had claimed many a ship, not least, the supposedly unsinkable Titanic.

The she in question was Mrs. Hyslop; Rhonda Barnett-Hyslop though, it should be pointed out, she rarely uses the Hyslop bit; only on cruises to make sure sex starved, fellow passengers leave her mate alone.

"The Atlantic," I said, "North or South?"

"Southampton to New York," she replied, leaving no doubt that she'd already packed her bags, and getting my nod was a mere formality.

The North Atlantic, I thought, knowing full well I hadn't coped too well with a 'mill pond' South Atlantic, on a previous expedition.

What do I mean by not coping too well?

Well, and I certainly didn't feel that at the time, rather than describing in too much detail a projectile vomiting session that could well have matched any in the Guinness Book of Records, I had a wee bit of trouble controlling the contents of my stomach. Yes, I was seasick!

Here's the thing. A male ego is a fragile, vulnerable little mechanism and what it dreads most are those difficult questions, which bring into sharp focus its owner's ability to be manly.

"Oh no, I can't possibly do that, I'll get sick!"

Now, I don't know about you, but I certainly couldn't allow that pitiful admission to escape my very masculine lips, especially when you have a wife who can eat, drink and sing her way through a force 5 hurricane.

And so, I looked at her, my rheumy eyes, not for one moment showing any trepidation whatsoever and said, "That's sounds wonderful, darling, when do we go?"

So, how did I go?

Well, I went, and in the interests of anyone who may fear the thought of the mighty Atlantic Ocean, I'll chronicle the measures and the psychological tools I employed to get through the bloody experience!

Upon our arrival, Southampton was bathed in a warm, summer sun. The same sun, which no doubt shone centuries ago on brave sailors who launched their daring voyages of discovery in ships made of wood. They were far more crudely constructed than our six-star ocean liner which positively shone, white and glistening and made of steel.

Lesson one: Steel versus wood. You have to feel better about that!

This will get you into a positive frame of mind. Don't read too much or else you'll find that compared to the big cruise ships, for example, the Queen Mary 2 at 150 thousand tons, your delightful, little ship weighs only 28 thousand tons. This is information you don't need to know, and only serves to make you apprehensive about the upcoming cruise across huge, potentially rough seas.

Nor should you search out any extended weather forecasts. This is a mistake, but to a news junkie like myself it is also unavoidable. So, when I heard the East Coast of America was battening down for a big hurricane, I started conjecturing at what point in our Transatlantic cruise we would bump into the killer storm.

I was not the only one equipped with this vital bit of intelligence. A group of American gentlemen of quite senior years smiled and winked at me, muttering something along the lines of, "should be interesting; nothing like a bit of sea!"

Can you imagine there are bloody idiots out there who welcome 'a bit of sea'! Thank-you very much Barney and Charlie, or whatever your names were!

A little bit of knowledge is a bad thing. I was already imagining the Italian Captain's first announcement over the crackling intercom.

"Ah, welcome to you all, Ladies and a Gentlemen. This is your Capitan speaking, Stefano Stromboli is my name and a battling cyclones is a my game. Donta a worry about nothing. We have a put plenty of buckets in the rooms and all the beds have gotta restraints."

Well, he didn't exactly say that, but in his first public announcement he did try to allay our fears by saying he believed all the bad weather would be over as we approached the North American continent.

My first question: How would he know? Is he a weatherman, a hurricane watcher?

No, he's the bloke who drives the boat, and he's sure as hell not going to tell you that you're in for a real, rough ride, is he?

"Most of you will spend the journey with your heads down the toilet." No – that's not what he's going to say!

So, yes, this was all a little unnerving. Of course, the missus didn't blink an eye, holding the view that seasickness is all in the mind. Now, she had witnessed my pathetic seasickness on a previous crossing so she must have known there was considerably more in my stomach than my mind, but she steadfastly stood by this well-worn maxim.

As for my previous bout of seasickness, I must explain. It wasn't as though I was bedridden for the entirety of the cruise. I was struck down only once, but such was the ferocity of the attack, it will forever remain a vivid and shameful episode in an otherwise unblemished record.

One moment I was dressing for the Captain's party, the next picking pieces off the front of my once immaculate tuxedo, after removing my head from the toilet bowl. I mean, it didn't happen straight away. I can remember walking arm in arm with the good lady wife towards the party, when I sprang a leak. That's right, a leak. No, I did not pee myself, but from every pore of my body sprang what felt like litres of fluid. My hair, ordinarily held in place by a liberal coating of spray, hung in my eyes, a sodden mess. I was assailed by the most shocking sense of disorientation, short of consuming massive doses of LSD (not that I'd know what that feels like!) I fled back to the suite, to perform my body-emptying act, leaving a clearly concerned wife to tell fellow revellers that her husband's seasickness was all in his mind. God knows most of it ended in the toilet bowl, but probably too much information.

So, against this backdrop, which incidentally occurred in the South Atlantic, I prepared myself for the more notorious stretch of ocean between Ireland and Newfoundland, the final resting place of countless intrepid sailors. I'd survived the Irish Sea crossing from Southampton without incident, making sure to stay 'three sheets to the wind', so as not to think about being sick. It worked!

But on departing the mist and rain shrouded Emerald Isle, the dark, seemingly angry seas took on a more menacing quality, and I found myself asking that inevitable question. Not if I'll be seasick, but when!

I think this is what my wife was suggesting when she said it was all in the mind.

I had, however, come prepared. I proudly sported my seasickness wristbands, designed to stimulate the P6 acupressure point, thus mysteriously countering the effects of huge, rolling seas. A day out of Waterford, I could feel my wristbands start to lose their secret powers.

A familiar clamminess came over me. Perspiring like a leaking faucet, I was forced to go urgently in search of a toilet bowl and bed, lest I hurl the contents of a lavish dinner down a three-metre stretch of pristine carpet. Thankfully, it was a one-day wonder.

I was back in the bar within hours of my recovery, sheepishly relating 'my adventures at the porcelain', but I was preaching to the converted. My bar pals, mostly chaps in the older age demographic, were veteran sailors who'd thrown up on every sea known to man and God. They smiled benignly as I regaled them with lucid details of my own disappointing episode. They pointed to little patches oddly positioned behind ear lobes, and swore blind they stopped similar inconvenient trips to the 'head'. I absorbed all this valuable information like a sponge, stowing it away for future action.

But thank the most merciful God it was not needed, as the cruise continued sailing on untroubled waters. Yes, the Capitan was indeed correct, the hurricane that had battered the east coast of America had fizzled out and my two American mates were denied their rough bit of sea!

As for the missus, she still believes it's all in the mind. No comment!

CHAPTER 28
BEEF JERKY AND BLACKJACK

"The name's Art, son, and this is the wife, Frieda, from the great state of Washington".

It was a proclamation that hung ominously in the air like a rain squall about to let loose.

"DC?" I asked, looking at the little guy with a mixture of condescension and incredulity as had, I guessed, a good percentage of people who had met him over the years.

"Washington State, son, the Pacific North West, Portland, and the Beef Jerky Capital of America!" he proudly asserted.

With this proclamation he thrust a fat, ballpoint pen into my hand; one of those functional writing utensils with four coloured inkwells encased in a shaft adorned with the name of a company, I guessed, was his.

This was not the first time I had laid eyes on old Art. He'd been regularly pacing the deck of the cruise liner since we'd boarded in Hong Kong four days earlier, and to say he stood out like 'canine familiaris genitalia' among the six hundred odd cruisers was a glaring understatement!

He was a tiny, stooped, ancient man who wore overly large spectacles with lenses as thick as coke bottles, and a straw, 'pork pie' hat that was a permanent fixture, atop what I guessed was a freckled, hairless dome.

Earlier in the cruise, I'd watched him on the top deck of the ship, clinging desperately to his hat, as a stiff wind threatened to whisk his 60-kilo frame from the walking track into the churning sea. He was one of the most strikingly ridiculous figures I'd encountered during a lifetime of encountering strikingly ridiculous figures. Childhood memories of the television cartoon 'Mr Magoo' flooded back!

I was shaken from these musings by the sight of Art, sitting opposite me in the main dining room of the '*MS Nautica*', removing his hat with a flourish to indeed reveal a smooth, freckled dome. With Frieda and four other diners, also the proud owners of new ballpoint pens, the diminutive fellow launched into what sounded like an effortless and rehearsed diatribe to acquaint us with his life story.

"It wasn't always easy" he intoned, his little brown eyes jumping energetically around the table.

"I mean, I had to educate Americans to eat jerky back in the 70s."

No kidding, I thought, remembering my first tussle, decades ago with the stringy, noxious, brown substance that looked and tasted like shit-flavoured leather.

"How the hell did you prize them away from their hamburgers and hot dogs?" I interjected, justly proud of the incisive brilliance of the question.

"Well son" he said, "it's all about marketing. I bought eighteen VW bugs and roamed the North West on selling campaigns, getting them used to the idea of eating the stuff".

It wasn't hard picturing this Magoo-like figure behind the wheel of a quaint German car, flogging jerky to the masses. He could well be the same guy who got Californians to buy 'pet rocks' back in the seventies.

"By the late eighties I was the biggest jerky producer in the country", he proudly proclaimed, looking around the table at the rapt expressions on the faces of a spellbound audience.

"In the nineties, I got an exclusive deal with Costco to take jerky to the world."

Good God, I thought, he could buy the bloody ship! He's a genius. I mean to get people to wear out a set of teeth, munching on a disgusting packaged food that looks and tastes like the sole of a shoe is no mean feat.

As if reading my thoughts, Frieda, interjected. Her upper lip was sprinkled with dark hair and quivered, as her big brown eyes sparkled with the proud emotion of the moment.

"Art doesn't work no more. We just travel. The kids run the business."

This piece of news was greeted with understanding nods around the table.

"How old are you, Art?" I asked, my voice failing to disguise the warm reverence with which I'd come, in the last few minutes, to view the man.

"I'm 79, son," he informed me, justly proud of the declaration.

"And you put your longevity down to eating jerky?" I smugly asked, allowing him a chance to bask in the glory of his creation.

"Well son, to tell you the truth, I'm not partial to the stuff, but it sure has made me a truck load of money!"

It was at this point, while I watched those at the table explode into uncontrolled laughter, I made up my mind to never again judge a book by its cover.

The fact is, cruise ships are an oasis of some very strange people. You just don't know with whom you'll share a table. I well remember when Rhonda first raised the subject of taking a cruise on the high seas. I'd just turned fifty and looked at her as though she was having a very senior moment.

"What do you mean a cruise", I asked indignantly, "That's for old farts about to die!"

"You're talking through what you sit on", she responded, "You've never been on one!"

Well, that was five years and six cruises ago, and it's only now dawned on me just how fertile they are in hosting genuinely interesting characters, who in their twilight years show a perverse fascination with trolling the world's oceans.

This was never more forcibly rammed home than two days after meeting the colorful Art and Frieda.

Again, we were about to stick our quivering snouts into the trough to savour what we had been assured was some of the 'best damned food afloat', when I spied him across the opulent dining room being led by a uniformed maître d'. He was a little fellow with a pronounced hunchback who looked 'older than God', and was feeling his way with the aid of a formidable wooden walking stick.

I found myself thinking, somewhat cruelly, who in the packed dining room would find themselves saddled with the onerous task of trying to entertain this funny little fellow.

I think it was the smile of the maître d' that gave it away. Looking up from the overpriced wine list, I blanched as he loomed over me while pulling out a chair for our new guest. So long had it taken them to reach our table that I'd forgotten seeing the old man, and thinking those unkind thoughts. It was God's punishment!

"Hello there", he squeaked, "The names Reginald".

Bloody hell, I thought, this is a conspiracy; first Art, the jerky man and now Reg, the bloody 'Hunchback of High Seas'.

Always quick to recover, and hoping he was half as interesting as the Jerky King, I jumped in with the introductions.

"G'day Reg, the name's Ian, my wife Rhonda and this is Phil and Maude from your neck of the woods".

"Well, what a pleasure to meet you all," he politely offered, showing off a stunningly white set of false teeth, that somehow stayed firmly planted in his mouth. On taking a seat, however, his age showed as he let out an audible expulsion of air, akin to a death rattle.

Stay with us, Reg, I thought!

"Where are you from then?" asked Phil, the other Englishman at the table.

"I'm from Edinburgh", he said without the slightest hint of the thick brogue commonly spoken in the Scottish capital.

"You certainly don't sound like a Scot," I quickly offered.

"Very perceptive of you, and you don't sound like an Australian, if you don't mind me saying so," he replied, his twinkling eyes sending out a clear challenge.

It must have been the g'day greeting, I thought, while being struck with a premonition that this old gentleman was a lot sharper than he looked.

"Actually, I hail from Essex" he offered, "But we moved to Edinburgh in the 90s. I lost my wife there four years ago".

With this solemn bit of news, the conversation took on a serious note. Death will do that, I thought, assuming of course he hadn't lost her somewhere in the suburbs, while on a short walk with the dog. All eyes fell on the crumpled little guy in the seventies suit, and one could acutely feel the compassion and embarrassment of the moment, but as is often the case, there was a rush to dispel the sombre mood.

"So, have you cruised before, Reg?" asked Maude, who was also from the south of England.

"No, this is my first cruise. I've just turned 89 and I thought it was time to spend some of the winnings," he offered, again showing off a brilliant smile, I suspected, may have also been purchased with some the mysterious winnings.

"Winnings?" inquired Phil, a little too quickly.

"Yes, you see I'm a professional gambler, and I tend to win a lot of the time," he declared giving us his best poker face.

Now, after my experience with Mr Jerky, I was fully expecting to hear that Reg was richer than the Aga Khan, and had cut a swathe through the gambling capitals of the world, reducing the likes of Steve Wynn to a pauper.

"What's your game, Reg?" I asked, sensing the old fellow was about to shanghai the conversation. He was making a mockery of my earlier concern about some poor bugger having to entertain him.

"Blackjack and poker," he replied, his eyes lighting up and threatening to set fire to the tablecloth.

"That's right, I thought I saw you at the tables the other night. You was playing blackjack wasn't you?" proffered Phil, in his peculiar distortion of the English language.

"Yes indeed, I won nine hundred pounds, but that was a fraction of what I won in a poker tournament in London just before boarding," he proudly proclaimed.

Bloody Hell, I thought, here I am lucky some nights to count to ten and here's this old codger with the 'marbles' to gamble professionally.

"But you haven't always been a gambler, have you Reg?" I asked, failing to keep the awe out of my voice.

"Oh, good gracious no!" he giggled, "I was an actuary for over forty years; rather good with figures I was, hence my move into cards."

And so, let me reiterate; never again will I fall into the trap of judging a book by its cover, and never again will I underestimate the sage-like powers of the aged.

CHAPTER 29
BARGING IN BURGUNDY

It was a breathtaking sight, as my focused gaze settled on a petite derrière wrapped in a tight-fitting pair of white denim cutoffs.

She could not have been a day over twenty. Her pretty, tanned face beamed a warm welcome as the words fell from a sensuous mouth.

"Bonjour Monsieur, Bonjour!

"Bonjour," I enthusiastically replied, happy with my practiced French accent, knowing full well I probably had not fooled her into thinking that I was anything but a large foreigner, probably an American.

The fact that I was sitting on the barge, 'Art De Vivre', on a narrow canal in Burgundy, an overweight sixty-year-old, slurping a glass of the region's famous 'rouge', was probably hint enough. Add to that, the shockingly decadent sight of my better half, Lady Barnett, a woman of discerning taste and prodigious appetites, immersed in a bubbling jacuzzi, sipping champagne, then the young woman should have been in no doubts about our lack of French genes.

I watched in fascination as she plied her craft as an 'eclusier' – a lock keeper – an occupation that for centuries had been essential to the health of the French economy. In modern times, however, food and produce are transported overland, and the canals are generally reserved for tourists. They churn up the shallow, narrow waterways in small self-drive boats or larger, exclusive barges that charge a fortune. Guests are offered a slow and outstanding view of the French countryside, while hoovering up sumptuous feasts and fine wine.

The girth of my now fast-growing belly bore ugly testament to the expertise of a delightful chef who toiled tirelessly in the small, hot galley, whipping up an impressive selection of gastronomic delights.

He explained to me that the young lady was probably a student, making a little money in the busy holiday season. She stood in stark contrast to the other professionals who manned the dozens of locks through which we'd already passed. No gender barrier here. There were fat, chain smoking monsieurs, ageing overweight madams, and skinny whippet like chaps, who all had one thing in common. They smiled and 'bonjoured' us to death, rarely showing ill temper or bad manners; a perfect advertisement for grand French hospitality.

For all I knew, they may well have been cursing us under their breath, mercilessly slagging off at the indulgent, wine swilling bastards who parade past them in vast flotillas, making them feel hopelessly overworked and underpaid.

Ah, barging through Burgundy, or the Loire, or Bordeaux! Could anything be more appealing to a culturally deprived antipodean looking to discover the charm of history-rich France, and the promise of apparently superior vintners and fine cuisine?

Why then are we Australians, and Americans for that matter, suckers for this type of holiday option? The cynics may contend that it has everything to do with the plonk! Hold on though, the stuff we drink and (rarely) spit back home is not half bad either. Our fusion cuisine, which has benefited from a vast multi-cultural mix, is also bloody good! Surely, it is not simply a matter of what we put into our mouths.

Now, don't laugh, but I think I know why, and it is all to do with the eyes. The thing is, Australians are just not attuned to taking in lush, green, countryside and verdant forests. It is a vastly different aesthetic for those of us who hail from the bottom of the world. The bush back home has a rugged beauty, which appeals to some; that's if the flies don't pick you up and carry you off, the glare doesn't blind you, or a deadly snake or spider doesn't take a bite out of you. In France, you aren't likely to meet a grisly end, short of liver cirrhosis, as they have few venomous snakes, and their bite is rarely fatal.

Not to disappoint the adventurous types, however, there is wild boar that roam the forests in huge numbers, ravaging the countryside. However, according to a knowledgeable French friend, the only way you're likely to die, is at the hands of a hunter and his stray bullet.

So, there you are, an Australian in France is going to be considerably safer and a tad more comfortable surrounded by nature. Add to this, the lure of the long and exotic history, and you may glean some clues as to why barging holds such appeal to the average Aussie.

Everything is so bloody old, medieval even, in stark contrast to the 'land girt by sea', where the oldest dwelling dates back to shortly after Jimmy Cook planted his stockinged feet on the sands of Botany Bay in 1770.

Yes, we are in awe, even intimidated by the frogs' rich history, which has seen them hone their culinary skills, churn out plonk to an extremely high standard, and successively snub their collective nose at the rest of the world.

And here we are downunder, still boasting about the quality of our four and twenty pies, and outstanding taste of our very beautiful beers.

Is it any wonder that Australians fancy a holiday on the barges in Burgundy or Bordeaux? Vive La France!

CHAPTER 30
CHECKING OUT THE CHEF

They must feel as exposed as a bare bum on sun-soaked Bondi Beach.

I refer to that small, rotund bunch of celebrity chefs, who seemingly infest our television screens, and influence a good deal of what we thrust into our eager, salivating mouths.

Where am I going with this you may justifiably ask?

On a recent trip to France and the United Kingdom, which was always going to be an energetic exploration of the good life, I persuaded the better half, Lady Barnett, to visit the quaint Cornish coastal village of Padstow.

The visit came after three weeks in France, where we ate and drank ourselves to a standstill; firstly, in the scrumptious restaurants of Paris and then on another gourmet barge cruise through the famous Burgundy wine region. A spirited search for succulent seafood followed on the Brittany and Normandy coastline.

Needless to say, when we finally made it to Padstow we were gastronomically jaded, wine soaked, travel weary and perhaps understandably, several kilos heavier! Yes, I know it's a tough life, but someone's gotta do it!

At any rate, a trip to this seagull infested fishing village had been on my bucket list, since I first spotted a native of the area, spruiking its unique charms on a television program.

I refer, of course, to that rumpled, rambling TV chef, Rick Stein.

Now, Mr Stein is one of those strange fellows who, because of his rough head and engaging, effervescent personality, has a magnetic power to get you in; to make you intensely interested in what tumbles from his mouth. He used to be the struggling chef of his own modest little restaurant, until someone in the BBC tapped him on the shoulder and suggested he stick his head up on TV and talk about food. He did, and twenty years later, he oversees a veritable epicurean empire and syndicated television presence in countries across the globe.

In that time, I have watched him steadily get fatter, balder and more accomplished in the complicated art of television presentation. He is a passionate man, and it comes across in spades, as he animatedly talks about his favourite subject – food!

He does so without a hint of ostentation, snobbery or pretension. He is what I call a natural, and I am a fan of the likeable, loquacious lump!

Therefore, we found ourselves driving into the once-sleepy little town Stein has helped make famous. You know you've made it when they call the place 'Padstein'. It was certainly not asleep; the joint was heaving! Lily white, bare legged, holidaying Brits, screaming children in tow, swarmed all over the place.

The sun was miraculously out, and a reservation awaited us at Stein's up market eatery simply called, The Seafood Restaurant.

Life was good!

It was with no small amount of anticipation we approached the TV chef's renowned restaurant, only to be comprehensively overwhelmed by evidence of his notoriety.

First, there was Rick Stein Fisheries, a long, low building housing huge fish tanks and refrigerated slabs of fresh seafood, doing a booming business. Next door was another asset bearing his name and best described as an up-market deli, selling a dazzling array of produce again emblazoned with his autograph. There was Rick Stein wine, Rick Stein preserves, Rick Stein pates!

God almighty, I thought, could this be the same seemingly shy, self-effacing bloke I'd been watching on television all these years.

But wait, there's more! There was a Stein's fish and chip shop, no doubt for the frazzled Poms, Stein's hotel, Stein's patisserie and another restaurant bearing the name St Petroc, also a Stein asset.

By the time we reached the front door of Rick's restaurant, I was all-Steined out!

Now, don't get me wrong; I have nothing against rampant success, but I was left with the impression that my mate, Rick was spreading himself a wee bit thin. As Lady Barnett put it, "I wonder if he has a golf apparel range". A tad unkind maybe, but I trust you get the idea!

The fact that Mr Stein had also travelled to our homeland to set up another high profile eatery in Mollymook, on the New South Wales south coast, goes to prove he is no slouch as an entrepreneur looking for far-flung opportunities.

Such was our eagerness to savour some of Rick's fine food that we were among the first to 'darken his door'. We were shown to a table in the centre of the restaurant, close to a large circular bar, (someone knew we were coming). It was bustling with staff preparing to do battle with what was obviously going to be a packed lunchtime sitting. There was an impressive, no nonsense body language about the waiters from the get go. There were certainly plenty of them, translating into a not inconsiderable wages bill.

My attention was drawn to the Polish waiter who hovered over me with the concentrated concern of a doctor looking after a seriously ill patient.

"Do you have any questions, sir?"

A brief conference with Lady Barnett ensued and the critical decisions made.

We settled on a couple of little tasters before the entrée. Large plump local oysters and a couple of langoustines, not much bigger than our Australian king prawns. They passed the test, though quite a bit of work was required to prise the wee morsel from its shell.

Entrées followed; mussels in a white wine and garlic sauce for me and courgette flowers stuffed with prawn and pork for the blushing bride.

Now, after savouring moules (mussels) regularly on our gastronomic tour of France, I had the perfect opportunity for comparison and fair dues to Mr Stein, his won the contest. They were plump and tasty. Lady Barnett also applauded her zucchini flowers and the world was at peace.

Our polish waiter, Voytek, meanwhile, ran around the table like a small bantam rooster on the hunt. He knew his stuff and proved it conclusively when he solved a vexing problem that had plagued my better half. She hadn't been able to find a chardonnay that met her demanding requirements and refined 'Aussie palate.' Even the French had often failed in their offerings. On more than one occasion, she threatened to spark an international incident when describing a Chablis offered to her as insipid and thin.

"I like an oaky, buttery chardonnay," she explained to Voytek, my now second best friend.

The little fellow's brow furrowed in deep concern and concentration before his face lit up with a satisfied smile.

" Madam, he said," I think I have the one."

Good God no, I thought, my natural cynicism expecting the recommended offering to cost somewhere over the 200 pound range.

"It's a Sicilian chardonnay – a Planeta," he said, clearly trying to reign in his excitement over the brilliant suggestion.

I quickly focused on the wine list looking for this Sicilian gem and more particularly its cost.

There it was; 50 pounds, about 85 Aussie dollars.

Acceptable, I thought, Voytek was looking good!

He ran off like a scalded cat to fetch the fine wine he was convinced would bring a satisfied smile to Lady Barnett's face. By the time he returned a loud drum roll was pulsating in my expectant head.

"Here it is madam, the wine that will change your life!" he proudly proclaimed.

You little bullshitter, I thought. Nevertheless, I watched on with no small degree of perverse fascination as Rhonda lifted the glass to her expectant lips.

Now, I could simply say she appeared to like it, but that would not do the startled reaction justice. Her head snapped back, her eyes appeared to roll and a radiant smile, the likes of which I have rarely seen, creased her flushed face.

It appeared my wife's search for an oaky, buttery chardonnay in Europe had come to a 'happy ending'!

I don't know who was happier, Voytek, who looked like he'd just won lotto or Lady Barnett, who seemed to have been transported into something resembling a post orgasmic state.

Well, as you could imagine, after that proceedings went extremely well, lobster thermidor for the bride, seafood pie for me, and of course another bottle of Planeta Chardonnay.

My search for Rick Stein continued, but sadly, he was not to be seen.

Probably at the fisheries, I thought, helping out, or maybe in the deli signing autographs.

However, in the end, you know, it didn't matter because the standard of this fine celebrity chef's establishment was not at all compromised by his obviously busy schedule.

CHAPTER 31
BRUISED BUTTOCKS, BATTERED TESTICLES

"You're just too bloody old to do that!"

Now, they don't say it, but there can be no doubt it's exactly what cruise lines mean when they tout their highly priced excursions, designed to add a little adventure to the genteel pastime of cruising the world's oceans.

'Not for the wheelchair bound', they say, going so far as to give a fitness rating required to indulge in the activity. What they don't appear to understand, though, is you don't have to be confined to a wheelchair to be woefully ill suited to some of the 'Action Jackson' activities they offer. Many of their largely geriatric clientele are quite delusional about the state of their health.

It is a minefield for both cruiser and cruise line. For many an 'old timer' an ill-considered excursion could lead to a large refrigerator located in the bowels of the ship. This is where his or her body is quietly kept, until it's offloaded at the next port.

Passengers dying of old age and natural causes is a sad fact of life for cruise operators, but they try to minimize the carnage, and need for more refrigerator space by advising their guests to be careful in their excursions choices.

A recent experience in the Azores, a few specks of Portuguese rock in the North Atlantic, illustrates how careful one has to be. My wife, Lady Barnett to those who know her well, is an energetic lass, who fancies herself and her hubby to be first class adventurers and up for anything.

Waking me from a deep slumber, she informed me we would be going on a 'whale and dolphin watching cruise' when we arrived in the Azores. How hard could that be, I thought. I nodded agreement to her suggestion, and so set in motion a day that will be forever remembered.

Along with the other 'grey nomads', we made our way to the marina area, to board the super-fast 'zodiacs' that would take us to observe one of nature's great mysteries, the migration of the Sperm Whale. We would also be treated to playful dolphins, cavorting in the waters off the small islands; on paper a rather enticing prospect.

We had been warned, of course, that the activity was on the high side of difficult. A picture of three figures meant to illustrate on a scale of 1 to 3 that this was the toughest activity available.

How tough could it be watching a bunch of large mammals from a boat, I thought.

I would soon find out!

We had also been cautioned that no guest with back/neck/joint problems/mobility concerns or pregnant women should indulge in this activity; though the likelihood of a pregnant passenger being found anywhere near the ship was beyond remote.

However, the warnings were there to be taken seriously. A quick perusal of the old folks who signed up for the excursion didn't convincingly persuade me that all of them were up for the job. Just getting into the bloody little zodiacs would test more than a few of them, I thought.

Equipped with waterproof coats and bright orange life vests, the adventurers were dispatched to their respective craft after being given a 20 minute briefing on the possibility of seeing absolutely nothing. Nature, they told us, could not be manipulated or controlled to magically produce these denizens of the sea, who boast the largest brain of any creature known to have lived on Earth.

It was not what we wanted to hear, but certainly reasonable to cover their arses.

The first hint of trouble came with loud groans from Helen in the seat behind me. The boat was still tied to the dock and the male driver and female guide were attempting to get her to straddle the seat on which she would sit to 'enjoy' the 3-hour experience.

"My legs won't work," she told them, something I related to as I had almost fallen out of the craft trying to get one leg over the 3-foot high seat. It was not an auspicious start to the adventure. Lady Barnett achieved the feat with less fuss, a discernible amount of pride and a small smirk after her accomplishment.

After a struggle of some five minutes, Helen was lifted upon the high bench that bore little resemblance to a seat. It was nothing more than a seven-inch-wide piece of solid padding positioned between the legs, which for both sexes was hellishly uncomfortable. It contradicted every definition of a 'seat' designed to accommodate a bum, more like a saddle and, scarily, the rodeo was just about to begin.

It was explained to us that spotters with military grade binoculars were positioned on high points around the island to call in sightings of the huge, amazing creatures. Then the pursuit began, and the problems started.

The staccato burst of excited Portuguese language over the craft's radio alerted Manuel, the skipper of the flimsy craft, to the presence of a pod of sperm whales not far away.

Within seconds, the brutal attack on my testicles and buttocks began.

The boat accelerated to an impossibly swift speed and the chase was on. However, this was not a serene lake with a glassy surface. It was the bloody Atlantic Ocean, full of white caps and relentless swells. The little boat hit each wave crest and became airborne before crashing into a watery trough with a loud bang, accompanied by the frenzied screeching of excited and, no doubt, terrified elderly adventurers. My baseball cap went overboard in the first hour leaving my thinning 'scone' to the ravages of a hot sun.

Inner thighs had never had such a workout, private parts a battering, but there was nothing erotic about this experience and the groans were not orgasmic.

The guide and skipper were, however, thrilled to come up with the 'aquatic goods', and no time was wasted in getting the intrepid tourists to the next pod of whales and dolphins. The battering continued unabated, our pain momentarily ameliorated by the sight of these majestic mammals and playful antics of the dolphins. It was bloody fantastic! But please, go easy on the balls!

"Are you comfortable and happy," the delightful guide would bellow from time to time.

"No, we are bloody well not," screamed the bride, who was showing the first signs of wearying of the adventure.

It may have been the assorted groans of the old folks and heartfelt expressions of appreciation that resulted in our adventure coming to an end. "We will head back now," declared our guide, encountering no opposition to the suggestion.

We raced back home to the mothership, to lick our wounds (not literally) and tend to our respective bruised and battered private parts, after our adventure on the Atlantic Ocean.

CHAPTER 32
GETTING DOWN AND BROWN IN DC

Of all the ingredients that go into shaping the complicated make-up of a human being, I believe the most interesting characteristic or trait is vanity!

I came to this conclusion on a recent trip to Washington DC, throbbing U.S. capital, seat of government and hiding place of George W Bush, or the 'Moron in Chief', as political opponents liked to call him.

Weather conditions in the city were surprisingly mild, but in general the harsh winters are renowned for producing some of the palest people on the planet, and an incessant exposure to politics cited as the principal reason for creating this phenomenon.

Therefore, I reasoned this would be a perfect environment to find a tanning studio. It was an opportunity to add a dash of colour to those lily-white legs some of my mates had made disparaging remarks about on the tennis court.

With another cruise looming large, it would just not do for two Aussies to board a luxury liner looking as though we'd just emerged from years inside a refrigerator, dispelling any notion that all Aussies are bronzed beauties.

So with a guiding hand from our hosts, Susan and Jared, exceedingly white Washingtonians, we located "Palm Beach Tans". Just days old and running specials, we were assured this was just the place to do the makeover. Upon our arrival we were greeted by a young, white, and I mean white (not even a hint of a healthy glow), freckled lass with a large metal bolt pierced through her left eyebrow.

Immediately behind this super sales girl was row upon row of a tanning product bearing the name AUSTRALIAN GOLD, along with a picture of a prancing kangaroo. Suppressing the urge to laugh, I reflected on the idiocy of a very white couple from 'downunder' coming ten thousand miles to get a fake tan.

Stunned by the discovery of a truckload of Aussie tanning products,

I immediately adopted an American accent, not wishing to shatter the staff's perception of 'all things Aussie'.

In the meantime, Rhonda briefed the lass on our upcoming cruise and warned her we had no wish to come out 'the other end' looking like a couple of dark, wrinkled walnuts. After her chat, she was led off to be introduced to the magic of the 'mystic super tanning booth'.

While I waited, I pondered which of the numerous, young nubile staff was going to get the honour of disrobing me and spraying my elderly, pale body using, I guessed, a similar technique to that employed in a smash repair shop.

The question would be very quickly answered.

Rhonda was soon back, and directing me to the booth at the rear of the salon.

There I received the shocking news. I would not be undressed by anyone! I would have to do that myself, and what's more, in my naked, lonely state, I was expected to smear a white, creamy goo between my fingers and toes (for what reason I had no idea).

The next step involved standing on two footpads, about three feet apart. Now, if you are a male over the age of fifty, you would understand that this is not a particularly easy feat. With sagging genitalia, just inches from the floor (because of your splayed position, not the size of said appendages), you are then expected to hold your arms out in front, wrists rotated, fingers pointing to the floor, resembling the "karate kid" or a giant praying mantis!

If this is not ridiculous enough, you are forced to stare at three rotating nozzles, disconcertingly close to your penis! And then, hoping there are no two-way mirrors or cameras in the booth, the magic tanning process begins.

With a fine, cold mist, which you can't see because your goggles (that make you look like a mad 'kamikaze') have fogged-up, you feel your trembling body being coated and coloured.

For all of fourteen seconds this goes on. And then you're expected to pivot like a bloody ballerina, and point your rectum, much the same as you did your penis, at those three rotating nozzles. All the time remembering to reverse the angle of your wrists, this time pointing the fingers to the ceiling in an effort to achieve an even coating.

Ah, the indignity of it all!

What, you may well ask, was the result? Well, in the words of my now-bronzed bedmate, describing her appearance after the session: "I look like a bloody zebra with orange socks!"

"Not enough 'white goo' on the feet" I said, knowingly!

CHAPTER 33
ROYAL RAT

Anyone who knows my wife, Rhonda, will not be surprised by the following story.

Ever the one to seek the exotic holiday destination with a difference, she informed me that as part of a trip to the United States, organized to attend Adam and Faith Skolnik's wedding in Florida, she had booked a seven-day cruise to the Mexican Caribbean.

Suppressing the urge to rush to the medicine cabinet, to retrieve my anti-seasickness wristbands, I nodded and agreed it sounded wonderful.

Now, I could have told her I had absolutely no interest in going to the bloody Mexican Caribbean, but again, anyone who knows Rhonda, knows that would have had little effect. After all, she had spent long hours researching this trip, and besides I'd always enjoyed her elaborate itineraries in the past, hadn't I?

"Belize," she announced, "it should be great!"

Belize, I thought; that mosquito infested country at the top of South America, that I had briefly visited on assignment in 1986.

Rhonda knew this, of course, as I had regaled her with the story many times; one of the dozens of fascinating yarns told by an old journo living on past glories.

"This time you can get a proper look at the place," she told me, excitement lighting up her always-enthusiastic face.

And so, after eating and drinking our way across North America, we found ourselves eating and drinking at a furious pace on the high seas. We joined hundreds of large Americans in loud Hawaiian shirts, breasting the bar on the *'Regent Voyager'*.

I sat with them at the poolside bar for the first two days, clad in the loudest shirt I could find, and sporting my colour coordinated wristbands. They were doing a fabulous job of countering the effects of flat seas! I waited patiently for the supposed highlight of the cruise – our arrival in Belize.

"Know anything about Belize?" I asked one chap, who I'd watched drink close to a bottle of vodka in the space of twenty minutes.

"Goddamn hole," he replied, "won't bother getting off the ship!"

Why would he, I thought, the booze onboard is free, though his words, I must admit, didn't do much to titillate my anticipation of our much-touted visit to the exotic, tropical destination.

We arrived in Belize after visiting Key West, Ernest Hemingway's old stomping ground, and Cozumel, popular among American college kids, for getting pissed and raising hell.

My first glimpse of the former British Honduras came shortly after the anchor dropped; its noise waking me from my deep slumber. I opened the drapes of our impressive stateroom to take in the view, but there wasn't one. I mean nothing! A bloody flat bit of uninspiring scrub across the water, about five miles away.

Not a good start, I thought, only to be told by Rhonda that we would be tendered off the ship, because of a large barrier reef, second only to our own 'Great' one off the Queensland coast.

Understanding totally the green implications of our intrusion into this coral paradise, I helped my wife into the small tender to take us to the shore and our encounter with Belize, the compelling reason for this 'delightful' Caribbean cruise.

We were supposed to have joined a cruise line tour, which would have taken us whizzing across the mangrove swamps on airboats, a la CSI Miami, but a cock-up with the tenders sent the rest of the group whizzing and us going it alone.

"Leave it to me!" Rhonda cautioned as we waded into a group of hungry tour guides, assembled dockside to rip valuable dollars off the gringos.

She threw herself into the pack like a pit bull, while I loitered like a bad smell, ready to jump in, should any of the locals take umbrage to her enthusiastic negotiating style.

Ten minutes passed and the group thinned markedly, their faces showing despair, their dark eyes defeat at the hands of this relentless woman with a strange accent.

"What will it be, Ian, howler monkeys in the jungle, or the Mayan ruins?" she yelled across the crowded square.

"Your choice, darling," I mumbled, my eyes betraying the exhaustion of watching her manipulation of these potential tour guides.

In the end, there was one man standing and he would be our guide for a day at the Mayan ruins.

"My name is Rudolf, call me Rudy," he said, in perfectly accented English, as he led us to a large, jungle scarred van that had seen better days.

It would be the start of a memorable trip. Memorable for many reasons, not least, the expertise of this charming Belizean guide with an encyclopedic knowledge of his country and its inhabitants.

We sat like a couple of besotted parrots on a perch, hungry for the facts expounded effortlessly by this man, whose ability to feed his children had been somewhat compromised by my wife's pruning of his daily rate.

By mid-morning, I could see the guilt written all over her face. Rudy was in for a big tip. However, it was his next action that absolutely guaranteed it.

While discussing some the country's unique flora and fauna he pulled out colored photographs, including a large rodent-like creature called an 'agouti paca'.

"This animal we fed to Queen Elizabeth when she visited in 1985," he told us. "It caused quite a stir. British journalists travelling with her reported she had eaten 'Royal Rat' in Belize."

We giggled like small children in appreciation of this shocking tale, but my wife took it one step further when she asked Rudy, "Where can we get some of this agouti paca?"

Yes, folks you guessed it. If it was good enough for the Queen, it was bloody good enough for Lady Barnett and her royal taster, Moi!

This time Rudy giggled like a small child, threw the truck into second and sped off like a man possessed. He was on a quest, and I'm telling you, it wasn't hard for him to track down one of these agouti pacas!

We found it in a small roadside restaurant of not surprisingly modest appearance. I half expected to see a large heavily whiskered black rat staring out from an advertising awning, but no, our agouti paca came to us in the form of, surprise, surprise, a stew.

What did it taste like?

You've heard it all before – chicken!

CHAPTER 34
AND YOU THOUGHT YOU WERE FIT

"Jesus, you're joking!"

The blasphemy erupted from my constricted throat, as I looked up impossibly steep stone steps, disappearing into the tangled, green canopy of impenetrable jungle. We were on the Aberdeen side of Hong Kong Island.

I'd found myself there, chest burning, anus twitching, at the invitation of a dear friend and local resident, Michael Tobin, an extremely fit, sixty-year-old, who no doubt secretly wanted to show up his younger mate with a 'little walk'.

I, of course, the younger man by only a few years, was no stranger to the challenging topography of Hong Kong Island, and knew this was not going to be a cakewalk.

Equipped with a healthy ego and an inflated sense of my own fitness level, I was up for the challenge, despite a number of niggling insecurities.

I stood there watching my friend's 'bobbing, little bottom' effortlessly ascending the stairway, through eyes that were disconcertingly blinded by the sweat cascading down a wrinkled, troubled forehead.

I tried desperately to suppress the sound of my rasping, ragged breath, lest my mate think I was having a massive heart attack. Even though he was a trained nurse, the thought of him performing the "kiss of life" on me held little appeal.

Michael became a blurred figure, but every so often he would thoughtfully stop, turn back and inform me, "Not long, now!"

"Yea right, you bastard," I muttered, under my laboured breath.

To be fair, he had made it clear from the outset, the walk would last about two hours. It would take us from the low-lying area of Aberdeen, up over the famous, scenic peak and down into the chaotic centre of bustling Hong Kong, where, waiting for us was his favourite bar and several cold, frothy beers.

There it was – the magic word – beer!

However, what he didn't make clear was the lung crippling extent of the climb needed to reach the peak. On the surface, my friend was a delightful, gentle human being, but had I missed an underlying mean, sadistic streak. Was this payback time for some past unintended sleight on my part?

I returned my tortured thoughts to beer.

To many an Australian, it is the wonderful elixir of life, for which he'll undergo almost any physical challenge or frightful indignity. But to this Aussie, the thought of a beer only raised the spectre of projectile vomiting.

I cast the thought of alcohol from my addled brain, as I focused on the task ahead. This should be fun I kept saying to myself. Fabulous scenery, bearable temperatures, and a good mate to share it with, so why was it hurting so bloody much? And, why did the little bastard look like he was doing it so easy?

Had I bitten off more than I could chew?

The indignity of failure was not an option. It was a notion I quickly dismissed, despite the fact that it felt like one of my testicles had become unanchored and my liver was in the process of making its escape from my anus.

The narrow dimensions of the ever-ascending steps kept the two us trudging along in Indian file, a relief, lest Michael see the agony etched into my profusely sweating face. Conversation was sparse. Even if I wanted to chat, few words could be shaped through the ragged expulsion of air, but as is often the case, pain brought inspiration.

"Oh look," I panted "what a view!"

It bought me a couple of vital minutes to recover, without the loss of face. I walked to the grassy fringe of a rocky precipice and feigned intense interest and wonder at the extraordinary scene that lay below. Dozens of cluttered apartment buildings lining Aberdeen Harbour rose skywards like skinny, white, fingers reaching for the clouds. The sparkling South China Sea played host to dozens of huge ships and tankers navigating their way through a sprinkling of jade-coloured outer islands. It was a beautiful sight, but one which seemed to quickly bore Michael, as he urged me onwards and upwards – the bastard!

I cast my mind back to my weekly gym sessions in Sydney, where I often found myself watching attractive women and their shapely backsides work out on stair master machines. Step up; step down, again and again. Stupid bloody things I'd always thought.

Not now!!

It came to me in a rush, the blinding realisation that I had been living in a cloud of self-delusion, and was not as fit as I thought. My morning walks around the northern foreshore of Sydney Harbour, the gym sessions, meant little now as I tackled this 'death march' through the dense jungle, with a man I fantasized was intent on killing me. Funny how pain and paranoia walk hand in hand!

The first hour passed, and for a brief period we found ourselves on level ground under a cool, luxuriant umbrella of tropical vegetation. My breath returned to something resembling normal and my usual, cocky self-assurance emerged as I engaged my mate in conversation.

"Shit, it's tough mate, how often do you do this?" An insightful question, I thought, in my present condition.

"A couple of times a week," he replied, his voice normal and not a bead of perspiration in sight. Quite sick, really!

It was a quick exchange, for as we rounded a bend another stretch of steep steps came into sight. My eyes bulged, my heart sank, my legs trembled as this bloody nightmare continued.

When the famous peak finally came into sight, there was no euphoric sense of victory, no chest swelling inflation of self-esteem, no warm embrace of shared achievement. We took but a few seconds to view the fabulous city bathed in bright sunshine on this perfect winter's day, before launching ourselves into the descent leg.

And, yes, it hurt too!

Did the beer make up for it?

It helped!

CHAPTER 35
JURASSIC PARK

It was marked clearly enough, but I still had difficulty accepting that we could become a bird's lunchtime snack.

The sign loomed into sight seconds after entering a huge, netted bird aviary in the tangled, green jungles of Borneo's west coast.

It read "BEWARE OF ATTACKING BIRDS".

Now, this was a tad unnerving given the fact that we'd already remarked on how this nature reserve, once a British rubber plantation, bore an uncanny resemblance to Jurassic Park, of movie fame. The thought of some gnarly old prehistoric raptor sweeping down from high in the jungle canopy to swallow us whole (no easy feat given our respective sizes – it would have to be one bloody big raptor) sparked nervous giggles at first.

But, as the bride and I moved further into the shaded depths of this seemingly impenetrable jungle environment, we were overwhelmed by an eerie sense of foreboding, keenly sharpened by the cacophony of piercing bird screeches. One could feel hundreds of beady birdy eyes watching our every move, and being the only two tourists in this enormous cage, only served to increase the prickly discomfort of the experience.

There were tall, elegant egrets wading in the creek bed on the jungle floor, peacocks parading their colourful plumages, and brilliant, exotic parrots sweeping through the netted tree line, screeching profanities known only to them.

Baseball cap firmly planted on my sweating scone, I moved carefully, scanning the treetops for an imminent attack or more likely, a giant bird dropping, which had the potential to knock me off my feet. I giggled briefly to myself at the sight of my hatless bride, a prime target for some feathered friend intent on dumping a load.

Then we saw him, at least I think it was a he, sitting on a slightly elevated tree branch behind a long bulbous beak, following our every move.

"Look!" Rhonda screamed over the raucous utterances of this large, horrible hornbill. Clutching her newly purchased camera to a sweating face she didn't see the attack coming.

I did!

He left his perch and swooped and in one of those moments of blinding clarity, I believe our eyes met. Time was suspended, the seconds felt like hours, as he came inexorably closer.

Renowned for my quick responses in times of crisis, I did what few would not have had the wits to do. I pirouetted with the agile grace of a ballerina, crouched in the manner of a Kung Fu master and stuck my arse into the air, to intercept the angry intruder.

But, instead of feeling the stinging sensation of meat being stripped from bended buttocks, I recoiled at the sound of high-pitched laughter emanating from a familiar source. Yes, the bride!

There she stood, camera happily clicking, recording the potentially newsworthy event as the attacker came to rest just feet from my feet. His feathered head slightly cocked, his huge beak opened to affect the slightly ludicrous pose of a sly grin. He stood peering at me, his feathered form betraying the cocky assurance of a killer. I readied myself to deliver a wicked kick to his colourful head. But then, something strange happened. He turned his evil head to face the bride and in four or five jerky little hops, he made his intentions clear. Her giggles over my plight turned to nervous shrieks as the avian 'beak on legs', still screeching loudly, advanced.

"Ian – DO something!" she screamed.

Now, it was my turn to laugh, and laugh I most certainly did, though I must say, I don't know who was making more noise, the bird, the wife or me!

Squawking, screaming and laughing combined to drown out all other sounds in the oppressively humid jungle, as this dance with death played out. Finally galvanised into action at the thought of appearing to abandon the bride in her hour of need, I stepped in to show this 'would-be raptor' who was the boss.

It took some harsh words to make our feathered friend abandon his aggressive pose, but in the end, man prevailed over bird. He took flight to reclaim his haughty perch from which he could no doubt prepare his next attack on two legged intruders.

As we departed the bird enclosure, leaving our potential assassin in his huge wiry jail, we reflected on the term, 'free as a bird'.

We later discovered that it was a female Wreathed Hornbill, an omnivore, eating fruit, insects and 'small' animals. Luckily, we were a tad too large! The native tribes of Borneo consider it very lucky to have hornbills fly over their huts – obviously they don't poo while in flight!

CHAPTER 36
GOPHERS IN PARADISE

"Jeez man, you're joking, right! You don't know what a fucking gopher is?"

"We don't have 'em in Australia, mate – aren't they those hairy little buggers that dig up the ground, like in the movie, Caddyshack."

With this less than informed reply, I watch as my friend William's face turns apoplectic purple, his words producing a sudden ejaculatory explosion coating my face in warm saliva.

"You can say that again, ya dumb shit. My damn ranch looks like the Klondike after the fucking gold rush!"

This man is passionate, I conclude, and shows no sign of calming down, while warming to the annoying subject of gophers. They have systematically wreaked havoc on what's left of the lawn at his ranch house, which sits on 42 acres on the coast of central California.

"The ugliest little critters you can get, man, fucking huge front teeth that smile at yer while they're sucking the life out of yer plants and destroying yer land – little bastards!"

With this last expletive, his words trail off, his eyes glaze over and his face becomes a sad mask showing graphically the depths of despair to which he's fallen because of the dreaded gopher!

Now, to an Australian who (A) doesn't know what a gopher is (B) is a city slicker anyway and (C) never ever gets excited about any form of wildlife, William's reaction does seem a little over the top. Then I reflect; here's a guy who has lived in Tokyo for more than twenty-five years, immersed in the high-pressure world of television production with one all-consuming dream; to return home with his delightful Japanese wife, Carole, and buy a ranch. I mean, they don't have gophers in Shinjuku! It's not as though he's used to them fucking with his life, so I guess it's understandable he'd be somewhat put out when he sees the little bastards tearing up his lawn, and making his life a bloody misery.

I look at my friend, again, armed with a new sense of warmth, sympathetic to his dilemma and decide to extend a reassuring hand.

"So, mate, what are you doing about the little bastards?" I inject into the use of the last word a bit of "oomph" to impress him with my heartfelt concern.

"Shoot the little fuckers, that's what I'm doing! Got a twenty-two up there on the veranda. They stick their fucking little heads out of the hole and BANG!"

With that imaginary gunshot resounding in our ears, William's eyes light up, a flicker of smile lends to his face a look of sublime peace and contentment, but that soon disappears as I doggedly continue to probe the subject.

"How's your shot, mate, get 'em all the time?"

Before he gets a chance to answer, Carole, who I've noticed has followed the conversation closely, interjects.

"He's a dead eye – a great shot!" She too seems to have been transported into a state of gleeful anticipation, at the thought of another dead gopher littering the backyard.

"Not all the time", William declares sadly, "But I'm fixing that, I've borrowed my Dad's shotgun. It's got a bit more firepower, so the little bastards will get the message. And if that doesn't work, I've got flares to stick down the holes."

Jeez, I think, talk about being goaded by gophers. But then a quick glance at the lawn and all the ugly little mounds of dirt, testimony to the little critters industrious endeavours, I start to get it. You see, to Australians, or at least urban Aussies, the thought of resorting to gunfire is a bit dramatic, but then I reflect, who am I to judge this man? I haven't just paid millions of dollars to watch some "hairy little fuckers", in my friend's vernacular, chew up my back lawn.

"I don't know why you're getting so worked up," I helpfully proffer, "We've got wombats 'downunder' that make these little holes look like pinpricks!"

As soon as the words escape my mouth, I regret it. After all, why would he care about bloody wombats digging up half of Australia when here, before his eyes, gophers are making his lawn look like Baghdad after the bombing. He confirms my suspicions.

"Who gives a fuck about what the wombats are doing in Oz. The place is a fucking desert anyway!"

In response to this outburst I look at William sternly, but before I get a chance to vent my indignation over this rude outburst about my beloved country, my concentration is disturbed by a high pitched pulsating buzz.

"What's that?" I ask, glad to a have the potential flashpoint avoided.

"Another counter measure to get rid of the little fuckers. They're supposed to come out with their hands up, but as you can see it's not working."

And with this sad proclamation William's face clouds over, accentuating glassy eyes and tired, defeated features.

Ever sensitive to a mate's less than rosy predicament, I put my arm around his sagging shoulders and scramble to say something to lift his battered spirits.

"C'mon mate – fuck the gophers. Let's go and have a beer!"

CHAPTER 37
OUT OF AFRICA

Did you know an African Dung Beetle pushes shit backwards, careful to keep its head away from the offensive odour while propelling the precious cargo toward its ultimate destination?

It's amazing what you learn on the first day of a safari into the Dark Continent!

Our 'informant' was a big bellied, bare footed, bearded Boer guide, who drew our attention to this little-known gem by standing on his brakes, rudely jolting a number of safari folk from a deep slumber.

"Shit, have we lost the trailer?" I asked, as the van slid to the dusty shoulder of an isolated road.

"No man, I'm going to show you something special in Africa!" he responded, slamming the van into first gear and performing a dramatic U turn to get us back to one of great mysteries of the African animal kingdom.

"There," young Ettienne pointed to a section of hot bitumen, his voice filled with awe, "He's pushing shit backwards!"

"My God, look at the little bastard go," I replied enthusiastically, as a little dung beetle did his thing in the middle of the road.

I mean, how did I know this was not going to be the absolute high point of the whole safari; I'd never been on one before. And how did our guide know the beetle was a he?

My ten fellow 'Dr Livingstones', including Lady Barnett didn't seem too worked up about the little critter pushing shit five times his size, whether it was backwards, forwards or sideways. It wasn't as though he qualified to be in the "Big Five".

Ah, life on safari!

It had all started some eight hours earlier under the cover of darkness when we were picked up from our lodge in Johannesburg at 5 am, after a 13-hour flight from Sydney, and only four hours' sleep.

We weren't exactly 'bright eyed and bushy tailed', and certainly not expecting the day from hell that was going to take as long as the flight from Australia.

Our vehicular conveyance was an aging, non-air conditioned, 15-seater, Mercedes Sprinter van, with over one million kilometres on the clock. How did I know it had passed this milestone?

Ettienne proudly announced it, assuming I'd be impressed by the vast experience of his vehicle, incidentally called "Trouble". Now, that was a confidence builder!

I personally would have liked to have seen a sparkling new vehicle with a little more rubber on the wheels, but this was Africa.

Sharing 'Trouble' with us was a mixed bunch of considerably younger tourists – two Kiwis, two Poms, two Yanks and five Aussies, including Lady Barnett and myself. The average age was probably around thirty. This was not an Abercrombie and Kent all-inclusive African romp for the rich and famous.

An essential part of this newfound freedom we were to discover was music – loud music. A speaker, just inches from my head produced a sound akin to a sonic boom, leaving my shoulders coated in ear wax and my sphincter twitching. Got a lot of exercise over the years, that sphincter!

For 12 solid hours our senses were comprehensively assaulted by every conceivable genre of head-banging music; reggae, hip-hop, rap, electronic and raucous rock. They all got a go!

Where were Perry Como and Nat King Cole when you needed them?

Six hours into Day One and Lady Barnett and I shared one of those rarefied moments when our eyes and minds met and we were in complete sync (yes it is possible). No words necessary, because her formidable antenna picked up my telepathic attempts to communicate.

"Don't look at me, you researched and bloody well booked it!"

Thirteen interminable hours on the road on top of thirteen in the air, with bugger all sleep and two hot and dusty 'old farts' emerged from 'Trouble' looking like they had just undergone an intensive session of electric shock treatment.

Seconds after pulling up at the Elephant Sands Lodge in Botswana, almost a thousand kilometres from Johannesburg, we naturally fled to the bar for a cold beer.

A burning, red African sun was in the final phase of warming the earth and a bright, full moon was looming large, as more than twenty huge elephants crowded around the waterhole, just metres away from us, quenching their thirst after a long day's march.

It was the quintessential African experience delivered to us on a plate on the first night of our safari.

Copius quantities of beer and a soft bed rounded off the dusty day on the road, but our Boer guide had plans for an early start and we soon found ourselves on a bushwalk through elephant country.

In the pre-walk briefing he told us with a straight face that, if we found ourselves, and it was a remote possibility, of being charged by one of the huge beasts, we were to stand very still. That's right, don't run! Elephants, he said have poor eyesight and hearing, but amazing smell. Great, I thought, I hadn't changed my clothes in 2 days, I was buggered.

A quick look around at fellow adventurers in the group and I had the distinct impression there were a few runners amongst us. I prayed no one would be tested as Lady Barnett and I were the oldest, and would be easily trampled by the huge beasts, not to mention our fellow travellers. But first, we would have to find the noble creatures, and to that end our guide carried a small stick, which he took great relish in plunging into the huge mounds of elephant poo scattered around the area.

"This", he told us, "will tell me how long ago the herd passed by."

Ingenious, I thought, but I was hoping the smelly piles of dung were 'stone cold' as I had no wish to stare-down an elephant and stand very still, a concept I had great difficulty comprehending.

The Boer's bush craft was impressive as he explained all the tricks of the trade in tracking down Africa's vast array of animals. An avid reader of Wilbur Smith novels, I was well acquainted with such terms as spoor, and familiar with the many dangers lurking in the bush.

Not only could Ettienne examine the large, steaming piles and tell when the elephant had last passed, but he could discern its age and sex, a truly remarkable skill. He was a bona fide 'poo expert'.

His efforts on the walk, however, failed to produce one of these magnificent animals, so it was back to the van, and a drive to where he knew for certain there was a sizeable pachyderm population.

We found them, dozens of 'Dumbos' in all shapes and sizes, from old bulls to babies splashing about in a shallow river that cut through the dry bushland.

Camera's worked overtime, as the smiling faces in our little tour group could not disguise their delight at witnessing this extraordinary sight. But it was just the start!

We were instructed to re-board 'Trouble' to be taken to see one of the great sights in Africa, albino lions of which there were very few on the continent.

The enthusiastic group was handed over to another expert, a small African man, who had reared two of the albinos since birth. To assist him were another four young guides who formed a perimeter around us as we set off on a bushwalk, with the big white lions ambling alongside.

"They are reasonably tame," he assured us, but as an added precaution everyone was given a long wooden staff or pole to be carried on the walk.

I assumed this was just in case the lions got hungry along the way, and fancied a bit of white meat. I posed the question to our head guide who assured me he and his men were there to make sure that did not happen, a comforting thought.

"We haven't lost anyone yet," he said "but there's always a first time, I guess," he offered with a smile.

Ah, a man with a sense of humour, I thought, clasping my long pole a little tighter.

It was a truly unique experience. The huge lions were well-behaved, never wandering far from the walkers and obligingly letting out the odd roar for theatrical effect.

The safari was progressing nicely, but on balance, on a weight for age basis, it was hard not to award the African Dung Beetle top points.

Certainly not as impressive or large as members of the 'Big Five' but most assuredly one of the world's great wonders!

CHAPTER 38

A HOLE IN NONE

So, you're in the United Kingdom and fancy a spot of golf.

Where better than the birthplace of the ancient game, Bonny Scotland, that windswept, frosty, heather patch; home to fierce mountain clans that have, since the dawn of time, spurned the advances of the English heathens, in the same way a young virgin repels the fumbling fingers of an eager lad – with a wee hatchet!

The birthplace of scotch whiskey and an unintelligible brogue that defies all attempts to resemble the English language; the homeland of Robbie Burns, the famed poet, who once described the game of golf as "that bloody silly pastime where grown men go in search of hole in which to place their balls."

It was in defiance of Mr Burn's cynical view that we went in search of not a Scotsman, but a wee Welshman, recently domiciled to this barren, northern Celtic stronghold. The husband of my cousin Trish, he was a man among men, who, because of a perverse genealogical coincidence, had been fated to live in the shadow of well-known actor, Omar Shariff.

But, that fact aside, I'd heard from the grapevine, that since swapping his rugby ball for a golf club, he'd made admirable headway in reducing his handicap to single figures.

He was the boyo, I decided, who would give me an insight into the legendary Scottish golf scene.

Upon our arrival in the historic village of Aberdour, perched perilously close to the turgid waters of the Firth of Forth, I commenced my search. Without an address I was at a distinct disadvantage, however, equipped with sharp, deductive powers, I made my first stop. The pub!

Just minutes earlier, I had dropped Rhonda, at a local B&B to exercise her supreme negotiating skills, and find a warm bed for the night.

In answer to my query at the pub came the reply, "Aye, we know 'im; that be Omar of the Vallies" thundered patron, Bernard McTacky.

"Good lad for a Welshman too," he allowed.

"Yes, he'd be the boy with the 'come to bed' eyes," commented a barmaid, with a nose longer than John Holmes penis.

Rejoicing in the news, I settled down to taste the local brew and try to understand this ancient language that tumbled out of the locals' mouths like porridge from a cereal bowl.

"You like your golf around here then" I asked McTacky, whose ruddy face sported more potholes than an Australian outback track.

"Oh aye, we invented the bloody game, and we do ave an affection for it," he said.

"And where be St Andrews," I quizzed, imagining my silly singsong delivery was close to what this bloke could understand.

"A bloody long way from 'ere," he said, with the hint of humor creasing his weathered face.

"You wouldna wanta play it there, neither," he offered. "It'll cost ya a friggin fortune!"

Emboldened by this man's challenge of my capacity to pay for a round of golf, I shot back, "and how much would that be then?"

"Oh, close to a hundred quid, I should a think, and then there'd be the caddie, another twenty, and have you not got your own clubs? Aye, I thought not, that'll be another twenty quid".

With my face betraying the shock, I began the mental effort of making the conversion to Australian dollars.

"Shit, or should that be shite in Scotland", I thought, that's over three hundred and fifty bucks".

With his beady eyes twinkling, Bernard shot me a look of triumph on discovering he'd pricked my balloon.

"Bit rich", I conceded, "but you're only in Scotland once", thinking to myself, yea right – say goodbye to St Andrews.

At this point in the animated conversation there came a scream from the back of the bar, "Omar me boy, get in 'ere. There's someone to see ya, its yer cousin from Australia".

As I shook Christopher's hand and took him into a warm embrace I thought to myself, geez he does look a bit Arabic, I wonder if this is the right time to be consorting.

But then, that wonderful lilting Welsh accent hit me and I cast those unkind thoughts from my mind.

"I play off six now," he confirmed with the justifiably proud look of a man who'd worked a bloody miracle in the ten years since I'd last hit the links with him in Wales.

I, in stark contrast, had not improved my game and was forced to admit, shamefacedly, the fact that my handicap had stayed static. It had quite possibly blown out, but I wasn't going to tell him that over a beer. I'd let him discover that on the course.

With McTacky hovering in the background, I drunkenly suggested that he should take me to St Andrews.

"But Ian," he said, "it's bloody expensive".

With the potholed patron looking straight at me, I told Chris, "mate, money is no object – you're only in Scotland once!"

Two hours later, as we limped arm in arm from the bar, the thought of swinging a golf club in the foreseeable future caused the bile in my stomach to send warnings to my brain.

But that was not a new sensation. During the course of this grand tour it seemed we'd been in a perpetual state of 'pissiness'. A beer buzz had comfortably settled over me making deep thought a virtual impossibility.

So, the next day, nursing a wee hangover, we set out for St. Andrews, the Royal and Ancient Club itself; aptly named, I thought, by the look of some of the old geezers swinging a club on the first tee.

A closer inspection revealed that not one of the old gentlemen was under the age of eighty, and all of them, seemingly proud graduates from the school of 'shocking pants'. Americans, I thought. No doubt about it, as I jammed on a pair of sunglasses, to protect my eyes from the colorful assault of their garb.

And, striding alongside these old blokes were equally ancient, coiffured wives, babbling inanities, much to the consternation of bemused local caddies, who probably couldn't understand what the hell the old girls were saying anyway. They all looked terribly 'well to do', and likely candidates for mention in the latest Forbes world's richest list.

Old Bernard McTacky may be right, I thought. It was probably not worth asking how much to play.

As my perusal of the scene continued, another fact became abundantly clear. There appeared to be more Japanese gents here than in downtown Tokyo. They moved with casual ease, but they'd left the little ladies at home and unlike their American mates, donned a less garish golf garb.

But still, there was the unmistakable stench of money about them, reinforcing the view that it may not be the day to take on St Andrews.

Chris appeared more than happy to allow me to indulge my fantasy, all the while knowing his golf clubs would remain safely in the boot of the car.

As for Rhonda, there was never a doubt. Once the asking price for a round threatened to hit the fifty-pound mark, her Scottish ancestors no doubt sent out telepathic messages, advising against the financial imprudence of this rash action (her middle name's not Stewart for nothing!)

She became quite indignant, however, after being politely asked to vacate the Royal and Ancient Golf Club premises when she wandered in to 'spend a penny'. They apparently don't have 'ladies loos' in the clubhouse as women are not allowed! This was a rude shock to someone who has always considered herself 'one of the boys'. "Bloody Dickensian" she announced after her undignified expulsion!

So there we were, pathetically posing for pictures, with the rich guys in the background looking very smug.

It was at this point I shared with my companions a fantasy I'd nurtured for years.

It centered, I told them, on St Andrew's legendary eighteenth hole, lined with old hotels, on whose balconies, during the British Open sit serious spectators, nursing alcoholic beverages.

It had been my dream, I confided, to slice a ball out of play smack bang into the middle of these old pisspots and watch them scatter. A psychologist, I mused, would have a field day explaining this anti-social behaviour. But there it was, an undeniable example of playful Aussie tomfoolery.

Responding to this story, Chris suggested we make a move before I acted out my fantasy. He would take us, he said, to his club for a round. It was not up to the international prominence of St Andrews, he confessed, but it would offer us an unforgettable taste of 'hacking in the heather'.

And what was his club's name, I enquired.

"Burnt Island", he replied.

"Oh," I said, thinking I'd heard him say Burnt Island.

Strange name, I thought. What, I wondered, had burnt the bloody Island.

Soon to be my scorching iron play, I offered, without so much as a giggle.

As we drove past rolling fields of rape, a brilliant yellow flower that carpeted the countryside, I began the mental preparation needed to be on top of my game. Rhonda too, appeared to be concentrating, whispering to herself some secret mantra, which would propel her ball past her previous longest drive of a hundred metres.

Chris drove with the grim determination of a man ready to shoot a sub-par round, heavy rainfall making his task all the more difficult.

As we neared the golf course, which lay at the edge of the River Forth, slanting sheets of icy rain and gusting winds increased our anticipation.

Ah, golf in Scotland!

The sound of pounding rain assaulted our eardrums. "Don't worry about the weather," I offered. But as the words fell from my mouth, an ear-splitting thunderclap prompted three heads to hit the lined roof of the car.

"Nothing like a wee bit of weather to make a game interesting", said Omar.

Yeah right, I thought, as long as we aren't blown into the bloody river.

Now the game of golf for me has always held a fascination, as distinct from passion. I've played on courses all around the world. Sometimes well, most times poorly, but always with enthusiasm, and a barely controlled temper which surfaces usually after every second shot.

As I stood on the first tee of this minor Scottish golf course, watching the marvelously fluid swing of Chris Bradshaw, and the windblown figure of Rhonda, I couldn't help but feel exhilarated at the prospect of what lay ahead.

Of course, the driving rain and whipping wind obscured much of what did actually lay ahead, but we were certainly not going to let that put a damper on this day.

If golf wasn't hard enough, I thought, under clear blue Australian skies, it was certainly going to be a tester under these threatening black clouds, that looked like they held half the content of the nearby North Sea.

Peeking out of a flapping, water soaked, hooded wind jacket, Rhonda gave a brave smile, as mascara ran down her sodden face into a semi open mouth.

Chris, meanwhile, stood casually looking like this was another perfect day in 'golfing heaven'. No doubt an attempt to unsettle me, and gain a psychological edge, in what was shaping up to be a one-sided contest.

As I hooked my ball into a thick hedge bordering the roadway, that barely controlled temper I alluded to earlier, started to rear its ugly head.

The sight of Rhonda's ball consistently sailing short but straight didn't help, and Omar's two hundred-and-fifty-meter professional efforts left me shaken.

This was not a good start. And worse was to follow.

Much has been said over the years, about the difficulty of playing on Scottish links courses. American pros have been filmed shaking their heads, swearing never to return after shooting scores more commonly recorded on ladies day at the local goat track. And, for some reason a common hazard for golfers around the world, trees, refuse to grow on Scottish golf courses.

Nowhere can be heard that familiar 'thwack' of ball hitting wood, followed by a stream of expletives.

I had been told, however, that it is not uncommon to see small golfers being blown across fairways, no doubt cursing the lack of trees that may have supplied an anchor point, or at least some protection from torrential rain.

With this in mind, I watched Omar carefully, lest he be one of the links victims whose bodies are found washed up beside the river days later, still grasping a three iron.

This is just one of the hazards to be considered when playing golf in Scotland. There is another one, far more dangerous and demoralizing.

It's called 'The Rough' and believe me, rough it is!

We call it grass in Australia. We mow it, cows eat it, dogs crap on it, snakes slide through it, but in Scotland, they grow it to make golfers' lives a misery.

Waist high in many places off the fairways, this grass provides an impenetrable barrier to even the strongest of the male species.

Nurtured by heavy rainfall and gale force winds, it possesses super strength and can be seen grabbing players' golf clubs, twisting them, and penalizing the hapless hacker to a point where suicide is often the preferred option, over a drink on the nineteenth.

Caught in a patch of this high grass myself, I am still at a loss to explain how, after a lusty swing and contact, my ball ended up fifty yards BEHIND me. It simply defies the law of physics.

To a Scotsman, of course, this is 'par for the course'. But to my Welsh cousin-in-law, it was the source of enormous mirth, not matched in his fifty odd years on earth.

How he had time to control his laughter and swing a golf club, I'll never know. The sight and sound of me cursing from the depths of the rough, to the image of Rhonda being dragged along behind an out-of-control motorized golf cart, made for a load of merriment.

All this in the midst of torrential rainfall not seen since Noah led the animals onto the ark.

Ah, golf in Scotland!

CHAPTER 39
BEER O'CLOCK IN PRAGUE

More than five decades have passed since the ominous roar of Russian tanks resonated through the cobbled streets of Prague, the capital of the Czechoslovakia.

The sound of Soviet subjugation has been replaced by the happy chatter of tourists, crowding the historic streets to experience what is undoubtedly one of Europe's most beautiful cities.

For those who remember Prague as the dreary backdrop for cold war espionage thrillers, be assured, the Czech capital has moved out of the dark shadows of communism, to unashamedly embrace tawdry, but colourful capitalism.

It's seen on every street corner, in every restaurant and bar, famous for the strong local beers, which have garnered the Czechs an international reputation as brew masters. However, the amber fluid is just one reason tourists now flock to Prague.

In all of Europe's tourist offerings, cities like Paris and London may be mentioned more often, but Prague in recent years has carved out a reputation as a sleeping gem; a city offering visitors rich history, grand architecture, friendly locals and yes, good, cold, cheap beer.

However, not even the superior flavour of its brews succeeded in attracting much attention from tourists in the dark years of political oppression and unrest. Czechoslovakia was largely closed to the west, firmly oppressed under the iron-fisted domination of its neighbour to the north. Then in 1989, a popular uprising known as the Velvet Revolution (because there was practically no carnage) swept the communists from power. The once dour, local population, schooled by their Russian masters to reject the excesses of the democratic bourgeois, soon discovered the value of a market economy. The Czech Republic's experiment with capitalism started in earnest and in the intervening years, there has been ample evidence of a dynamic revitalisation, leading to an explosion in tourism numbers.

So what is it about Prague that makes it such an enjoyable tourist destination?

Visitors quickly fall under the exotic spell of the city, which boasts a rich history dating back to the ninth century, when Prague Castle was built, the largest ancient castle in the world.

They trek up quaint narrow streets from the old town on a muscle-crunching journey to St Vitus Cathedral, at the centre of the ancient castle grounds, and surrounded by a number of Palaces occupied by Czech Kings through the ages.

However, for those just out for a good time, few experiences match the colourful walk over the ancient stone span Charles Bridge on a fine summer's day. Equipped with a wiener roll in one hand and beer in the other, one can savour the offerings of dozens of street musicians and artists exercising their creative juices, for a price, in true capitalistic fashion.

Exhausted casualties take refuge and sustenance in cafés and bars that make this city a positive boon to the alcoholic. The all-pervading aroma of pork knuckle and goulash, remind the weary visitor that a meal can't be too far away and liquid refreshment even closer.

Denied access to the country for more than forty years, the Czechs' foremost Cold War adversary, Americans, now come in their droves to discover the origins of 'Budweiser'. It's a name well known back home, but a brew that fails to measure up to the 'Real McCoy' in Prague. As one takes a leisurely walk through the city, you can hear the sound of many European languages, including Russian. Ironically, they have discovered a thing or two about capitalism in recent years, and have plenty of roubles in their pockets to prove it.

Entrepreneurial activity has blossomed, with some locals finding a lucrative market in exploiting the city's dark past.

The brochure described a visit to one of the city's nuclear fallout shelters, and the former headquarters of the despised secret police, responsible for the death of thousands of opponents of Russian sponsored communism. Our guide for the day, 20-year-old Jan, was obviously far too young to remember the atrocities of the past. However, he enthusiastically painted a picture of a time when political intrigue and espionage dominated the daily life of a population isolated from the west.

"And it was from that balcony, looking down on Wenceslas Square, that Havel was declared Prime Minister, thus ending those dark years," intoned Jan with admirable dramatic flair. "And now we go to the fallout shelter, where we can enjoy a quiet beer."

Now there's a good idea, I thought, looking forward to telling the family that I'd sucked on a bottle of a beer in an underground nuclear bunker, 16 metres below the surface of the earth.

The tour participants were led to a tram for the ten-minute trip to a huge hole in the ground, built in 1955, at the height of tensions between the nuclear superpowers.

Upon our arrival, it was apparent we'd been beaten to the bunker by a generation or two of graffiti artists, whose colourful work was plastered over a large, flat, concrete wall dug into the side of a hill.

Our guide removed a huge metal key from a pocket, explaining his company rented the fallout shelter from the 'authorities' and unlocked a massively thick, lead-lined door, guarding the top of spiralling stone steps which dropped dramatically into the earth.

Given the background of this unique tourist attraction, I don't mind admitting that I was filled with an eerie sense of foreboding, mixed with a healthy dose of wonder, at how some of my overweight tour companions, including myself, were going to be able to climb back out of this underground hole.

Did they have an arrangement with the local fire brigade for rescue services, I thought. Would travel insurance cover the cost of our retrieval? In the end, I brushed these negative thoughts from my mind and focused on the task ahead, including the consumption of a good Czech beer.

With each step down into the bunker the temperature dropped noticeably, in stark contrast to the unusually warm summer's day in downtown Prague. The sound of nervous giggling, creaking knees and odd anal explosion distracted everyone's thoughts from the fact that a little over sixty years ago, the world teetered on the brink of nuclear war.

This bunker, Jan explained, was designed to hold 2,500 people, and was built not long before the Bay of Pigs standoff in Cuba, between Russia and the United States, which threatened to tip the world into a devastating nuclear conflagration.

After the lengthy descent, which succeeded in altering the facial colour of a number of our group, we found ourselves walking along a frigid dimly lit tunnel, from which other tunnels snaked into darkness.

"And this is one of a number of the very essential toilet areas built for the short-term inhabitants," Jan informed us, pointing for emphasis.

The fact that there wasn't row upon row of basic squatters meant I had seriously underestimated the former communist regime's concern for their comrade's comfort level.

More surprises followed.

Such was the paranoia of the 50s and 60s that locked beneath the earth with the lucky inmates, was a huge array of gasmasks and flimsy plastic body coverings to be donned by survivors upon their emergence from the bunker after the feared, deadly atomic explosion.

Propaganda lined the walls, extolling the likely conditions in a post nuclear war. Dozens of serious-looking mannequins stood in glass cases dressed in police and military uniforms, holding threatening wooden batons, no doubt a symbolic reference to how, in the day, they would beat the living daylights out of non-compliant residents.

Our enthusiastic guide directed the group to racks of uniforms and hats, inviting us to dress up, so as to have recorded for posterity, ridiculous images of ourselves in drab, eastern bloc, military garb.

Like sheep, we did this, even going so far as to pull gas masks over ours faces to hide the silly grins and feelings of gross stupidity.

"This is a fantastic photo to put on your Facebook site," our young guide told us, looking squarely at two of the more senior members of the group.

Yea right, I thought, they'll have it up on the net tonight!

And then, Jan uttered those magic words. "Now for a beer," he said, looking directly at me, sensing somehow, it was the main reason I'd come on the tour.

He sidled over to a stack of crates set against the wall and with a flourish whipped out a local Czech beer, not much smaller than an Australian long neck and handed it to perhaps the eldest female member of the group.

Oh, he's got to be taking the piss, I thought, but as all attention focused on the dear old senior, she raised the bottle to her lips and took a healthy swig.

My turn soon followed, and as I savoured the taste of this fine Czech beer, I thought to myself, this surely must be the strangest place I had ever bent the elbow!

CHAPTER 40
TERRIBLE TRAVEL 'TAILS'

Life is full of embarrassing moments!

A disproportionate number of mine have happened while travelling the globe in search of adventure, with and without my loyal bride, Lady Barnett by my side.

They are ugly stories full of squalid detail I would normally not share, but occasionally one comes along, and the urge to shock and horrify is too much to resist.

For those who are easily offended, you may want to skip this chapter, and save yourself the dreadful experience of reading my sordid 'tail'.

This embarrassing misstep is indelibly etched into my tortured psyche. The story starts in the sleepy coastal town of Concon, on the Chilean coast north of Valparaiso. The bohemian port city was our launching point in 2016, for a 24-day cruise to Antarctica, South Georgia and on to Buenos Aires in Argentina.

For several days, I and my two travel companions, Lady Barnett and eminent Canadian legal eagle and prodigious poser, Sheldon Sherman, had explored Santiago, before heading west through verdant vineyards to the mighty Pacific Ocean.

Eating and drinking had featured heavily in our Chilean odyssey and that was not to change. After a warm greeting from the manager of the superb Hotel Casadoca, our eyes feasted on the numerous seafood restaurants lining the charming coastal fringe, and in clear sight of our elevated patio area.

The sound of crashing waves and the piercing screech of seagulls set the idyllic scene for what I anticipated would be a perfect interlude, offering all sorts of gastronomic delights and fine wines. A contraction of the word 'gastronomic' would come back to haunt me!

Bear with me, I beseech you, as I flesh out this terrible tale and examine what to do, should you be confronted with a similar dilemma. The mishap in question occurred after a short walk to a seafood restaurant recommended by the hotel manager. An exhausted Rhonda begged off dinner, leaving the boys to it.

A delightful, full-bodied Chilean red wine arrived in short order. However, the selection of food proved to be more problematic. English was a language rarely spoken in this sleepy little town, and an encounter with Aussies and Canadians even rarer.

The sartorial elegance of our Canuck mate also introduced an element of confusion to proceedings, as the waiters had no doubt gone through life ignorant of the high fashion stakes embraced in Toronto. After lengthy deliberations and good-natured attempts to communicate, a plan was formulated.

"That, that, that and that," I instructed, pointing at the tattered menu having no idea what it all meant. No, I lie; I cleverly comprehended the word "risotto" which I'd encountered on menus around the world.

Generous smiles followed and we prepared ourselves for an onslaught of delectable seafood dishes. Alas it was not to be.

The breaded calamari tasted like it had been fried in local petroleum from a nearby refinery. The swordfish ordered by Sheldon was quickly sniffed and poked, before he imperiously summoned the owner, to tell him his fish stank, and was overcooked besides.

I cringed and waited for an angry reaction and a fight with the eight or so beefy waiters 'sneaking a peek' at what looked like a looming confrontation. But, wonder of wonders, the owner raised his hands in defeat, and ran to the kitchen to produce another less malodorous offering.

"Gracias, Gracias," I babbled, feeling my sphincter momentarily contract, only to watch in horror as our Canadian friend poked the subsequent piece of fish and pulled a face as if he had been presented with a small dog turd. I prepared to kick him viciously under the table, but was interrupted by the manager, who returned with the offer of free wine to appease these strange foreigners.

More smiles followed, and when it became apparent my friend was not going to eat the newly presented offering, I reached over and surreptitiously concealed it in a napkin for later disposal.

Surely, I thought, this sophisticated man of the world would desist from applying the same high standards encountered in a Michelin star restaurant, but he showed no sign of doing so, increasing tension to boiling point.

It was a truly terrible meal, but by the end of it, we felt no pain, as our host had filled us with a generous amount of free vino. After an effusive and heartfelt farewell, we waddled and weaved our way back to the hotel, my pocket filled with soggy swordfish!

A short time later, I was to experience one of life's truly embarrassing moments.

I quickly fell into a deep alcohol-fuelled slumber, only to wake a couple of hours later, racked by severe stomach cramps. The pain was excruciating, though in my fuzzy state I had little hope of reacting quickly to the horror that was seconds away from erupting.

It came in the form of another painful cramp and then it happened, an explosion of volcanic proportions. It was a sensation hard to describe, but for the purposes of clarity, I will try. My bowel simply let go, resembling a runaway garden hose, my sleeping bride oblivious to what had just happened.

I returned sometime later, to hear the gentle rise and fall of her breathing, but when I looked down at the pristine white Egyptian cotton sheets my heart sank, and I could feel the colour rise in my cheeks. It was as though Jackson Pollock had laid out a monochromatic masterpiece on a blank canvas, just inches away from my sleeping beauty.

What to do now, I thought. Should I wake her from a deep slumber? I quickly rejected this, fearing the shock would prove too much. God help me if she rolled over to my side of the bed!

My now razor-sharp brain raced, as I looked for a way out of this humiliating dilemma. Had the restaurant owner laced our wine with rat poison after Sheldon's rejection of his seafood?

I could always pack my bags and do a runner, but I knew that was the coward's way out.

Instead, I cleaned as best I could, covered the offending area with a towel, and adopted the role of 'ceiling inspector', far too scared to sleep lest I experience another volcanic eruption.

I later watched as Rhonda stirred, and immediately let out a series of pathetic and pitiful groans.

"Food poisoning," I croaked, "I haven't slept all night and, darling, I'm afraid I've made quite a mess."

To this shocking declaration, she made comforting and sympathetic noises, reinforcing my decision to make her my life partner.

"What are we going to do," I asked, "burn the sheets?"

"For God's sake, Ian, do you think it's the first time a hotel guest has had a little accident?"

A little accident, I thought, try a full-scale bloody catastrophe.

"What you're prepared to take the blame then, are you?" "No," she responded, "I'll just tell reception my husband is unwell after eating at the restaurant they recommended. That should do it."

The clarity and logic of her advice filled me with awe, but still I found it hard to come to terms with the fact that I had committed such a heinous and embarrassing act. Still there was no doubt the hotel was complicit in this sordid debacle. If I had not gone to the restaurant of their choice, I would not have soiled their sheets.

Then another thought occurred to me! What if we had 'double trouble'.

Had our friend Sheldon also had a similar experience? I found him on the balcony eating breakfast, gazing out at the sparkling blue Pacific.

"Good morning," I offered, "Are we well?"

To this he responded with a glowing affirmative and an endearing smile. "Yes," he said, "slept well."

There was a god, I thought.

"Leaving in thirty minutes," I declared, before making my way back to the room to complete the pack-up.

There, I bunched up the sheets in an effort to disguise my disgrace and very deliberately placed a business card on top.

It bore the name of the restaurant "Aqui Jaime", the architect of my embarrassing fall from grace.

Did I say life was full of embarrassing moments – try beating this one!

CHAPTER 41
COPING WITH A COLONOSCOPY

After spending much of my professional life as a news reporter in front of a camera, and being told on many an occasion to shove the aforementioned device up my 'you know where', it still came as a rude shock when actually exposed to this gross indignity.

I laughed the abuse off in the old days, not for one moment imagining it would be possible or feasible to have a camera thrust up one's behind.

But how things have changed. Yes, folks, I had a colonoscopy!

Now, for those readers who have not yet reached what is delicately referred to as 'middle age', this will probably not be a familiar procedure.

But for many of us who are bloody old (over sixty) and no longer protected by the bullet-proof lustre of youth, we are easy prey for a host of insidious diseases, looking for a home in our ageing bodies. Yes, even up the dirty back end colloquially called the 'chocolate starfish!'

"Yuck," the younger and more sensitive will scream in unison.

"Yuck," I reply, my heart and mind filled with revulsion at the thought and sound of a word I can barely pronounce – colonoscopy.

The first bit, of course, will give you a clue that this is not going to be pretty. The colon is that snaking one and a half metre long organ that is attached to the rectum, and it is in this region that the 'Big C' often chooses to reside.

Enter doctors called gastroenterologists.

They came up with the inspired idea of sticking a miniature camera into the colon through the rectum to detect any telltale evidence of cancer. A brilliant idea, and one which has saved many a patient from an agonizing demise. So why then does the word colonoscopy strike the fear of God into the heart of most blokes I know, including me?

Well, I will tell you! Because we are pussies, wimps, and big girl's blouses when it comes to dealing with medical issues. Give us a pill to swallow or an elixir to sip: no problem, but bring into question our nether regions and watch out, we are gunna run!

There's something incredibly unnerving about having someone, even a medico, meddling with that part of the body, through which some pretty nasty debris passes.

Women are far braver when it comes to invasive medical procedures involving private parts. Don't ask me why, perhaps because they are well used to internal medical invasions from an early age. My wife had a colonoscopy not long ago and she didn't miss a beat; in fact, she almost appeared to be looking forward to it. When I found out I had to have one, I went into a deep funk and started, as they say in the classics, to shit myself (and that was without the MoviPrep, which I'll deal with later).

How did I find out?

Well, here's the thing. I was forced to act after one of those Government sponsored bowel cancer kits arrived in the mail. It sat in the bathroom for more than two months before the little lady badgered me into taking a sample of my stool (a lovely little word) to send off to the government department in charge of looking at people's – how do I put this politely – waste!

Did I say "YUCK" before?

So relieved was I to finally post off my little package that I soon forgot all about it, until a letter arrived in the mail advising me that my test had come back 'positive'.

Now, to a bloke who's spent much of his life shying away from all things medical, this was not good news. What did it mean? Did I have the 'big C'? Was I not destined to sip martinis on an Acapulco beach to celebrate my 100th birthday?

Anyway, I didn't have long to think about it because before I could sneak off to throw down a couple of quick comforters, the better half had rung doctors, specialists, lawyers and I suspect, the local undertaker. Quite the organiser, the wife!

On Doctor Doug's recommendation, I was booked into see one of Sydney's leading gastroenterologists, Danny Stiel, the former head medico for the Australian Olympic Games. He was given the unique honour of looking up the back end of another finely tuned athlete – Me!

Was I apprehensive? Scared? You betcha!

So, before going off to see Dr. Stiel, I hit the books or more precisely, Google and then I got really scared. Not surprisingly, what was most worrying was the extraordinary length of the camera devise that would be used to deflower me. Did I mention the colon was well over a metre long?

That's five feet!

Casting these disturbing thoughts aside, I spent a number of uncomfortable days getting ready for my meeting with Doctor Danny. These guys must see some funny things in the eyes of their patients. In mine, he would detect nothing but sheer, unadulterated terror.

The questions came thick and fast, "Do you have a family history of colon cancer?" "No", I answered. "Any bleeding problems down below?" "No," I proclaimed, somewhat indignantly. All the questions you would expect, with me wanting to ask just one.

"C'mon Doc, what are the chances I've got cancer?"

That didn't quite make it out of my mouth. It didn't have to, because he did a pretty good job of calming me down, explaining the bowel cancer kit that gave a positive result was not the most accurate test. It detected blood, but that could be present for any number of reasons.

No doubt aware of my heightened state of uncomfortableness, to put it mildly, raw terror to be more accurate, he turned to humour, God bless him!

He called on Google and American entertainer, Lou Rawls, to give me a little chuckle. The sight of the renowned, black crooner posing as a doctor on YouTube and singing into a snaking 17-foot-long camera/microphone, similar to the one destined to be inserted into my back end was supposed to be funny.

"You'll never find someone who loves you tender like I do" Lou crooned. Yea right – thanks Doc!

Nonetheless, I left his office feeling better than when I first entered. I sincerely hoped that would be the case after he worked his magic in a few weeks' time.

I took with me some serious reading material and spent the next several days being nervous, and locating a product called 'Picoprep'.

My man, Dr. Stiel, preferred that brand to another nuclear laxative, MoviPrep, which could only mean one thing – I was in for a real rough ride!

He wanted a squeaky clean colon to play around in.

I wanted to know just how bad this bowel evacuation was going to be. I had heard terrible things in the past, a major reason for me assiduously avoiding the whole ghastly procedure for so long. And so on the eve of my date with destiny, after having fasted for the day, I was instructed to mix three sachets of Picoprep into about a litre of warm water and consume it over 4-hour period.

This was not easy, after reading American Pulitzer Prize winning humorist, Dave Barry's account of his experience. "MoviPrep tastes (and here I'm being kind) like a mixture of goat spit and urinal cleanser, with just a hint of lemon."

Now, there's something to look forward to, I thought.

He went on to write, "The instructions for MoviPrep, clearly written by someone with a great sense of humour, state that after you drink it, a loose watery bowel movement may result. This is kind of like saying that after you jump off the roof, you may experience contact with the ground".

With those shocking images firmly planted in my addled brain I started swilling the dreadful concoction. I soon found out there was Buckley's chance of me climbing Barry's imaginary roof, as I was spraying into the toilet bowl like the proverbial runaway garden hose.

And yes, the Picoprep did taste like goat spit!

But that was the least of my worries. After finally drifting off to sleep, feeling like I'd lost half my body weight, the dreams started.

There I was, in one nightmare scenario trying to get a pair of tight-fitting jeans over some leak-proof Huggies. One question kept running around my slumbering brain: will I still be spurting all over place when I wake up, and what if I give Danny Stiel a liberal spray when he's taking a peekaboo?

To be fair, I'd be surprised if that was not a serious concern of most colonoscopy candidates in the lead up to the procedure.

To make matters even worse, I was going to be one of the first out of the gate. I certainly didn't need an alarm clock to wake me for the action-packed day ahead.

Rhonda dropped me off at the hospital shortly after 8am with the promise that she'd be back to collect me, and the reinforcing comment "don't worry, darling, it's a breeze!"

Thank you, I thought, you're not the one up whose bum they're going to stick a 17-foot-long camera. I don't mind admitting I was scared.

You see, I had reached sixty years of age without ever having to spend time in hospital as a patient. This was unfamiliar territory.

First, I signed a mountain of forms, one of which pointedly asked for the name of my next of kin, presumably to notify in case I didn't make it. I was then led off to a small, curtained cubicle, told to undress and put on one of those silly hospital gowns, which allow your plump posterior to be exhibited to the world. I was then instructed to get into a bed on wheels and wait.

Oh, and the nurse said one more thing. If I wanted to go to the toilet, it was down the corridor to my left. Yea right, I thought, I'd love to go wandering out there with my arse hanging out. Only the threat of a major spurt would get me moving anywhere outside my relatively private little cubicle.

And yes – I am a wimp!

This was it! The culmination of weeks of anxious speculation.

I was wheeled into the operating theatre, and there to greet me were a smiling Danny, and a very pleasant lady called Elizabeth whose job it was to knock me out.

There was also a nurse present, presumably to clean up should I explode during the tricky procedure. I looked around furtively to see if I could track down the 17-foot-long camera devise, which was going to go where no man had ventured before, but they must keep it deliberately hidden until they knock you out.

God knows what I would have done it if I'd got a glimpse of it!

"Now I'm just going to give you a little prick," Dr. Elizabeth, whispered to me in a soft, soothing voice. I've already got one I was tempted to reply, but didn't because I was too terrified to speak.

Then what happened, you might well ask?

Well, I haven't got a clue because whatever Liz gave me worked a treat!

I woke up in the recovery room over an hour later, with the man who had violated me standing over my bed smiling.

"All good, Ian. I removed one polyp, but it looked pretty inoffensive to me". At least that's generally what I remember him saying in my woozy state. "We'll send it off for tests, but I wouldn't worry too much if I were you."

So there it is – I survived my colonoscopy!

But wait, there's more, and this is where I start to get serious.

A few weeks later, Danny rang me to say that the little polyp did indeed contain what he described as 'a tiny bit of cancer'.

"You are a very lucky man, Ian," he said, "we got it, but if you'd waited any longer then it would certainly have spread."

So, to all of you big wimps out there, do yourself a favour – go and have a colonoscopy, and don't wait until you're sixty!

CHAPTER 42
AND ON IT GOES!

Gophers, royal rats, battered buttocks and bobbing bottoms; hardly the most worthy of subjects to write about in the course of a career, but life after 'serious journalism' has been a blast.

As I enter my 70th year there have been dramatic changes in the way information is gathered and disseminated in both the electronic and print media. Coverage of breaking news has evolved, and been enabled by breathtaking advances in technology. Where, as a young news reporter, I would run to a public phone to file copy, newshounds are now instantly connected, to file both words and pictures.

Cameras in mobile telephones can take the highest resolution photographs and videos, to be broadcast live on television or emailed to the photo departments of major newspapers. In the space of forty years, these game-changing developments have been blithely accepted by a population that shows little surprise at the mind-boggling rate of change. Whole industries and businesses have disappeared, workforces decimated, as technology makes old, established practices obsolete.

Few industries have been impacted as much as broadcast and print journalism. As an old timer, I can well remember working as a foreign correspondent, and being temporarily denied contact with editors back in Australia. Telephone connections were patchy, live broadcast satellite trucks unreliable. Just getting things done was a major logistical nightmare. There were no 5G mobile phone networks guaranteeing smooth communications. When you pulled off a live cross from a breaking news location in Central or South America, it was cause for celebration! In those simpler times, I was ignorant of the technical marvels that allowed me to be standing in front of a camera on the other side of world, broadcasting news into homes around Australia. To achieve that feat required the efforts of a group of professionals;

a cameraman, soundman, editor and satellite truck technician, or wire bender as we called them.

On a recent walk along the foreshore of Sydney Harbour, I was reminded of just how much things have changed. I came across a young, female reporter from Sky Television, in the midst of a live cross, using the city skyline as a backdrop.

A solitary figure, she stood in front of a small camera perched precariously on top of a tripod, buffeted by high winds. She was grasping a microphone in one hand, an I-phone in the other, while confidently delivering a report, which was being streamed live, back to the studio.

This is the new reality of television news reporting, I thought. No cameraman to guarantee the quality of the pictures, no sound man, no bounce board to light up her beautiful features, and more importantly no one to look out for her safety. She had arrived in her own car and most probably would drive back to the Sky News headquarters to personally edit her report.

While I resisted the urge to congratulate her on an impressive multi skilled performance, I also dismissed the notion of regaling her with stories of my own glorious past in the news business. She had enough on her plate. God knows, she probably had to get back and prepare the news director's lunch!

I resumed my leisurely walk, thinking for the first time in a long time, of how lucky I was to be retired and out of a business that had changed so much. This, of course, had not come in a blinding flash. For years, the economic rationalists, bean counters and media moguls have slashed newsroom budgets, reduced staff numbers and used technological advances as an excuse to change the business model. No doubt it needed change, but doing it while upholding journalistic standards was another thing altogether. In this endeavor, they have failed miserably. For years after leaving mainstream journalism, I have resisted the urge to throw heavy objects at the television screen, after hearing appalling reports from poorly trained journalists. Many are hired by a management more concerned about the budget bottom line than the quality of the product.

It has become a familiar story in both broadcast and print journalism. Experienced editors and reporters forced out, because of differences with management over a mysterious 'new direction', designed by yet another incoming regime.

Admittedly, their hand has been forced by the emergence of social media, and the resulting effects on newspaper readership and television viewer numbers.

Facebook along with a growing number of new platforms now command the attention of the 'great unwashed' and the media world has been turned on its head. This has obvious consequences for the journalists who ply their trade in the fast-changing space; their voices and writings have lost the power they once commanded. The noise and divergent views expressed on social media have empowered whole populations, and removed the public's need to digest and focus on trained, professional analysts and reporters.

Mobile phones have enabled the general population to film breaking news, while television reporters are now tasked with locating private vision and paying for it. Powerful media moguls, given a clear insight into the views expressed on social media, are now tailoring coverage and political bias, in a bid to reclaim and build lost market share, compromising journalistic ethics and integrity in the process.

Look no further than the American media scene and coverage of recent Presidential campaigns. The Murdoch owned Fox Network lurched so far right in its support of Donald Trump, while the influential CNN cable news network leaned to the left, all making a mockery of the slogan, 'fair and balanced'.

Here in Australia, Sky News, owned by Rupert Murdoch's News Corp has followed Fox's right wing agenda, and on-air personalities unashamedly push a line, which could not be further from balanced journalism. It's all very depressing to a retired television reporter.

"It wouldn't have happened in my day" a common refrain from ex-professionals in many avenues of endeavour. Journalism is only one business affected by the technological revolution, irrevocably changing the workplace, and wreaking havoc on the aspirations of employees seeking long-term employment.

My sagely advise to a son leaving university and making his first foray into the workplace, was "prepare yourself for multiple changes in how you make a living."

Unlike his grandfather and father, who spent long careers in the same industry, his future could not be as assured. Almost twenty years later, that prediction has not yet come to fruition, but I have not changed my view. Certainly, it has been born out in the broader community.

But, enough bitching about the sad demise of the once noble field of journalism. The thing about retiring is, anything you say about the business you were once involved in, doesn't count. You are irrelevant, and any comment will only sound like sour grapes, or the murmurings of an embittered old fart.

So, I will concentrate on the positives and say my time working as a television news reporter was great fun. I was witness and recorder of significant events, in countries around the world. I got to talk to and interview celebrities, politicians, sportspeople and anyone who popped up in front of my microphone. It was a great ride!

Now as I slip into my dotage, I really can't complain about much. I can try to impart my vast bank of knowledge to my grandchildren, Jude and Delphine, who will grow up in a world probably ruled by robots. What they'll do I have no idea. I only hope it's something that will give them as much pleasure as their grandfather got from his humble existence.

Travels with Lady Barnett, of course, will continue, so do expect a continuation of silly epistles about such worthy subjects as bobbing bottoms and battered buttocks.

PHOTOGRAPHY CREDITS

All photographs in this book are copyright © and may not be reproduced without permission. All efforts have been made to trace relevant photographers and copyright owners, but in the case of non-attribution or error, please write to the publishers for correction. The author would like to thank all contributors to the photographic section as follows:

7. Qantas 'Connie' arriving in Cocos Islands in the mid-1950s. Photograph courtesy of Civil Aviation Historical Society.
9. French President, General Charles de Gaulle drops into Cocos for a visit in 1956. Photograph courtesy of Civil Aviation Historical Society.
11. Lyn's childhood home – 'The Oaks' in Abersychan. View from the Oak Tree. Photographer: Rhonda Barnett.
13. The Hodder Family home in Hanbury Road, Abersychan, South Wales. Photographer: Rhonda Barnett.
19. On the road in Africa with Producer, Nick Farrow and Cameraman, Scott Barnett. Photographer: Wayne McKelvie.
25. The crew getting to know the locals in Kenya, with Wayne McKelvie and Scott Barnett. Photographer: Nick Farrow.
27. Our Los Angeles home in 1988, with Daniel and Kathy. Photographer: Rhonda Barnett.
31. The fruit of my loins, Daniel and Morgan. Photographer: Rhonda Barnett.
32. A new start with Rhonda, AKA Lady Barnett – March 2005. Photographer: Star Shots.
33. The Hyslop/Edmonds/Coulson Clans gather at Christmas in Belrose, Sydney in 2010. Photographer: Morgan Hyslop.
34. My old boss and Best Man, Mike Worner joins the Wedding Party, along with niece Stephanie Edmonds. Photographer: Star Shots.
36. Proud Mum, Lyn with her brood – Ian, Diane and Janine. Christmas 2010. Photographer: Morgan Hyslop.
37. Another 'My Life My Legacy' documentary production, for the Szekely family in 2019. With sound recordist, David O'Rourke. Photographer: Rhonda Barnett.
39. Three generations of Hyslop men – Ian, Daniel and Jude. June 2017. Photographer: Rhonda Barnett.